THE ENIGMAS OF HISTORY

The ENIGMAS of HISTORY

Myths, Mysteries and Madness from Around the World

ALAN BAKER

MAINSTREAM
PUBLISHING

EDINBURGH AND LONDON

First published in Great Britain in 2008 by
MAINSTREAM PUBLISHING COMPANY
(EDINBURGH) LTD
7 Albany Street
Edinburgh EH1 3UG

ISBN 9781845963361

A catalogue record for this book is available
from the British Library

Typeset in Goudy

Printed in Great Britain by
Clays Ltd, St Ives plc

CONTENTS

INTRODUCTION

Mysteries have an eternal power to delight and fascinate. Some mysteries are earth-shattering in their implications. Others simply offer the mind a little intellectual exercise in the form of an intriguing puzzle to ponder while washing the dinner plates or walking the dog.

This book presents some of the most compelling enigmas of history, a few of which have maintained their grip on the imagination for centuries. That includes the mystery surrounding the lost continent of Atlantis, which is probably the most famous legend in recorded history. This fabulous civilisation, existing on a paradise island located somewhere 'beyond the Pillars of Hercules', has been the subject of speculation since Plato wrote about it in 360 BC. Protected by the mighty sea-god Poseidon, Atlantis conquered many lands before its people grew corrupt and began to worship other gods. Enraged by this betrayal, Poseidon punished the Atlanteans with 'a single day and night of misfortune in which the island of Atlantis disappeared into the depths of the sea'. There have been many theories on the location of Atlantis and many have pondered the nature of Atlantean society and the reason for its demise. But the key question remains: did Atlantis really exist?

Other mysteries revolve around the lives of eccentric or enigmatic individuals, such as Count Alessandro Cagliostro, a poor Sicilian peasant who became the toast of European society in the eighteenth century. Cagliostro was, in modern parlance, a 'superstar' of magic and the occult and his celebrity still captivates the imagination today. Historian Lewis Spence (1874–1955) called him 'one of the greatest occult figures of all time', while the famous writer on ghosts and the supernatural, Peter Underwood, stated that 'while he seems to have been party to a number of disgraceful intrigues and forgeries, he was nevertheless a true wizard'. Who was Count Cagliostro, and why does his life maintain the power to fascinate us to this day?

History is replete with artefacts that defy rational explanation. What, for instance, is the truth behind the mysterious sixteenth-century book known as the *Voynich Manuscript*? What is the secret of the indecipherable script and bizarre diagrams which cover its pages? Why does the book contain carefully drawn illustrations of plants that do not exist and objects that look like galaxies? What is the nature of this strange document that retains its mystique to this day, in spite of the efforts of countless linguists and cryptologists to decipher its extraordinary text?

And the world is full of mysterious places as well as artefacts. Some are real and some are the stuff of complex and beautiful myths. The fabulous realm of Shambhala is a case in point. Legends tell of a mysterious kingdom somewhere beyond the Himalayas, an oasis of advanced science and culture inhabited by ascended Masters who secretly work towards the spiritual enlightenment of humanity. The mysterious city of Shangri-La in James Hilton's classic novel *Lost Horizon* was inspired by the stories of Shambhala and its hidden community of perfect beings guiding human spiritual evolution. Is there any truth to these legends? Were Jesus Christ, Buddha, Apollonius of Tyana and other great teachers sent from the hidden realm of Shambhala with the means for every human on Earth to attain a higher state of consciousness?

These are just a handful of the mysteries that will be examined in this book. Immerse yourself in the enigmas of history for an hour, a night or even a week and feel your imagination go into overdrive as you share the esoteric knowledge within.

1

ATLANTIS

The Search for the Lost Continent

A Magnificent Civilisation

It is without doubt the most famous of all legends: a fabulous island-continent lying somewhere 'beyond the 'Pillars of Hercules', home to an advanced and enlightened civilisation that dominated the world long before the first cities took root in the distant lands of Mesopotamia to the east. From deep in the night of prehistory comes Atlantis and its mysterious people, reaching through the millennia to the present, to inspire wonder and fascination to this day.

First to write of Atlantis was Plato, who described the lost civilisation at length in two of his dialogues, *Critias* and *Timaeus*, in which he takes on the role of a young student listening to conversations between Socrates and a group of friends. One of them, Critias, speaks at length of the land of Atlantis and its people, describing its location, history, society, its beliefs and customs – and its total destruction in 'violent earthquakes and floods in a single day and night'. Even in classical times, however, there were many who believed that Atlantis was merely Plato's invention; no less a figure than Aristotle believed that Plato had concocted the whole story, that the wonderful land had only ever existed in his imagination.

Today, most archaeologists and historians hold the same belief: that Atlantis never existed and was, in fact, an allegorical description of the fabulous Minoan civilisation in Bronze-Age Crete. In his book *Lost Continents*, L. Sprague de Camp suggests that 'the most reasonable way to regard Plato's story . . . is as an impressive if abortive attempt at a political, historical and scientific romance – a pioneer science fiction story', which expressed Plato's idea of an idyllic community.

Is it possible that the sober community of orthodox archaeologists are mistaken, that Atlantis did exist and that its relics still lie in the depths of the ocean, waiting to be discovered?

Whether striving to be a master of fiction or seeking to present evidence for the truth, Plato provides us with information on the origin of the Atlantis story. He states that Solon, an elder statesman of Greece, was told of Atlantis by the Egyptian priests of Sais; he had even planned to immortalise the tale in a poem. Of equal renown was Critias (the grandfather of the Critias who appears in Plato's great dialogue), to whom Solon related the story of Atlantis.

Following his retirement from public life, Solon travelled widely throughout the Mediterranean and, around 600 BC, he visited Egypt. A celebrity of the ancient world, it is highly likely that he would have been granted an audience with the Egyptian priests, and those who believe that Atlantis was a real place, not a philosophical invention, maintain that it was at this time that the priests shared with the illustrious Greek their tradition of the lost continent. (Plato affirms the truth of what he is writing several times: 'The fact that it is not invented fable but a genuine history is all-important,' he says.)

Plato gives a location for Atlantis that, at first sight, seems unequivocal: it lay, he says, beyond the Pillars of Hercules – in other words, the Straits of Gibraltar, which separate the Mediterranean Sea from the Atlantic Ocean. However, there is an entire world 'beyond the Pillars of Hercules' and this has led later writers and investigators to propose all manner of locations for the site of Atlantis, from Africa to the Americas, from the Middle East to Scandinavia, from the Indian subcontinent to Antarctica.

What was Atlantis like? To answer this, it is worth quoting fairly extensively from Plato's own account of the island's central region, a lush, flat plain which contained the fabulous capital city:

> At the centre of the island, near the sea, was a plain, said to be the most beautiful and fertile of all plains, and near the middle of this plain about fifty stades [one stade is equal to just over 606 feet] inland a hill of no great size . . . There were two rings of land and three of sea, like cartwheels, with the island at their centre and equidistant from each other . . . In the centre was a shrine sacred to Poseidon and Cleito [his mortal wife], surrounded by a golden wall through which entry was forbidden . . . There was a temple to Poseidon himself, a stade in length, three hundred feet wide and proportionate in height, though somewhat outlandish in appearance. The outside of it was covered all over with silver, except for the figures on the pediment which were covered with gold . . . Round the temple were statues of all the original ten kings and their wives, and many others dedicated by kings and private persons belonging to the city and its dominions . . . The two springs, cold and hot, provided an unlimited supply of water for appropriate purposes, remarkable for its agreeable quality and excellence; and this they made available by surrounding it with suitable buildings and plantations, leading some of it into basins in the open air and some of it into covered hot baths for winter use. Here separate accommodation was provided for royalty and commoners, and, again, for women, for horses, and for other beasts of burden . . . The outflow they led into the grove of Poseidon, which (because of the goodness of

the soil) was full of trees of marvellous beauty and height, and also channelled it to the outer ring-islands by aqueducts at the bridges. On each of these ring-islands they had built many temples for different gods, and many gardens and areas for exercise, some for men and some for horses . . . Finally, there were dockyards full of triremes and their equipment, all in good shape . . . Beyond the three outer harbours there was a wall, beginning at the sea and running right round in a circle, at a uniform distance of fifty stades from the largest ring and harbour and returning in on itself at the mouth of the canal to the sea. This wall was densely built up all around with houses, and the canal and the large harbour were crowded with vast numbers of merchant ships from all quarters, from which rose a constant din of shouting and noise day and night.

The Antediluvian World

Several writers have equated the Golden Age of humanity represented by Atlantis with the biblical Garden of Eden and this is surely one of the reasons why the legend still retains such a profound hold on the modern mind. However, serious research into the legend of Atlantis did not begin in earnest until the seventeenth century when the scholar Athanasius Kircher placed the lost continent in the middle of the Atlantic Ocean. It would be more than another century before public interest in the legend really took off.

The man responsible for this was Ignatius Donnelly, a formidable figure in North American history. Following his qualification as a lawyer at the age of 22, he became Lieutenant-Governor of Minnesota at 28, and entered Congress six years later. In 1882, he published the first modern study of the Atlantean legend, *Atlantis, the Antediluvian World*, which became a huge bestseller. One of the main arguments he presented in support of the existence of Atlantis was the ubiquity of deluge myths, which he claimed had their origin in a single event.

He believed this catastrophe, which overwhelmed the lost continent and its people, occurred approximately 10,000 years ago. Donnelly also claimed that all the main features of advanced civilisation were invented or discovered in Atlantis, including writing, paper, gunpowder, navigation and agriculture.

In his *World Atlas of Mysteries*, Francis Hitching notes that Donnelly's monumental research influenced the hundreds of later books which place Atlantis in the mid-Atlantic. 'Unfortunately,' he adds, 'our new-found knowledge of sea-floor spreading and continental drift, and other scientific advances, has weakened most of the arguments put forward.' Hitching goes on to provide a few examples, which are worth repeating here.

Donnelly claimed, for instance, that the presence of certain plants on both sides of the Atlantic is evidence for an ancient land bridge between them. However, seeds can be carried great distances on the winds and can also float for thousands of miles on the ocean's surface. Hitching continues:

> The many cross-Atlantic cultural similarities (e.g. pyramid building, mummification) must be derived from a central source. Or because people were much better navigators than had been supposed. Greeks, Egyptians, Celts and other Europeans all had legends of fairy-tale land-masses in the Atlantic; the Aztecs of Mexico believed they had migrated there from an island called 'Aztlan' – very close to the word Atlantis. Impossible to deny this evidence, which remains the strongest corroboration of Plato. However, some of the legends seem to be purely symbolic, and the Celtic paradise islands may well have been the Canaries. The Aztecs themselves dated their departure from Aztlan to AD 1186, and whatever date you put on Atlantis, it requires the Aztecs to wander around for several thousands of years before their arrival in the American archaeological record.

With regard to Hitching's point about the similarity of pyramid use, the shape is the most stable for large structures and was almost certainly developed independently by the Egyptians and the indigenous inhabitants of the Americas.

Another piece of evidence presented in favour of the mid-Atlantic as the location of Atlantis is the Mid-Atlantic Ridge, the great chain of mountains that scars the ocean bed, running roughly north to south. The peaks of this vast range protrude above the ocean surface in places such as the Azores, which are, so the theory goes, the last vestiges of the lost continent. This might seem a powerful argument . . . until one considers the fact that the ridge is actually getting *larger* as new material slowly issues from the Earth's interior. In addition, it is geologically impossible for large parts of the ridge to have been above sea level as recently as Plato's Atlantis is said to have existed.

Atlantis in the Mediterranean

In 1939, the Greek archaeologist Spyridos Marinatos published a book entitled *Antiquity*, in which he presented his theory that the legend of Atlantis arose as a result of a natural disaster that was barely imaginable in its ferocity, and that the true site of the lost civilisation was not some mythical continent in the middle of the Atlantic Ocean but rather a place in the Mediterranean Sea.

Today, the island of Santorini in the southern Aegean Sea is a popular holiday destination. Its beautiful villages cling to the sides of steep mountains and the strangely chaotic lunar landscape, tinged with hues of ruddy ochre, tumbles down to the warm and gently lapping ocean waters. Seen from the air, the island has a curiously irregular crescent shape, as if a large portion of it has been gouged away by some angry god. This impression is closer to the truth than one might imagine: Santorini was once much larger than it is now. Around 1500 BC, when the island was known as Thera, it was almost completely annihilated by a truly colossal volcanic eruption. Spyridos Marinatos estimated the eruption that destroyed Thera was perhaps four times more powerful than that of Krakatoa in the Pacific, which erupted in 1883. As Hitching notes, Krakatoa:

> set off a series of tidal waves 15 metres high that devastated neighbouring islands, unleashed an enormous cloud of ash and colossal volumes of lava that covered the whole island and killed 37,000 people; it was so deafening that the explosion could be heard 6,300 kilometres away in Australia – the loudest historically verified sound in Earth's history.

When Thera blew itself apart in 1500 BC, Marinatos suggests, tidal waves and debris travelled 100 kilometres to Crete, where they decimated the advanced Minoan civilisation. Marinatos equated the Minoans with the great civilisation about which Plato wrote so evocatively, and found that by taking away one zero from 9000 BC (Plato's date for the destruction of Atlantis) and adding 900 BC to 600 BC (the date given for the conversation between Solon and the Egyptian priests), one arrived at a date of 1500 BC, the date of Thera's destruction. Marinatos concluded:

> Thus the myth about Atlantis may be considered as historical tradition which, in the manner typical of the distortion of such events, grew from the fusion of various disparate episodes. The destruction of Thera, accompanied by terrible natural phenomena felt as far away as Egypt, and the simultaneous disappearance of the Cretans trading with Egypt, gave rise to a myth of an island, beyond all measure powerful and rich, being submerged.

This would seem to put paid to the idea of Atlantis as a real civilisation thriving in the deep, millennia-shrouded past. But the search for Atlantis is not quite so easily abandoned. For instance, evidence emerged in 1977 that the eruption of Thera happened much earlier than 1500 BC; two German scientists, Hans Pichler and Wolfgang Schiering, demonstrated that the cataclysm had little if any effect on Crete. In fact, Minoan civilisation continued until 1380 BC. According to the archaeologist Peter James:

> The Minoan centres of Crete survived Thera by about 50 years and, in the case of Knossos, by over 100 years. The basic archaeological premise for Crete/Thera/Atlantis has therefore been proved shaky, quite apart from all the other weaknesses in the evidence. The original story of Atlantis as told by the Egyptian priests can't have been about the destruction of Minoan civilisation by a volcano on Thera, because no such thing happened.

As for the subtraction of a zero from the 9000 BC date, James considers this both arbitrary and unjustified, especially in view of the fact that the Egyptian priests noted that many great deluges took place in the previous 9,000 years, 'for that is the number of years that have elapsed' since the time of which they spoke.

According to the priests, a great war was fought between the Atlanteans and the Greeks 1,000 years before the 'institutions' of Egyptian civilisation were founded. Since Egyptologists agree that the beginning of Egyptian civilisation can be dated to c.3100 BC, the date for this war can be tentatively established as 4100 BC. This is, of course, much more recent than 9000 BC, but Peter James explains this by pointing out that ancient civilisations (for instance, the Egyptians, Babylonians and Phrygians) tended to exaggerate their own antiquity. The Egyptians did this by adding up the number of years their various kings reigned; however, since many of their kings reigned simultaneously, this resulted in wildly inaccurate figures. Hitching notes that 'the Greek historian Herodotus, visiting Egypt a mere 150 years after Solon, was given by this method an authoritative date of 12,040 BC for the founding of Egyptian civilisation'.

Given that what the Egyptian priests told Solon was
similarly exaggerated, it would seem possible at last to arrive
at a sensible date for the destruction of Atlantis: 3100 BC
(the archaeological date for the beginnings of Egyptian
civilisation) plus about 500 years (halving the priestly '1,000
years').

If Atlantis did exist, then where might it have been, and what was it
like? One of the most notable of Atlantis scholars was the Scottish
newspaper editor Lewis Spence (1874–1955), who published
his *Problem of Atlantis* in 1924. Like Donnelly's book, it became
enormously popular amongst a public that was still hungry for
information and speculation on the nature and location of the
fabulous lost continent.

Spence, who was also a widely respected scholar of Babylonian,
Egyptian and American history (and whose *Encyclopaedia of Occultism*
remains a standard text on the subject), suggested that there is
evidence of a vast continent existing in the Atlantic region in the
Miocene epoch, approximately 25 to 5 million years ago. Over many
millions of years, it gradually broke up until all that was left was
several smaller land masses, some close to the Mediterranean, and a
larger island in the region of the West Indies. Spence claimed that
the western land mass 'still persists fragmentally in the Antillean
group'. Since the sea around them is shallow, it seems logical to
suggest that during the last Ice Age, when sea levels were lower, a
much larger area of land may have been above the surface.

Atlantis Discovered?
One of the most famous commentators on Atlantis and its history
was the American psychic Edgar Cayce (1877–1945), who gave a
series of 'life readings' of 1,600 people between 1924 and 1944 in
which he 'saw' their past lives as members of the lost civilisation.
Cayce claimed that Atlantis had extended from the Sargasso Sea to
the Azores and was comparable in size to the continent of Europe.

The ancient Atlanteans, he said, used crystals to generate electricity and other forms of power and to rejuvenate bodily tissues. However, through rampant materialism and arrogant self-indulgence, they became irredeemably corrupt and ultimately destroyed their continent.

Cayce also made several predictions, including that Atlantis would rise again in 1968 or 1969. Needless to say, this prediction was not fulfilled. However, another event occurred which could, at a stretch, be considered a symbolic fulfilment of the prophecy.

In late 1968, a Bahamian fisherman called Bonefish Sam took archaeologist J. Manson Valentine to see a strange collection of stones lying about seven metres beneath the surface of the ocean off the coast of Bimini. When Valentine explored the site more fully, he was astonished to find two parallel lines of regularly placed stones approximately 600 metres long.

Valentine was honorary curator of the Museum of Science in Miami, and he wrote a report of his findings in the museum *News*. In part, he wrote of:

> An extensive pavement of regular and polygonal flat stones, obviously shaped and accurately aligned to form a convincingly artefactual pattern. These stones had evidently lain submerged over a long span of time, for the edges of the biggest ones had become rounded off, giving the rocks the domed appearance of giant loaves of bread or pillows of stone.

Not surprisingly, opinion on the origin of the so-called 'Bimini Road' has been divided ever since, with some archaeologists and researchers claiming that the stones were laid by human beings and thus represent evidence for a vanished civilisation, and others dismissing them as nothing more than 'Pleistocene beachrock erosion and cracking' – an entirely natural phenomenon.

As J. Manson Valentine himself notes:

> The difficulty is that the stones could be at the same time both natural in form, yet put in place by man. Fractured beachrock on Bimini certainly exists, as for instance on the west coast of South Bimini. What if this had been used to form the causeway. . . ? There are many precedents for this type of megalithic construction, including the transport for unknown reasons of the blue stones at Stonehenge from the Prescelly Mountains in Wales 200 kilometres away.

During their initial 1975 expedition, Valentine and his team spent several months mapping, measuring and taking geological samples of the Bimini Road, which consists of 'huge stone blocks about 5 × 5 × 1 metres in size, extending more than 1,000 metres distance on the seaward leg, which is aligned north-east'. At the southern end of the 'road', there is an arc where it doubles back on itself in the shape of a 'J'. Valentine continues:

> Apart from four or five exceptions where there are two or more blocks resting vertically on top of each other, the structure consists of one layer of blocks. Although they are not of standard size throughout the structure, we derived through statistical analysis a theoretical building unit of 1.15 metres, based on a number of stones with dimensions clustering around 2.30 metres and 3.45 metres. Exact measurement on rounded stone blocks underwater is necessarily imprecise. The closest unit of measurement in the ancient world to the supposed Bimini unit would be a module of two Phoenician cubits, equal to 1.14 metres.

The team found other evidence arguing against a natural origin for the Bimini Road, including the fact that the joints between stones on the top layer do not coincide with joins in the bedrock beneath, which would be expected if the stones were merely the result of geological processes. In addition, no beachrock in the area runs in a straight line for more than 50 metres (considerably shorter than the 600-metre length of the Road); jointing in the bedrock is, on average, approximately twice the width of the top layer; and the arc of the 'J' turns precisely through 90 degrees.

Following the end of the last Ice Age, the sea rose in the area, and did so quite rapidly around 5000 BC. 'The best estimates are that the upper layer of stones would have been above the surface of the ground by 10–12 metres in 6000 BC, and 2–3 metres below sea level in 2000 BC. This gives us an approximation for its most recent human occupancy, if it was so used.'

Valentine states that conclusive proof of human habitation around the Bimini Road could only come from an artefact discovered in a secure archaeological context, that is, beneath the top layer of the Road. He also concedes that no such artefact has been found – although several intriguing objects have been uncovered in the area, including a fragment of worked stone with a tongue-and-groove joint and several fluted marble columns. 'The question is whether the marble and the tongue-and-grooved stone may come from a lost civilisation, or are ballast from wrecked ships.'

In spite of many theories, both plausible and outlandish, and several unusual archaeological discoveries, the question of whether Atlantis ever existed remains open. However, the archaeological record of our world is far from complete. There are doubtless many more strange and wonderful discoveries to be made. Perhaps, one day, one of those discoveries will be the ruins of Atlantis.

2

FABULOUS FEMALE WARRIORS
The Legend of the Amazons

Diodorus Siculus wrote in the first century BC of a tribe of formidable female warriors, who once lived 'in the western parts of Libya, on the bounds of the inhabited world'. It was a society, he said, unlike any that had been heard of before:

> For it was the custom among them that the women should practise the arts of war, and be required to serve in the army for a fixed period, during which time they maintained their virginity; then, when the years of their service in the field had expired, they went in to the men for the procreation of children, but they kept in their hands the administration of the magistracies and of all the affairs of state.

Today, the Amazons are one of the most famous and enduring of Greek myths; but did they really exist and, if so, did they really cut off their right breasts to make it easier to wield their bows and throw their spears, as many still believe?

It is often claimed that the very word 'Amazon' means 'without breast', being derived from the Greek 'a' ('without') + mazos, variant of mastos (breast). Although this etymology looks fairly neat and unequivocal, the truth is a little more complex. For instance, the 'a' prefix can be read in two ways, so Amazon could mean 'without breast' or 'full-breasted'.

To make matters more complicated, there are several other possible meanings of the word 'Amazon', deriving not only from Greek but also from Old Iranian, Hebrew, Mongolian, Gothic, Sanskrit, Armenian, Phoenician and Slavic. The possibilities include:

Unapproachable

Without man

With honour

With belts for cinching armour or dresses

Living together

All women

Warrior

Youth

Strong

Fallen woman

Excellent woman

Virgin

Children of the moon goddess

Mother lord

Masculine woman

The legend of breast mutilation comes from Hippocrates (c.460–c.370 BC), who stated that while the Amazons were babies, their mothers cauterised the right breast with a red-hot instrument, 'so that its growth is arrested, and all its strength and bulk are diverted to the right shoulder and right arm'.

Although the Amazons first appear in Homer's *Iliad*, that great epic only mentions them in passing as fighting women, whose skill in battle was fully the equal of any man, and makes no mention at all of the dubious practice of breast mutilation. This myth regarding them had gained wide circulation by the fifth century BC although it seems that no one could quite agree on why the Amazons should do such a thing. Some suggested it was done so that a bow could be drawn or a javelin hurled with greater ease, while others believed that the life-force of the excised breast would be diverted into the throwing arm.

Other claims for their ferocity were also made, including that they kept men as sex slaves and that they killed their male children (or left them in the wilderness to fend for themselves).

One of the lengthiest accounts of the Amazons' exploits appears in the *Histories* of Herodotus (*c.*484–*c.*425 BC), in which he tells of how a group of Amazons was blown across the Sea of Azov into Scythia. They had been taken prisoner by the Greeks but had risen up against their captors and had slaughtered them all (living up to their Scythian name 'Oiorpata', or 'slayers of men'). Knowing nothing of ships or seafaring, the Amazons were unable to control the vessel and were blown towards Scythia and made landfall at a place called Cremni.

Coming upon a herd of horses, they seized them and rode further inland, plundering the settlements they encountered. The Scythians were nonplussed: they had never seen the like of the strange, fierce warriors who had invaded their territory. Assuming them to be men, the Scythians met them in battle, after which they examined the bodies of those who had fallen and discovered to their astonishment that their new enemies were, in fact, women.

Resolving to kill no more of them, the Scythians sent a detachment of young men, equal in number (as near as they could guess) to that of the invaders, with orders to camp nearby but on no account to engage them in battle again. If the women approached, they were to retreat and when the women halted they were once again to pitch their camp nearby. The reason for this was that the Scythians wanted to have children born of this brave and noble race.

The young men departed and did as they had been commanded and, by degrees, the two camps gradually approached each other. When the Amazons saw that the men wished them no harm, they allowed them to approach yet nearer.

Then it happened that one of the youths came upon an Amazon woman alone 'and she did not repulse him but allowed him to lie with her'. Although they could not speak each other's language, by means of signs she made him understand that she wished him to return to the spot the next day and to bring another man with him.

The man returned to his camp and told what had happened. The next day, he did what the Amazon had asked, appearing with one of his fellows. The Amazon also returned with one of her own comrades and by this means the two groups finally came together. Although the men could not learn the Amazons' language, the women quickly learned the Scythian tongue.

The men told them that they had parents and possessions, and that they wished to return to their people with the Amazons as their wives. But the Amazons replied that they would not be able to live with the Scythian women, who 'stay in the wagons and work at the works of women, neither going out to the chase nor anywhere else'. The Amazons shot with bows, hurled javelins and rode horses and knew nothing of domestic life and duties. They knew, therefore, that they would never find themselves in agreement with the Scythian women. So a compromise was proposed. The men should return to their families and take their share of the property and then they and their Amazon wives should go and live by themselves.

The men agreed and went to claim their inheritance from their fathers. But when they returned, the Amazons said to them that they were both ashamed and afraid to dwell in this place, for they had done much harm to both the Scythians and their country by their plundering. 'Since then you think it right to have us as your wives, do this together with us – come and let us leave this land and pass over the River Tana.'

The men agreed to this also and together they crossed the Tana and travelled eastward for three days, and then northward for three more. Herodotus concludes the story thus:

> [H]aving arrived at the place where they are now settled, they took up their abode there: and from thenceforward the women of Sauromatai practise their ancient ways of living, going out regularly on horseback to the chase both in the company of the men and apart from them, and going regularly to war, and wearing the same dress as the men. And the Sauromatai make use of the Scythian tongue, speaking it barbarously however from the first, since the Amazons did not learn it thoroughly well. As regards marriages their rule is this, that no maiden is married until she has slain a man of their enemies; and some of them even grow old and die before they are married, because they are not able to fulfil the requirement of the law.

According to Herodotus, the Sauromatians were the descendants of the Scythians and Amazons; however, although there is some archaeological evidence that some Sauromatian women were warriors, there is no evidence that they were descended from a tribe of women who originally lived entirely without men.

Although the Sauromatians might be seen as good candidates for the source of all the later myths regarding the Amazons, the archaeological evidence does not seem to support this. In fact, there is no evidence for female warriors on the Eurasian steppe until two centuries after the Amazons first appear in Greek art and literature. It seems likely, therefore, that while the Sauromatians may have influenced legends of the Amazons, they are not its ultimate source.

The fact is that no one knows where the legend of the Amazons originated, or if they really existed. It is possible that the Amazons constitute a vague and distant memory of an unknown society ruled by (and perhaps consisting entirely of) women; or perhaps they represented the unknown and untamed realms that existed beyond the male-dominated societies of the ancient world.

3

SIRIUS

The Mysteries of the Dog Star

Between 1946 and 1950, two French anthropologists, Marcel Griaule and Germain Dieterlen, lived with the Dogon tribe of Mali, West Africa. During that time, the two Europeans managed to persuade four of the Dogon head priests to share the tribe's most secret traditions with them. The anthropologists were astonished at what they were told.

Central to the Dogon tradition was the star Sirius, about which they knew far more than seemed possible. For instance, they knew that Sirius has a twin – the white dwarf Sirius B, invisible to the naked eye on Earth – and also that Sirius B is extremely heavy. According to the Dogon priests, it is made of a substance 'heavier than all the iron on Earth'. In addition to this, not only did they know that the white dwarf's orbit around Sirius A takes 50 years, but also that the orbital path is elliptical; they even knew the position of Sirius A within the ellipse.

Griaule and Dieterlen were also astounded to learn that the Dogon knew of Saturn's ring system, the four main moons of Jupiter, the revolution of the planets around the Sun and the spiral shape of our galaxy, the Milky Way.

There is no doubt that Sirius holds a pre-eminent position in the mythology of human civilisation. The brightest star in the heavens, Sirius is a binary system in the constellation Canis Major and is approximately 8.7 light years from Earth. Around Sirius A revolves the white dwarf star Sirius B, which is believed to be nearing the end of its life. Unlike its bright companion, Sirius B is invisible to the naked eye and was seen through a telescope for the first time in 1862 by the American astronomer Alvin Clark. Since Sirius B is 100,000 times fainter than Sirius A, it was not possible to photograph it until 1970. White dwarfs are extremely dense objects, so dense that a cubic metre of Sirius B weighs about 20,000 tons.

What is yet more astonishing, however, is the explanation given by the Dogon themselves for this knowledge. They believe that their ancestors were visited in antiquity by spacefarers from a planet in the Sirius star system. According to Robert K.G. Temple in his book *The Sirius Mystery*, the Dogon are the last people on Earth to worship this race of amphibian beings who landed in the Persian Gulf at the dawn of human civilisation. Temple suggests that memories of this event are represented not only in the culture of the Dogon but also in the myths, legends and art of Babylonia, Egypt and Greece.

The Dogon priests told the two French anthropologists that they called the alien visitors 'Nommos'. These creatures, they said, needed to spend most of their time submerged in water, a trait they shared with the Babylonian god Oannes. The priests described 'the spinning and whirling of the descent of the ark' (the Nommos' spacecraft), and the noise of thunder it made upon landing. Reference is also made in the legends to the ark 'spurting blood' – perhaps a rocket exhaust. The Dogon also spoke of an additional star-like object that remained in the sky while the ark descended to Earth, which may imply the presence of a larger mother ship.

> The whole body of the animal was like that of a fish; and it
> had under a fish's head another head, and also feet below,

similar to those of a man, subjoined to the fish's tail. His voice, too, and language, were articulate and human; and a representation of him is preserved even to this day . . . When the sun set, it was the custom of this Being to plunge again into the sea, and abide all night in the deep; for he was amphibious.

This is not a Dogon description of a Nommo but an extract from the surviving fragments of the *Babylonian History* of the priest Berossus. It refers to the ancient civiliser-god Oannes, who taught the Sumerians mathematics, astronomy, agriculture, social and political organisation, and written language.

In *The Sirius Mystery*, Temple argues beyond this initial connection between the Nommos of the Dogon and Oannes of the ancient Sumerians and attempts to demonstrate a connection between Oannes and Sirius and the classical mystery religions, which were recorded in a coded form that represented an arcane system of knowledge available only to initiates of the mysteries. There are, however, occasional clues pointing to the connection with Sirius, including the repeated motif of the number 50, representing the orbital period of Sirius B, and a dog-headed deity, representing Sirius A, the 'Dog Star'.

In his book, Temple attempts to back up his theories concerning amphibious explorers from Sirius with reference to the mythology of the ancient world. Aside from the Annedoti ('Repulsive Ones'), of whom Oannes was the most famous, there are Dagon and Atargatis, who were worshipped by the Philistines, and had fishes' tails and human bodies. At the Pharos off Alexandria rested the amphibious god Proteus, known as 'The Old Man of the Sea', who rested in a cave, sheltering 'from the heat of the star Sirius'. Lake Triton in North Africa was the home of another amphibious god, Triton, who helped the Argonauts (of whom there were, perhaps significantly, 50).

The Aegean Sea was home to Nereus (like Proteus, a shape-changer), who had 50 daughters, each of whom was half human, half fish. At Phigalia on the Mediterranean there was an ancient sanctuary described by Pausanias, where an image of Artemis was kept. The representation of the goddess was that of a woman down to the waist and, below that, a fish. The amphibian gods known as the Telchines lived on the island of Rhodes. After they were scattered from the island by Zeus, some of them fled to Greece, where they became the 50 'hounds of Actaeon'. The Telchines had dogs' heads and flippers in place of hands.

In classical mythology, Sirius is closely associated with the constellation Orion, at whose heel it lies. In Greek myth, Orion's ascent into the sky was the result of his death at the hands of the goddess Artemis. There are a number of versions of how this occurred. One has it that Artemis shot Orion by accident at Apollo's instigation; another that he had incurred her wrath by boasting that he had killed all the wild beasts in Crete; yet another that, after he had attempted to ravish her, she produced a scorpion from the earth, which killed both Orion and his dog, Sirius, both of whom were subsequently transported into the sky.

The Greeks were not the first people to be fascinated by Sirius. The ancient Egyptians identified the star with Isis, the wife and sister of Osiris, and mother of Horus. Isis was identified by the Greeks with Demeter, Hera, Selene and Aphrodite, and eventually she absorbed all the qualities of the other goddesses. She is also credited with performing the rites of embalmment for the first time in history, upon the corpse of her husband, who had been murdered by Isis and Osiris's violent brother, Set. The murdered god was thus restored to eternal life.

Are researchers such as Robert Temple correct in asserting that the reason for Sirius's significance in human mythology is that it is home to space travellers who visited Earth in the distant past, and perhaps kick-started our civilisation? At first sight, the evidence seems compelling: there is the Dogon knowledge of Saturn's ring system and Jupiter's four largest moons, not to mention their understanding that Sirius B is made of the heaviest substance in the Universe. How could a poor tribal people in West Africa have come by this apparently detailed astronomical knowledge if not from beings from the stars?

The answer, unfortunately, is rather less romantic and astonishing than we might be led to assume. The NASA scientist James Oberg includes a chapter on the 'Sirius Mystery' in his book *UFOs and Other Outer Space Mysteries*, in which he calmly demolishes the argument for extraterrestrial intervention by beings from Sirius.

For instance, he notes that the Dogon claimed knowledge of Jupiter's four largest moons and questions why they only knew of four, when the planet actually has at least 14 moons, plus a ring system (although far less spectacular than Saturn's). Wouldn't extraterrestrial visitors have told them of the true extent of the Jovian system? The Dogon also spoke of Saturn as the farthest planet from the Sun; once again, we know this to be untrue: beyond Saturn lie Uranus, Neptune and Pluto. Surely the Dogon would have known this if they had received their astronomical information from visiting aliens.

While it is true that Sirius has always been of great significance to the Dogon and many other ancient peoples, their myths could still have been contaminated from outside (but very earthly) sources. Oberg writes:

> So what is the alternative to the extraterrestrial hypothesis for the Dogon myths? The Dogons could have learned of European Sirius lore in the 1920s from traders, explorers, and missionaries, many of whom are avid amateur astronomers . . . The Dogons were not isolated. Many served in the French Army in World War I and some of them could have returned years later with colorful embellishments for their native legends.

No radio signals have been detected emanating from the Sirius system (which is hardly surprising, given that Sirius is a hot, young Class A star, and as such is extremely unlikely to be home to an advanced form of life – at least, a form of life which we could comprehend). But is it possible that there are intelligences in the system that may be capable of communicating across the light years with certain human beings?

Anyone familiar with the work of the late American writer Robert Anton Wilson (author, with Robert Shea, of the bestselling *Illuminatus!* trilogy) will know that he claimed to contain 24 'selves', each with different beliefs and agendas, and any of which could be brought into play in order to deal with a particular situation. In his semi-autobiographical book *Cosmic Trigger: Final Secret of the Illuminati*, he describes how, following an intense study of the occultist Aleister Crowley, he 'entered a belief system, from July 1973 until around October 1974, in which [he] was receiving telepathic messages from entities residing on a planet of the double star Sirius'.

Unwilling to wholeheartedly accept the idea that he was literally in contact with extraterrestrials, Wilson, after a meeting with the famous computer scientist and ufologist Dr Jacques Vallée, began to formulate a new belief system based on the theory that 'otherworldly communication' has been going on for centuries, and in the end may not turn out to be the result of a non-human presence from beyond Earth.

However, no sooner had Wilson begun to think of his Sirius experiences as merely a modern interpretation of a phenomenon that has always been with us, than he came across Temple's *The Sirius Mystery*, which seemed to lend considerable weight to his initial feeling that he really was in contact with Sirius.

On 23 July 1973, Wilson awoke from a dream that he could not quite remember; the only piece of information he had brought back from his dream state he quickly scribbled down. The 'message' was:

'Sirius is very important.' He proceeded to look through his library of occult books and, on pages 15 and 50 of Kenneth Grant's *The Magical Revival*, came across the following:

> Phoenix was [Aleister] Crowley's secret name in the Ordo Templi Orientis . . . The Phoenix was also an ancient constellation in which Sothis, or Sirius, was the chief star . . .

> Crowley identified the heart of his magical current with one particular Star. In Occult Tradition, this is 'the Sun behind the Sun', the Hidden God, the vast star Sirius, or Sothis . . .

The component of his being which Wilson called 'the Skeptic' was intrigued but unconvinced by this, so he went to the public library and made another interesting discovery: 'This very day, July 23, when I had received the message "Sirius is very important", *is the day when, according to Egyptian tradition, the occult link (through hyperspace?) is most powerful between Earth and Sirius.*' (Wilson's emphasis.) In Egypt, the Sirius celebrations began on 23 July and continued through to 8 September. This is the origin of the expression 'dog days' (from 'Dog Star days'), since it is in this period that Sirius rises and sets with the Sun.

According to Wilson, even the Skeptic was impressed by this, and he found himself wondering whether his Crowley studies had opened up a channel of communication between Earth and Sirius, a channel used by 'adepts since ancient Egypt'.

Is it at all possible that Robert Anton Wilson and other occult adepts have actually been in contact with intelligent entities in the Sirius star system? In *Cosmic Trigger*, Wilson draws our attention to a Norwegian radio engineer called Jorgen Hals who, in 1927, received signals 'which have never been explained; in the 1950s, various Russian scientists tried to prove that the Hals signals were of interstellar origin, but this theory is still being debated and no consensus has emerged'.

However, in 1971 an American electronics engineer called L. George Lawrence was investigating 'the Backster effect' (telepathy in plants) near Mount Palomar in California. Using his own special equipment, Lawrence apparently picked up signals that seemed to be emanating from the sky in the region of the Big Dipper. After checking his equipment for bugs, he wrote a report to the Smithsonian Institution in Washington:

> An apparent train of interstellar communication signals of unknown origin and destination has been observed. Since interception was made by biological sensors, a biological-type signal transmission must be assumed. Test experiments were conducted in an electromagnetic deep-fringe area, the equipment itself being impervious to electromagnetic radiation. Follow-up tests revealed no equipment defects. Because interstellar listening experiments are not conducted on a routine basis, the suggestion is advanced that verification tests should be conducted elsewhere, possibly on a global scale. The phenomenon is too important to be ignored.

As Wilson states, these findings do imply that there is a certain amount of interstellar communication going on that does not use radio, on which the proponents of SETI (Search for Extraterrestrial Intelligence) are relying, but rather utilises the 'biological or cellular level of consciousness'.

Although he tried to maintain a healthy scepticism about the true nature of his Sirius experiences, Wilson admits that in the end he couldn't help wondering whether it were all literally true – if there were, after all, some 'strange cosmic link' between Earth and the Dog Star. In common with many theorists and investigators of the paranormal, he wondered whether quantum physics might hold any clues. His eye was immediately caught by the so-called Einstein-Rosen-Podolsky (ERP) demonstration, which indicates that, if quantum mechanics is true, 'some particles are in instantaneous contact even if at opposite ends of the universe'. There is a serious problem with the ERP, however, namely that instantaneous contact implies action at a speed greater than that of light, which is forbidden by Special Relativity.

A possible solution to this problem has been put forward by Dr Jack Sarfatti. Wilson writes:

> [Dr Sarfatti] assumes that ERP transmissions (faster than light) are 'information without transportation'. Limiting our view to a local universe – to transmissions at, or less than, the speed of light – is 'electromagnetic chauvinism' . . . Information without transportation is information without energy, without 'signals' in the ordinary sense. The rule of Special Relativity is, thus, not challenged but merely reduced to a definition of locality; it applies only to *signals* and *energy systems*. Pure *information* can take the form of ERP transmissions not limited by signals or the speed of light. [Wilson's emphasis.]

On the third anniversary of his original Sirius experience, Wilson attempted to repeat it through occult means, using the invocation of Hadit (the Intelligence identified with Sirius in Aleister Crowley's symbolism). The following week, *Time* magazine ran a full-page review of Temple's *The Sirius Mystery*.

4

AN ANCIENT OBSERVATORY?

The Mystery of Stonehenge

Standing in majestic isolation on Salisbury Plain in Wiltshire, the enigmatic complex of Stonehenge has stirred the imagination of the countless thousands of people who have visited it over the centuries.

The most famous megalithic site in Britain, it is unsurprisingly still seen by many as a place of powerful magic, a nexus of ill-understood forces where the mysteries of the remote past live on to bewilder and perplex the modern world.

One of the more romantic myths associated with Stonehenge is that it was built by the Druids as part of their mysterious religion. This was first suggested by the famous seventeenth-century English antiquarian and diarist John Aubrey, who spent a great deal of time investigating the site and who discovered the ring of 56 shallow holes (now known as Aubrey Holes) which surround the outer circle of the monument.

Aubrey disagreed with his contemporary, Inigo Jones, who had declared that the ancient Britons were too primitive and savage to have constructed such a 'stately structure' as Stonehenge and that it must have been designed and built by the Romans in the first or second century AD. At the request of Charles II, Aubrey made a detailed examination of the monument and wrote a lengthy account in which he suggested that both Stonehenge and the vast stone circle at Avebury (which he also investigated) were pre-Roman and had in fact been constructed by the Druids, the priests of the early Britons. He added: 'It is most likely that these monuments were the temples of the priests of the most eminent order, the Druids, and it is strongly to be presumed that they are as ancient as those days.'

However, while Aubrey was certainly on the right track as far as the antiquity of Stonehenge and Avebury was concerned, he was still off by a considerable margin, as was Dr William Stukeley, who took up Aubrey's theories and elaborated upon them in the next century. In his highly influential book *Stonehenge, a Temple Restored to the British Druids*, Stukeley declared his own belief in the Druidic origin of the monument and suggested that it was built around 460 BC.

In fact, Stonehenge is much older than the Druidic religion (although the Druids may conceivably have used the monument in their ceremonies). In the 1960s, radio-carbon dating of artefacts around the site revealed that construction work may have begun as early as 3000 BC, during the Neolithic period, and continued in stages for a period of about 1,500 years.

But why was Stonehenge built, and what was its use? Many archaeologists suggest that it was in fact built by a culture known as the Beaker Folk, named after the pottery vessels they left behind. Others are still unsure whether such a primitive society would have had the wherewithal to build such a complex and magnificent structure.

And complex and magnificent it certainly is, consisting of two circles, the outer one composed of sarsen (sandstone) monoliths, and the inner one of bluestones. Each circle was once surmounted by a ring of lintels with peg-and-socket joints, although only six lintels now remain on the outer circle. This arrangement is echoed to an extent at the centre, which contains two horseshoe-shaped series of stones, the outer one composed of sarsens and the inner of bluestones. Within the inner horseshoe is a single stone, now broken in half, known as the Altar Stone. Many of the stones have fallen, and most of the lintel stones are missing, but it is not difficult to imagine how magnificent Stonehenge must have been in its mysterious heyday.

While the sarsen stones are of local origin, the inner bluestones were quarried from the Prescelly Mountains in southwest Wales, some 200 kilometres away. Legend has it (particularly in the work of the great twelfth-century chronicler Geoffrey of Monmouth, who wrote the *History of the Kings of Britain*) that the stones were transported through the magic of the wizard Merlin. Modern archaeologists, however, make the more plausible suggestion that the stones were transported by means of great platforms riding upon wooden rollers.

The sheer scale of this task, and the perseverance required to complete it, remains astonishing. The larger stones weigh as much as 50 tons each, and their transportation and erection must have required the combined effort of thousands of people.

As to its actual purpose, weird and wonderful theories abounded until 1963, when the British astronomer Gerald Hawkins noticed that certain stars and planets rose and fell over certain stones. Gathering astronomical data from the putative period of the monument's construction, Hawkins suggested that the stones may have been used as a gigantic calendar to observe various celestial events, including the summer solstice, which was of great significance to agricultural communities.

One of the strangest theories concerning the origin and function of Stonehenge is that, like many other megalithic constructions, its stones contain mysterious healing powers. The ultimate source for these beliefs lies, once again, with Geoffrey of Monmouth, and they have since entered the realm of folklore.

The researcher Paul Devereux, who has intensively investigated the theory of 'earth energies', was intrigued by these folkloric beliefs, and in 1978 he began the so-called Dragon Project, named after the 'dragon paths' of mysterious energy in which the Chinese have believed for many centuries. Devereux demonstrated that several of the Rollright standing stones in Oxfordshire (which are also steeped in strange legend) exhibited striking fluctuations in magnetism. In his book *The Unexplained*, Karl Shuker notes that:

> What is so interesting about this is that for centuries local people with broken or fractured limbs have visited the Rollright Stones in the belief that the stones will mend them – and modern hospital therapy has revealed that electromagnetism does accelerate the healing process of bone fractures.

Shuker wonders whether this is mere coincidence and suggests that such forces were known to the builders of Stonehenge and other megalithic structures. Did these mysterious builders site their monuments in places where the Earth's natural energies flowed most freely and powerfully? Devereux's Dragon Project has demonstrated that many such structures are located on or near geological faults, where such energies may be concentrated.

For centuries, these patterns of earth energy have been believed to follow the so-called ley lines that link sacred sites and pre-Christian monuments, and which (as noted) are known in China as 'dragon paths'.

Before leaving Stonehenge, we must note that such earth energies are apparently not always beneficial. It seems that the air of magic and mystery that surrounds the monument turned sinister and terrifying one night in August 1971. The depressing wire fence that now surrounds the monument had yet to be built, and on that night a group of young hippies decided to camp in the centre of the stone circle.

They lit a campfire, rolled some joints and began to sing songs, doubtless wishing to partake of the mystical atmosphere of the place.

At two o'clock in the morning, a powerful thunderstorm rolled in across Salisbury Plain, and the stones were illuminated by bright flashes of lightning. According to two witnesses, a farmer and a policeman, the monument lit up with an eerie blue light that was so bright they could not look at it directly. They heard screams coming from the campsite, and rushed there, expecting to find injured people. To their surprise and horror, they found no one. All that remained were a few smouldering tent pegs and the waterlogged remains of the campfire. Of the campers themselves, there was no trace.

5

THE LAST WONDER
OF THE ANCIENT WORLD

The Great Pyramid of Cheops

The Great Pyramid of Cheops at Giza is the last of the Seven Wonders of the Ancient World still in existence. Composed of more than 2,300,000 blocks of stone, it originally stood 482 feet high at the time of its completion around 2600 BC. It covers 13 acres and weighs in excess of six-and-a-half million tons. It is one of the most enigmatic objects on Earth and has captivated countless thousands of visitors over the years with its monumental elegance and profound mystery.

In addition to investigation by archaeologists, that mystery has of course given rise to much fevered speculation by many writers over the years – some of it interesting and plausible, some no more than science fiction and fantasy masquerading as 'truth'.

The two most popular fringe theories are that the Great Pyramid of Cheops – along with the two other, smaller pyramids comprising the Giza necropolis, the Pyramids of Chephren and Mycerinus – were built with the aid of extraterrestrial visitors, or that they are artefacts from an unknown and very ancient civilisation that was at its height 10,000 years ago. These theories have their genesis in the mistaken assertion that the ancient Egyptians did not have the technical expertise to construct such colossal objects and that the objects themselves contain encoded information that was likewise unavailable to the Egyptians.

While it is true that we are not absolutely sure how the pyramids were built, we can make some fairly confident guesses that do not require the presence of super-intelligent aliens wielding anti-gravity beams to move the massive stone blocks into place.

The first priority, of course, would have been to choose the site. A large area of solid rock would have been needed, along with close proximity to water-borne transport. A large workforce would certainly have been needed, although it was almost certainly not as large as the 100,000 labourers described by Herodotus, who visited Giza about 2,000 years after its completion. Nor were the pyramids built by slaves, as Hollywood would have us believe. The work crews were probably taken from the surrounding population, taking time away from small farms to work on the pyramids in exchange for exemption from taxes.

The site would also have to be made perfectly flat and level, and this was probably achieved by constructing grids that were then flooded with water. As the water gradually drained away, its level would reveal even slight bumps and irregularities that would then be chiselled away. In order to align the sides of the pyramid precisely, observations of the stars, in particular the Pole Star, would have been made.

There is no mystery as to the location of the quarry from which the builders took the stone for the pyramid: it is immediately around the Sphinx. The white limestone for the facing stones came from the Tura quarries on the eastern bank of the Nile. Once quarried, the stones were carefully shaped with a variety of instruments, including plumb bobs and T-squares, and were then cut with copper saws and chisels.

The main contention of the ancient-astronaut and unknown-civilisation theorists is that the pyramids could not have been built with the technology extant at the time (c.2500 BC). Without ropes and rollers, and without sufficient grain to feed the workforce, the construction of the Giza necropolis could not have been achieved, and could not even be achieved today with the combined resources of every continent.

The facts are somewhat different. Ropes and rollers were available in the Fourth Dynasty (2575 BC–2467 BC) and, while archaeologists are unsure as to exactly what lifting devices were used to haul the blocks to the upper reaches of the pyramids, they have one or two theories which do not require the involvement of advanced extraterrestrials or an unknown and long-lost human civilisation. It is most probable that a ramp of reed and mud bricks, either linear or spiralling up around the rising form of the pyramid, was used. As to there not being enough grain available to feed a large workforce, the highly fertile Nile Valley would have been well able to satisfy their requirements.

As noted, many researchers claim that the dimensions of the Great Pyramid are encoded with astonishing scientific data, much of which could not have been known to the ancient Egyptians. These theories are sometimes known collectively as 'pyramidology' – although orthodox archaeologists have a rather less flattering term for them: 'pyramidiocy'.

In his book *The World Atlas of Mysteries*, Francis Hitching neatly summarises the most frequently made claims and equally neatly demolishes them. For instance, there is the Pyramid/Earth weight ratio, which states that the weight of the Great Pyramid (5,923,400 tons) equals the weight of the Earth divided by 10^{15} or 1000,000,000,000,000. In fact, the precise weight of the Great Pyramid is unknown, since no one knows exactly how many blocks were used in its construction, nor the exact weight of each one. 'Estimates: 2.3–2.6 million blocks, 5.75–6.5 million tons. The Earth weighs about 6.6×10^{20} tons. The equation doesn't work.'

It is also claimed that the height of the Great Pyramid, multiplied by 1,000 million, is equal to the distance between Earth and the Sun. However, this cannot be true, not only because the top ten metres of the pyramid are missing but also because the Earth's orbit around the Sun is slightly elliptical and so the distance between them varies by as much as three million miles.

In the nineteenth century, the most famous of the alternative researchers into the secrets of the Great Pyramid was Charles Piazzi Smyth, the Astronomer Royal of Scotland, whose many years of devoted study resulted in a series of complex books on the subject. Smyth claimed that the length of the pyramid's perimeter equals the length of the solar year. Unfortunately, this isn't true, and in order to arrive at his conclusion, Smyth was obliged to invent a new unit of measurement, the 'pyramid inch', which is 0.999 of an imperial inch. Smyth claimed that the perimeter of the pyramid was 36,520 pyramid inches in length, which equates to 365.20 days (he had to bump the comma one place to the right and change it to a point in order to make his figures fit). If all this sounds a little too contrived for comfort, there is worse to come: as Hitching notes, the great archaeologist Flinders Petrie conducted his own survey, using Smyth's pyramid inch, and found the perimeter to be 36,276 inches.

Another oft-mentioned curiosity of the Great Pyramid is that its height stands in the same relationship to its base as does the radius of a circle to its area. However, as Hitching notes: 'The magic figure of π may well have been known to the pyramid architects, but they certainly did not use it in these dimensions; to make the mathematics work, you have to multiply everything by two even to arrive at an approximation.'

Although many of the pyramidologists' claims can be refuted, the Great Pyramid retains an air of intriguing mystery. Perhaps the most perplexing enigma is the lack of bodies: why, if it was intended to be Cheops's tomb, has his body never been found? The usual explanation is that they were taken by grave-robbers at some unspecified time in the past, but is this true? Although grave-robbing was a common practice in Egypt, thieves invariably went for the valuables – the gold and other precious objects that were entombed with the person in order to provide for him or her in the afterlife.

The King's Chamber of the Great Pyramid was discovered in AD 820 by workmen employed by the Caliph Abdullah Al Mamun, who believed that the vast building contained a hidden library containing many marvellous secrets. On finding the so-called Ascending Passage, the workmen discovered that it was blocked by three granite plugs, around which they had to tunnel before continuing on their way upwards. When they found the King's Chamber, they saw that the great stone sarcophagus that should have held the mummified body of the Pharaoh was empty and its lid was missing. There appeared to be no way in which earlier grave-robbers could have entered the pyramid, bypassed the granite plugs and removed Cheops's body without leaving any evidence of their activities – and yet the fact remained that the Pharaoh's body was nowhere to be found.

Some researchers have suggested that the architects of the Great Pyramid did not intend for it to be used as a tomb and that they either misled Cheops into thinking that the pyramid was for him (thus securing the necessary funding for the project), or that Cheops knew what they were doing, willingly funded it and arranged for his final resting place to be elsewhere. Many suggest that it was used as a sophisticated astronomical observatory, or as a geodetic marker in which the geography of the ancient world was encoded.

Other pyramidologists, however, have claimed that the pyramid (indeed all pyramids) possesses yet more mysterious attributes. In the 1930s, a Frenchman named Antoine Bovis visited the Great Pyramid, and noticed that the corpses of several small animals that had died there had not decomposed quite as much as they should have. Returning home, Bovis made a number of small pyramids from cardboard and placed vegetables inside them. He was astonished to discover that they remained fresh for longer than usual.

Some time later, a Czech radio technician named Karel Drbal learned of Bovis's research and decided to conduct some experiments of his own. He placed blunt razor blades inside his own home-made pyramids and found that they regained their sharpness. He later wrote:

> There's a relation between the *shape* of the space inside the pyramid and the physical, chemical and biological processes going on inside that space. By using suitable forms and shapes, we should be able to make processes occur faster or delay them.

Drbal remembered a trick his friends in the army used to play on each other. They would take someone's straight razor and leave it all night in the light of the full moon; by morning, it would be blunt. Drbal put a sharp razor under his model pyramid, but nothing happened. He then tried putting a blunt razor under the pyramid. It became sharp, and he found that he could shave up to 50 times with the same blade at the same level of sharpness.

So impressed was he with his discovery that Drbal tried to patent his blade-sharpening pyramid. The patent office in Prague was dubious and refused to issue a patent until it had investigated Drbal's claims further. When the office's chief scientist made a pyramid and found that it did indeed keep blades sharp, the office issued patent number 91304 on the Cheops Pyramid Razor Blade Sharpener.

In his book *Supernature*, Dr Lyall Watson speculates on the possible nature of the energy at work inside pyramidal structures:

> The edge of a razor blade has a crystal structure. Crystals are almost alive, in that they grow by reproducing themselves.

When a blade becomes blunted, some of the crystals on the edge, where they are only one layer thick, are rubbed off. Theoretically, there is no reason why they should not replace themselves in time. We know that sunlight has a field that points in all directions, but sunlight reflected from an object such as the moon is partly polarised, vibrating mostly in one direction. This could conceivably destroy the edge of a blade left under the moon, but it does not explain the reverse action of the pyramid. We can only guess that the Great Pyramid and its little imitations act as lenses that focus energy or as resonators that collect energy, which encourages crystal growth. The pyramid shape itself is very much like that of a crystal of magnetite, so perhaps it builds up a magnetic field. I do not know the answer, but I do know that it works. My record so far with Wilkinson Sword blades is four months of continuous daily use. I have a feeling that the manufacturers are not going to like this idea.

In *Psychic Discoveries Behind the Iron Curtain*, Sheila Ostrander and Lynn Schroeder describe an elaborate experiment that was begun in 1968 by the Ain Shams University near Cairo. The scientists placed cosmic ray detectors in a chamber at the base of the Pyramid of Chephren, which is nearly identical in size to the nearby Great Pyramid. Their intention was to try to detect any secret vaults within the six-million-ton mass of the pyramid, by recording on magnetic tape the amount of cosmic ray penetration.

The cosmic rays strike the pyramid uniformly on all sides and, if the pyramid is solid, should be recorded uniformly by a detector in the chamber at the bottom. However, if there were secret chambers above the detector, more cosmic rays would come through the hollow areas than through solid areas. Thus the scientists might be able to locate secret vaults or even the tomb of Chephren himself inside the pyramid.

For more than a year the recorders ran for 24 hours a day, until in early 1969 a state-of-the-art IBM 1130 computer was delivered to the Ain Shams University and analysis of the tapes began.

Finally, that summer, Dr Amr Gohed, the scientist in charge of the project, made a statement that was reported in *The Times*, London, in which he said that his team were utterly unable to make sense of the data they had gathered. The pyramid, he said, 'defies all the known laws of science and electronics'.

John Tunstall, a reporter for *The Times*, flew to Cairo to interview Dr Gohed. He watched as Gohed ran several tapes from the cosmic ray detectors, which recorded the patterns of ray penetration over different days. The recorded patterns were totally different, a result which Gohed described as 'scientifically impossible'.

Tunstall asked the obvious question: 'Has all this scientific know-how been rendered useless by some force beyond man's comprehension?'

Dr Gohed replied: 'Either the geometry of the pyramid is in substantial error, which would affect our readings, or there is a mystery which is beyond explanation – call it what you will, occultism, the curse of the Pharaohs, sorcery, or magic, there is some force that defies the laws of science at work in the pyramid.'

6

THE WORD OF GOD?

The Origin of the Bible

No other document has so profoundly influenced the course of Western history and civilisation as the Bible. Nothing has been read and studied as much by so many people . . . and raised as many profound questions about our cultural history and spiritual destiny.

And yet, there remains a question which devout Christians answer with ease and without the slightest hesitation, and which scholars and historians view with the utmost perplexity. It is a question which is at the very heart of Christianity.

The question is: who wrote the Bible?

The Bible is at the very centre of our cultural and spiritual awareness; it has been published in thousands of editions (in the English language alone), and has sold more copies than anyone can accurately say. And yet, ironically, we do not know who wrote it.

A devout Christian will say that, on the contrary, we *do* know the origin of the Bible: it is the word of God, passed down to humanity to guide us through our lives and towards salvation. But, if the Bible was written and compiled by human hands, to whom did those hands belong?

To answer this question is well beyond the scope of a single chapter in a single book. However, we can at least frame the question in terms useful enough to afford the interested reader some potentially useful directions for further study.

The first place to start is, of course, the Old Testament: more specifically, the Pentateuch or the Five Books of Moses. Traditionally, authorship of these books is ascribed to Moses himself, despite the fact it is never explicitly claimed in these texts that Moses was the author. For the last 2,000 years it has been considered tantamount to heresy to suggest that Moses did not write the Pentateuch, and yet even during the life of Jesus Christ certain Talmudic scholars wondered openly whether Moses was its sole author.

And here we come to one of the central points of this chapter. Many assume that some of the most potentially shattering of theories and assertions about the history of Christianity and Judaism have been made only in recent years, in books such as *The Holy Blood and the Holy Grail* by Michael Baigent, Richard Leigh and Henry Lincoln, and *The Da Vinci Code* by Dan Brown. The former book was a huge international bestseller when it was published in 1982, and, of course, the truly monumental success of *The Da Vinci Code* since its publication in 2003 is still causing intense debate across the world.

Many traditional Christians have been horrified by both these books, accusing their authors of a crass disregard for theological history at best and outright blasphemy at worst. When the film adaptation of *The Da Vinci Code* was released in 2006, many opined that it should be boycotted, and in Italy the Pope advised Catholics not to see it.

And yet this questioning of accepted religious truth is by no means a modern phenomenon, born of our cynical, materialistic age. It has always been thus. Scholars, theologians and historians have always (to a greater or lesser extent) questioned accepted doctrines and dogmas; the origin and authorship of the Bible is no exception. With regard to the Pentateuch, such scholars have wondered how the Book of Deuteronomy could possibly have been written by Moses when it describes his death and the period following.

Such questions were addressed by the seventeenth-century Jewish scholar Baruch de Spinoza (1632–77), who theorised that the Pentateuch might have been written by someone else (he suggests Ezra the Scribe), who was largely inspired by other writings of Moses, which are now lost. The Church was furious but he had sown the seeds of further inquiry and he could be called the father of modern critical scholarship of the Bible.

If Moses didn't write the Pentateuch, if indeed it was not written by any one person (Ezra the Scribe included), then who else might have written it? The most widely held theory is the so-called 'documentary hypothesis'. Proponents of this theory believe that the Pentateuch may have been written not by one person, but by four.

This conclusion has been arrived at following many years of study by many scholars, which began with an examination of biblical doublets (in biblical study, the word 'doublet' has a very specific meaning: it is the repetition of the same event in two or more parts of the Pentateuch). One of the most striking discoveries was the inconsistency of the name of God as written in the five books: in various places, He was referred to as Jehovah and also as Elohim. The initial implication was that the Pentateuch was written not by one person but by two.

Their identities were, of course, unknown and so the scholars who made these discoveries agreed to call the writer who referred to God as Jehovah 'J' and the writer who referred to God as Elohim 'E'. However, further study revealed that the text attributed to E contained numerous references to priests and their various functions. It seemed that E was not alone in his literary endeavours and that there was in fact another writer at work in these passages. Since he seemed so preoccupied with priests, he was named 'P'.

To complicate matters further, scholars decided that the Book of Deuteronomy was written in a markedly different style from the other books (which, incidentally, one might expect, considering that it describes Moses' death). So at variance was Deuteronomy with the style of the other books of the Pentateuch that a fourth writer was suggested, who was duly given the letter 'D'.

If it is true that the Pentateuch was written by four individuals, then their identities will probably never be known. However, if their names are lost to us for ever, we can still make educated assumptions regarding them. Something about their backgrounds, for instance, can be deduced from the ways in which they tell their stories, the concerns they express and the ways in which they express them.

Scholars have suggested, for instance, that D and E were Levitical priests from the city of Shiloh, and that E may have been a descendant of Moses. P was probably an Aaronid priest from Jerusalem, who wrote before the city's sacking in 587 BC, and J was probably of the tribe of Judah, and lived sometime between 1200 and 722 BC. Perhaps most interestingly, scholars have been intrigued by J's emphasis on female characters, and many have wondered whether J was, in fact, a woman . . .

The true authorship of the New Testament is also shrouded in uncertainty. Traditionally, of course, each of the gospels is attributed to one of the apostles, Matthew, Mark, Luke and John; however, many scholars have questioned this assumption. They believe, for instance, that the Gospel According to Matthew is actually of anonymous authorship, using a collection of Jesus's sayings perhaps written down by Matthew himself.

Although it follows Matthew in the New Testament, the Gospel According to Mark was probably written first. Here, scholars are divided on the question of authorship: some believe that it really was written by Mark, in Rome, and was intended as a summary of the teachings of Peter regarding Jesus's life and sayings, while other scholars believe that Mark was not a real historical personage, and that his gospel must have been written by someone else.

Opinion is similarly divided on the authorship of the Gospel According to Luke, which emphasises the compassion of Jesus and the presence of the Holy Spirit in his life. While some accept that

Luke did write this gospel, others claim that he could not have done so, and his name was attached to it in accordance with the practice, prevalent in the late first century, of attaching an apostle's name to a text to lend it greater weight and legitimacy.

Finally, the Gospel According to John reads very differently from the first three gospels, and is far more mystical in nature, presenting historical events in metaphorical terms. Many scholars agree that John could not have written this gospel and that it was most likely composed by one of his followers, perhaps around AD 90.

While research and debate as to the origin and true authorship of the Old and New Testaments of the Bible is a fascinating and worthwhile pursuit, one wonders whether it has any real bearing on the fact that the Bible has offered comfort and guidance to countless millions over many centuries. Does it really matter who wrote it? The answer has to be a resounding 'Yes', for while many have been guided along a path of goodness and compassion in their lives, many others throughout the last two millennia have used Christian teachings as a justification for the most appalling acts of cruelty and repression.

The American writer Robert Anton Wilson once stated that belief is the death of thought. Once you truly believe something, there is no further need for analysis of the belief or acceptance of the possibility that there might be any alternative. Notwithstanding the great beauty of the Bible, and the monumental inspiration afforded to humanity by the life and teachings of Jesus Christ, it is essential that the Bible continue to be treated as what it is: a historical document that should be amenable to historical research and continued interpretation.

7

THE DELUGE FROM HEAVEN

Noah and the Great Flood

The tale of the Great Flood is told in many traditions around the world. For Westerners, of course, the most famous is that told in the Book of Genesis, in which God commands Noah to build an ark for himself and his family and to fill it with animals so that the sinful world might be re-inhabited following the Deluge. The story also appears in the mythologies of many other cultures, including those of Mesopotamia, Scandinavia, Greece and pre-Columbian America.

In fact, many historians believe that the flood story recounted in the Epic of Gilgamesh, related by the ancient Sumerians and dated at least 1,000 years BC, may have been the inspiration for the biblical account. There are certainly a great many similarities between the story told in the Book of Genesis and those written in the cuneiform language of Babylonia. These include the enormous vessel and its living cargo of animals, the sending out of birds to find land and the signal sent from Heaven to tell of the end of the Deluge (a rainbow in Genesis, a goddess's necklace in the Epic of Gilgamesh).

According to the Book of Genesis, Noah's Ark was a huge vessel 300 cubits (450 feet) long and 50 cubits (75 feet) wide. It is said to have made landfall on Mount Ararat (although the Bible does not give any specific location for it). Nevertheless, the Mount Ararat in Turkey is seen by many as the likeliest location, and the mountain has been reconnoitred many times in an effort to discover the Ark's remains.

The first European to climb Mount Ararat was Dr Johann Jacob Parrot, professor of natural history at the University of Dorpat, who scaled the mountain in 1829. In fact, he was not even looking for the Ark but had the good fortune to be shown relics from it that were kept in a monastery nearby. It seems, however, that the monks who took the professor into their confidence should perhaps not have done so, for their monastery was destroyed in an earthquake 11 years later.

Dr Parrot's expedition set the stage for the modern European fascination with the Ark and with the possibility of actually finding its remains. Such a discovery would be a monumental event in the history of archaeology; moreover, it would be of vast significance, not just to Christianity and Judaism but to all the world's major religions.

That the Ark's discovery would indeed cause a seismic shift in our historical and religious perspectives is implied by the testament of Archdeacon Nouri of the Chaldaean Church who searched for the Ark three times between 1887 and 1892 and who claimed to have seen it near the summit of Ararat on his final expedition in April 1892. Bob Rickard and John Michell, in their book *Phenomena*, quote Nouri's words from an article in the journal *English Mechanic* of 14 October 1892, thus:

> I was almost overcome. The sight of the ark, thus verifying the truth of the Scriptures, in which I had before had no doubt, but which, for the sake of those who do not believe, I was glad, filled me with gratitude.

Verification of the truth of the Scriptures would indeed have been the conclusion of many, had Nouri actually excavated the Ark's remains. His story, however, ends sadly: with his incarceration in a mental institution following the Turkish government's refusal of his request to ship the Ark to the Chicago World's Fair.

Did Archdeacon Nouri really see the remains of Noah's Ark near the summit of Mount Ararat? Perhaps, but the story is, in fact, of no more use than the many other claims regarding its sighting. These claims go back more than 2,000 years, to the time of the Babylonian historian Berosus, who claimed in 275 BC that the remains of the Ark could be seen in the Kurdish mountains of Armenia. Local people, he said, even scraped the bitumen from its vast hull, salvaging it for their own use.

Like any legend, Noah's Ark generates additional myths and half-truths, sightings that may or may not have occurred and additional events whose strangeness rivals that of the legend that gave them birth. For instance, Rickard and Michell cite the strange tale of a monk who searched for the Ark during the time of St Gregory the Enlightener, who is said to have brought Christianity to Armenia in the fourth century. On several occasions, the monk attempted to climb Mount Ararat, but each time he fell into a deep sleep, and upon awakening found himself magically transported back to his monastery at Echmiadzin near the foot of the mountain.

It seemed that unearthly powers did not want anyone wandering around that sacred place. Yet he was told in a vision that he would be rewarded with a piece of its timbers. Although it is unclear how the monk actually secured the sacred relic, it was given pride of place in his monastery, and Rickard and Michell speculate that this may have been the object that Parrot was allowed to see in 1829.

Before the invention of powered flight, searching for the Ark was a risky, expensive and time-consuming business, yielding little more than intriguing but unverifiable testimony from brave explorers who ventured up the mountain. However, the number of searches during the twentieth century increased dramatically. This is no more than one might expect given the ease of photographing the terrain. Nevertheless, the search for the Ark in recent years has rapidly become entwined with another set of legends, half-truths and wide-ranging speculations which are collectively labelled 'conspiracy theories' and which have muddied the historical waters still further (as conspiracy theories tend to).

For instance, an article in the August 1975 issue of the American journal *Christian Herald* tells of an Armenian immigrant (who died in 1920) who claimed that he and his father were hired by 'three foreign atheists' in 1856 to guide an expedition to Mount Ararat. The foreigners' intention, apparently, was to disprove once and for all the Ark's existence. In fact, they found it. To preserve their cherished theories, they attempted to destroy the remains of the Ark, but the vessel was too vast to succumb to such an unthinkable act of archaeological vandalism and instead the foreigners made their guides swear never to tell anyone of what they had found.

This story was apparently confirmed by a report in an unnamed newspaper of the deathbed confession of a British scientist, who said that the expedition really did take place and resulted in the discovery of the Ark. Rickard and Michell wryly note that while several people claim to have seen the newspaper item, no one has managed to produce it.

In 1953, an American oil engineer named George Jefferson Greene was flying in a helicopter at about 100 feet above the summit of Ararat when he saw something strange amid the rocks and ice at the edge of a cliff. The shape was that of a half-buried ship. Greene took several photographs and later tried to raise backing for an expedition. He was unsuccessful, however, and in 1962 he was murdered in Guyana. His photographs of the 'Ark' vanished and have never been seen again.

Other intrepid investigators have been more successful, including the French industrialist Fernand Navarra, who managed to excavate several pieces of ancient timber from an unknown structure buried in ice on Ararat in 1955. Fourteen years later, he returned to the region with another expedition and discovered more timbers, which radio-carbon dating revealed to be approximately 6,000 years old.

Satellite photographs of the region have yielded further mysteries, including a vast boat-shaped feature located about 20 miles from Ararat at the foot of Mount Judi in the Akyayla range. Intriguingly, this location is named in the Koran as the place where the Ark finally came to rest.

Unfortunately, this feature has since been identified as a fossilised mudflow bearing a striking resemblance to the outline of an ocean-going vessel.

Californian filmmaker Robin Simmons has collated numerous reports and tales of the discovery of Noah's Ark. Over the years, he has built up a network of contacts, some of whom have quite startling stories to tell. There is Ed Davis, for instance, who claimed to have been taken up Mount Ararat by a local guide in 1943 and to have seen a 'huge rectangular, man-made structure, partly covered by ice and rock, lying on its side'. He said that a 100-foot stretch of the vessel was visible and that he could even see inside it through a ragged hole in the broken timbers.

According to Rickard and Michell:

> Over many years of collecting accounts and stories about the Ark on Ararat, Simmons is convinced that not all has been revealed and that the 'truth' is considerably stranger than imagined. Much of his research contains elements that would not be out of place in a typical crashed UFO scenario, complete with recovered bodies and suggestions of high-level conspiracy. For example, he was told by a 'protected' source that an espionage team, returning across Ararat in secret in 1974, fell into a structure they took to be an ancient Byzantine shrine. When it was realised what this might be, a classified report went 'all the way to the White House'.

Others have apparently seen and photographed this object, including a military pilot who flew over the area in 1960 and took several photographs. Still more have claimed to have seen secret shipments of artefacts from Turkey, including a sarcophagus containing a body. The one thing that remains certain is the uncertainty surrounding Ark folklore.

8

THE ULTIMATE ARTEFACT

The Ark of the Covenant

It is said to have been constructed by the artisan Bezalel, who fashioned it from acacia wood and covered it, inside and out, with pure gold. Its purpose: to hold the tablets on which God had inscribed the Ten Commandments. It is one of the most powerful icons of biblical history and has been the subject of many books and films, including the worldwide blockbuster *Raiders of the Lost Ark*. Did the Ark of the Covenant really exist? Does it still exist today? If so, where is it and, if it were to be discovered, what would be its implications for humanity?

If the biblical account is to be believed, the Ark of the Covenant was an astonishingly beautiful object. It was surmounted by a heavy lid of gold bearing two cherubim, or winged sphinxes, and four golden rings were attached to the sides, through which poles were inserted so that it could be carried upon the shoulders of its bearers. The Ark was said to be representative of the pact between God and the Israelites, from which it derived its name: the Ark of the Covenant.

As the fictional Indiana Jones discovered to his terror and astonishment, the Ark contained more than the stone tablets upon which were inscribed the Ten Commandments. The Bible describes it as the sign and the seal of God's presence on Earth, implying that it contains the fantastic power of His divine energy. The Israelites took it into battle with them and it appears that the Ark was the equivalent of a modern weapon of mass destruction in that their enemies were instantly annihilated by it.

On one occasion, when the Philistines captured it, the Ark smote them with a horrible plague and cancerous tumours erupted on their bodies. This has led some to speculate that it may have contained a source of radiation. Not surprisingly, the Philistines quickly decided to return the Ark to its rightful bearers.

In 955 BC, King Solomon placed it within a sanctuary known as the Holy of Holies within the first Temple, which was entered once a year only, on the Day of Atonement.

Strangely, following the account of the Temple's destruction by the Babylonians in 586 BC, the Ark of the Covenant disappears from history. If it had simply been removed for safekeeping, one might have expected it to be returned when construction of the second Temple had been completed. But this seems not to have happened: the Ark seems to have vanished into the night of history, leaving nothing but legends and speculation in its wake.

In some legends, it was stolen by Menelik, Solomon's son, and taken to northern Ethiopia. As the story goes, Menelik was born of Solomon and the Queen of Sheba, and the elders of Israel, consumed with jealousy, demanded that the youth return to his mother in Ethiopia. Before he left, he took the Ark from the Holy of Holies and carried it to his mother's homeland, where it remains to this day in a church in Axum. In other legends, it was removed from the Temple by the prophet Jeremiah, who hid it in a nearby cave in Mount Jebo in present-day Jordan. Yet another story has the Ark hidden to this day in a cave beneath the Temple Mount in Jerusalem, close to its original resting place in the Holy of Holies. Of course, the possibility remains that it was simply destroyed during the sacking of the Temple.

One of the most colourful characters to dedicate himself to the search for the Ark of the Covenant is an American Baptist minister called Vendyl Jones, who claims to be the real-life inspiration for Indiana Jones. In 1992, while director of the Institute for Judaic Christian Research in Texas, Jones explored the Qumran Caves, where the Dead Sea Scrolls were discovered in 1947.

Taking clues from the so-called Copper Scroll, which was discovered in 1952 and contained a list of the items contained in the second Temple before its destruction in AD 70 (and reputedly including the Ark of the Covenant), Jones and his team searched the Qumran Caves and discovered what they believed to be incense from the second Temple. However, before they could take their investigation any further, the Israeli Antiquities Authority suddenly and unaccountably halted their excavations and refused to extend their research permit.

British journalist Graham Hancock, who achieved worldwide fame in the 1990s with his bestselling books *The Sign and the Seal* and *Fingerprints of the Gods*, conducted his own search for the Ark, which led him to Axum. However, Hancock came to believe that the story of Menelik's theft of the Ark was incorrect and that it was actually taken to Elephantine in Egypt by priests who feared that it might be destroyed by the Judean King Manasseh. When the temple which held it was destroyed in 410 BC, it was rescued again and taken to Lake Tana in Ethiopia. From there it was taken north to Axum by King Ezana in AD 350. Here, a new home was built for the Ark, the Church of St Mary of Zion. And it is here that the Ark is said to reside today.

In *The Unexplained*, Karl Shuker asks the obvious question: 'So why is it supposed to be lost? How can there be any mystery surrounding the Ark if it can readily be viewed in its present resting place?'

The answer is that a replica of the Ark is paraded in public (covered by a heavy drapery) during the Christian festival known as Timkat, but the Ark itself is kept hidden within the 'qeddusa qeddusan', the equivalent of the Holy of Holies, and the only person allowed into its presence is a person known as the Guardian of the Ark. There are several other replicas of the Ark, housed in various temples in Ethiopia, but to look upon these is likewise forbidden.

Historians and other researchers have speculated for many years on just what the Ark might actually be. Some of the more outlandish theories suggest that it might be some kind of immensely powerful machine – an artefact from a mysterious, long-vanished civilisation. Certainly the qualities attributed to it would seem to hint at something along these lines. However, we will never know unless the Ark is discovered and examined; and, as Shuker says: 'Bearing in mind that nothing created even by today's standards of technology can duplicate its formidable array of talents, will we be able to control the powers that our studies of the Ark may unleash?'

9

SECRETS OF CHRISTIANITY

The Cathars, the Holy Bloodline and the Gnostic Gospels

The Last Night of Montségur

Like a great stone sentinel, its walls crumbling into ruins, the fortress of Montségur perches high upon the summit of Mount Pueg in the Pyrenees. The fortress takes its name from the tiny village nestling upon the mountain's flanks, while the name 'Pueg' means 'peak' and is derived from the Occitan language that was once spoken throughout the Languedoc. About one-third of the mountain is covered with trees and grass, while the remainder is exposed grey-white rock, mottled with sparse vegetation. From a distance, this gives Mount Pueg a curious appearance, as if countless tons of ash have fallen upon that part of its vast, knuckle-shaped form, partially obscuring the green patina beneath. The analogy with ash is deliberately chosen, for the area around the mountain is still known to this day as the Field of the Cremated . . .

According to legend, this fortress is where the Cathars made their last stand against the forces of the Royal Catholic French troops in 1244. When all was lost, and the siege finally swung in favour of the attackers, the Cathars calmly walked out of their great redoubt and into the bonfires that had been ignited on all sides by the besieging army, sacrificing their lives for the sake of their beliefs, and to maintain the great secret that had come into their possession.

As with most legends, however, this is not quite accurate. The fortress that now stands atop the 1,200-metre peak of Mount Pueg was constructed long after the Cathars were destroyed. The original castle was pulled down by the victorious Catholic army, so that no trace of it remained; its replacement was gradually built over the next three centuries, a fact only grudgingly acknowledged by the French tourist board and largely ignored by a disparate group that believes the castle holds a mystical significance in the history of the region.

The latter consists of searchers for the Holy Grail, conspiracy theorists, maverick historians and amateur occultists, who wander the foothills of the mountain in the tireless hope of discovering some clue to the whereabouts of the Grail or the secret bloodline of Jesus Christ. They do the same in nearby Rennes-le-Château, another focal point of religious mystery in this legend-haunted region of southwestern France.

What is the attraction of Montségur, beyond the great beauty of the region, the mountain and the magnificent ruined fortress that stands upon its peak? To the people who live in the region, Montségur remains a stark reminder of the injustices and atrocities that were committed here in the thirteenth century by the Catholic Church; while others believe that the mountain holds clues to the fabled 'Cathar Treasure'. No one knows exactly what this treasure was (or is), but some researchers have speculated that it is intimately connected to the Catholic desire to exterminate the Cathars, to wipe them for ever from the face of the Earth.

For all intents and purposes, this desire was fulfilled by the mid-thirteenth century in what is known as the Albigensian Crusade, the first crusade conducted by Rome against fellow Christians on European soil. It took its name from the town of Albi, site of an ecclesiastical council in 1165, at which the Cathar heresy had been condemned. (Since Albi was a focal point for much Cathar activity, the heretics came to be known as 'Albigenses'.)

Many villages and towns in the Languedoc fell to the Crusaders, numbering about 30,000 knights and soldiers. The rules were the same as those covering other crusades: in return for their military service, the participants were absolved of their sins and were assured a place in Heaven; they were also allowed to loot and plunder as much as they pleased.

One of the most infamous episodes of the Albigensian Crusade was the siege of Béziers and its aftermath. The besieging army, commanded by the Papal Legate Arnold Amaury, had demanded that the townspeople hand over the 222 Cathars who were known to be living there. When the people refused, the Crusaders stormed Béziers and slaughtered more than 10,000 of its inhabitants. It is said that when one of his officers asked Amaury how the Crusaders should differentiate between the Cathars and the innocent townspeople, he replied (perhaps apocryphally): 'Kill them all. God will recognise his own.'

Following the fall of Béziers, the Crusaders swept like a fetid wind through the rest of Languedoc, taking all the larger towns such as Carcassonne, Narbonne and Perpignan. Thousands more were slaughtered, and the Cathars who managed to survive were driven from their homes and into hiding.

It is easy to understand the reason for the Church's hatred and fear of Catharism, although its antipathy had as much to do with politics and finance as with religious doctrine. In the early thirteenth century, Languedoc was not part of France: it was an independent principality with its own ideas on art, culture and religion. It was ruled by several noble families who deeply resented the tithes they were required to pay to Rome. In addition, they profoundly disliked the corruption that was so evident in the Catholic Church, as did the region's general populace.

For its part, the Church regarded the Languedoc as a place of heresy and evil, where philosophies and doctrines other than those of Christianity were openly explored and appreciated, where Greek and Arabic were studied and an atmosphere of enlightened religious tolerance prevailed. The region was wealthy and its people happy; they displayed no obvious need for the guidance of the Church and its priests and bishops, whom they regarded as corrupt and lazy buffoons who could offer little in the way of guidance towards spiritual salvation.

But it was against the Cathars that the Roman Church directed its most vehement fulminations. Although there were many variations amongst the numerous, loosely knit Cathar sects, their unifying philosophy was that of 'dualism'. While Christianity taught that there was one supreme God, whose adversary, the Devil, was inferior and would ultimately be defeated, the Cathars believed that the opposing principles of Good and Evil were exactly (or very closely) matched. They equated the concept of power (which to them was opposed to the principle of love) with that of matter; thus, the Universe, being composed of matter, was inherently evil and had been created not by the true God of love but by his evil counterpart, sometimes known as the 'demiurge'.

The Cathars also believed in reincarnation, in a long cycle of rebirth into the trap of sinful matter, and that only those who achieved enlightenment would be able to escape and to join the true God. Their sacrament, known as the 'Consolamentum' was only administered to a person on his or her deathbed, since continued existence presented the risk of experiencing impure thoughts, thus condemning the person to rebirth in the evil world of matter. For them, true enlightenment was, to put it simply, a matter between a created being and the God who had created that being; it was not necessary – indeed it was counterproductive – for priests to intervene in the relationship. In this belief, the Cathars were following the doctrine of 'gnosis', or the direct and personal knowledge of the true God.

To make matters worse (in the eyes of the Church), the Cathars understood the value of the feminine principle, and many of the priests and teachers (known as parfaits, or 'perfected ones') were women. The Cathars did not value marriage or procreation, since this resulted in the birth of children, in the bringing of more souls into the evil material world, condemning them to the cycle of reincarnation. For this reason, they practised contraception – further anathema to the Church.

To Rome, however, perhaps the greatest heresy of the Cathars was their beliefs regarding Jesus Christ, whose divine nature they could not reconcile with the concept of matter as inherently evil. The Son of the true God (the God of love and spirit) could not, they believed, have been incarnated in sinful flesh; thus, Christ was not a physical being but a nonmaterial phantasm. That is not to say there was anything 'unreal' about him: he was, rather, a spiritual essence with the outward appearance of a physical being. Of course, such a being could not be crucified, and many of the Cathars regarded the Crucifixion as irrelevant to Christianity, while others regarded him as an entirely mortal prophet.

In spite of the Cathars' simple and devoted life, which initially impressed even those who were sent to preach against their 'heresies' (in 1145, St Bernard had declared that no sermons were more Christian than those of the Cathars), the Church would not tolerate their continued existence. All that was needed for an all-out assault was a single catalyst, which occurred in January 1208, when a Papal Legate named Pierre de Castelnau was murdered in Languedoc.

Although there was no evidence that the crime had been committed by a Cathar, Pope Innocent III immediately ordered a Crusade and the fate of the Cathars was sealed. Aided by Simon de Montfort and Dominic Guzmán (the latter created the Dominican Order in 1216, which in turn created the Holy Inquisition 17 years later), the Albigensian Crusade destroyed virtually all opposition to the Roman Church and its doctrines in Languedoc. The Cathars were driven into hiding in several remote and well-defended locations, including the mountain citadel of Montségur.

When the besiegers, numbering more than 10,000, arrived at the foot of Mount Pueg, the castle was occupied by about 400 Cathar men, women and children. Two hundred of them were parfaits, or 'perfected ones'. The terrain made a straightforward storming of the castle impossible, so the siege dragged on for months. Some members of the besieging army from the Languedoc were sympathetic to the Cathars and, as a result, supplies were occasionally smuggled through the lines and up the mountain.

It was clear, however, that the 400 inhabitants of the castle could not all be evacuated without alerting the Catholic forces and, on 1 March 1244, the Cathars capitulated. In view of their heretical status, they were granted very lenient terms: the knights were informed that they would be allowed to depart with their arms and other possessions, and would receive a full pardon, while the Perfects would be allowed to go free with the penalty only of light penances, provided that they renounced their beliefs.

The Cathars replied to these terms by asking for two weeks in which to consider. The besiegers agreed. However, if they were expecting further capitulation, they were to be disappointed. During that two-week period, far from preparing to renounce their beliefs, the Cathars prepared themselves to go to their deaths.

It is at this point in their tragic tale that the Cathars did something that has perplexed historians for centuries. One night, under cover of darkness, a handful of Perfects left the castle and descended Mount Pueg using ropes, and carrying *something* with them. That 'something' has become known as the 'Cathar Treasure', and its nature is still unknown – and perhaps always will be – although some investigators have suggested what it might have been.

In their fascinating and highly controversial bestseller *The Holy Blood and the Holy Grail*, Michael Baigent, Richard Leigh and Henry Lincoln note that the Cathar Treasure could not have been anything as conventional as gold, silver and coin. While it is true that the Cathars possessed a great deal of wealth, it had already been smuggled out during the long weeks of the siege. In which case, what else was there that needed to be kept from the hands of the besiegers and their Catholic masters?

Baigent, Leigh and Lincoln write:

> Were the *parfaits* so committed to their beliefs that they willingly chose martyrdom instead of conversion? Or was there something they could not – or dared not – confess to the Inquisition? Whatever the answer, not one of the *parfaits*, as far as is known, accepted the besiegers' terms. On the contrary, all of them chose martyrdom. Moreover, at least twenty of the other occupants of the fortress, six women and some fifteen fighting men, voluntarily received the Consolamentum and became *parfaits* as well, thus committing themselves to certain death.

On 15 March, the two-week period of reflection granted to the Cathars expired, and they threw open the gates of their castle. They were taken to the foot of the mountain, where the pyres awaited them, and one of the most dreadful atrocities of the Middle Ages took place.

Are the writers of *The Holy Blood and the Holy Grail* (not to mention many other writers before and since) on the right track when they suggest that the Cathars possessed something that they could not, under any circumstances, allow to fall into the hands of their enemies? If it was not traditional treasure, then might it have been something altogether more valuable – a secret, perhaps? Historians of the Cathars maintain that we have absolutely no knowledge of what was smuggled out of Montségur on the night before the castle fell, while others (less orthodox and more speculative in their approach) point to various clues that suggest a possible identity for the fabled Cathar Treasure.

Many people assume that the story of the Holy Grail is as old as that of Christianity, and that it was the cup from which Christ was said to have drunk during the Last Supper, used to catch his blood during the Crucifixion and revered by his followers from the moment of his death. However, the Grail first appears in history centuries later in the writings of Chrétien de Troyes, who penned the *Conte del Graal* around 1180. In this, the *first* 'Grail romance', the knights of King Arthur embark on a quest to discover the cup of the Last Supper. Unfortunately, Chrétien died before he could finish his story, which was taken up and developed by other writers in the twelfth century, the most famous of whom is Wolfram von Eschenbach.

Although von Eschenbach is best known for his great Grail romance *Parzival*, he also wrote about the Grail in *Der Junge Titurel*, in which he states that the castle holding the Grail is in the Pyrenees. The lord of this castle, he wrote, was called 'Perilla'. Intriguingly, not only is Montségur in the Pyrenees but its lord, Raymond Pereille, signed his name in Latin, Perilla. Although some writers have (rightly or wrongly) pointed to this curious coincidence as evidence that the Holy Grail was kept at Montségur, and was in fact the Cathar Treasure, more cautious historians are not so sure. As Sean Martin writes in his book *The Cathars*:

> Such a strange coincidence does not, of course, mean that Wolfram knew something that later writers did not, but his account complicates any attempt to repudiate the Grail/Cathar myth entirely. It at least suggests that the Grail myth has been a part of the Cathar story since the time of the Good Christians, and is not just the invention of later writers.

In *Parzival*, von Eschenbach describes the Grail as a sacred stone (perhaps the Philosopher's Stone of alchemy), but other interpretations have been put forward over the years. One, in particular, has received worldwide attention thanks to the extraordinary success of a novel by a certain Mr Dan Brown . . .

The Holy Bloodline

While Dan Brown is the first to admit that the central ideas expressed in his mega-selling thriller *The Da Vinci Code* are not original, his novel has now sold upwards of 30 million copies and has been translated into more than 40 languages. Although the historical/religious mystery thriller subgenre already existed before Brown exploded onto the literary stage, *The Da Vinci Code* (and its predecessor *Angels and Demons*) has vastly increased the popularity of such books.

Whatever the book's technical literary merits, there is no denying that Dan Brown is a hugely gifted storyteller. But recently, Brown has had his own rather more mundane adventures in court, answering (successfully) various charges of plagiarism that have been brought against him by several writers, both of fiction and non-fiction. The most high profile of these cases was the charge of plagiarism brought against him by the writers of *The Holy Blood and the Holy Grail*, who claimed that Brown had stolen their ideas. Ultimately, Brown won the case.

The Da Vinci Code has also drawn intense criticism in other areas (besides those literary critics who are offended by its clunky dialogue and warped syntax). Various Christian groups have accused Brown of peddling historical inaccuracies at best, and outright blasphemy at worst, and some historians have been particularly offended by Brown's claim at the beginning of the book that: 'All descriptions of artwork, architecture, documents and secret rituals in this novel are accurate.' Like bulls who have spotted a red rag, many writers have seen this assertion as a challenge and have examined *The Da Vinci Code* in microscopic detail, pointing out the many inaccuracies in the novel.

Why has *The Da Vinci Code* caused such a worldwide furore? In short, the novel's controversial thesis is that Jesus and Mary Magdalene were married and that, far from being the prostitute so many believe her to have been, the Magdalene was actually Jesus's 'number two', his equal and counterpart, and the embodiment of the 'Sacred Feminine', whom he intended to continue his ministry after his death.

In addition, the book's supposition is that Mary Magdalene was pregnant with Jesus's child when he was crucified. Afterwards, Mary fled to France and their daughter, named Sarah, later married into the Merovingian line of French kings. The staggering implication of this is that there may be descendants of Jesus Christ alive today. To the general reading public who were unaware of the many other books that had already presented this thesis, *The Da Vinci Code* completely upturned their world view, presenting a new and totally unsuspected version of Western history.

Accordingly, the Holy Grail, so long thought to be the cup from which Jesus drank at the Last Supper and which was used to catch his blood during the Crucifixion, was, according to this theory, Mary Magdalene herself, the vessel which carried the seed of Jesus Christ and by which his holy line was continued.

In order to protect the descendants of Jesus and Mary, a secret organisation was created called the Priory of Sion, which in 1118 founded the Knights Templar, the order of warrior monks who themselves have been the subject of fevered speculation over many years. It may even have been subsumed by its offspring. Following the annihilation of the Templars by the forces of Philip IV of France in the early fourteenth century, the Priory of Sion continued in its sacred mission alone. Its list of Grand Masters included some of the greatest men in European history, such as Robert Flood, Isaac Newton, Claude Debussy, Victor Hugo, Jean Cocteau and Leonardo da Vinci. The Priory's duty was (and is) to watch over Jesus and Mary Magdalene's descendants, in preparation for the time when their existence will be revealed and they will reclaim the throne of France – and perhaps ascend to the rule of the entire world.

For Dan Brown's purposes, the most significant Grand Master

of the Priory of Sion is Leonardo da Vinci, whose great fresco *The Last Supper* forms the thematic centrepiece of *The Da Vinci Code*. (Incidentally, art historians intensely dislike the shortening of the artist's name to 'da Vinci'; his full name was Leonardo di Ser Piero da Vinci, which, if necessary, should be shortened to 'Leonardo'.) The fresco has been presented as evidence (specifically in Lynn Picknett and Clive Prince's book *The Templar Revelation*, another important source for Brown) that Leonardo was vehemently anti-Catholic and constantly hinted at the Priory of Sion's secrets in his work.

In one of the key scenes in *The Da Vinci Code* one of the novel's central characters, Grail historian Sir Leigh Teabing, explains the symbolism in *The Last Supper* to the two main protagonists, Robert Langdon and Sophie Neveau. The person sitting to Jesus's right, Teabing says, is not John (as is generally assumed) but Mary Magdalene, and the two figures are leaning away from each other, the space between them forming a 'V'. Teabing adds that this symbol represents the chalice or female womb, and that the opposite, 'Λ', represents the sword, or manhood. To the right of 'Mary Magdalene' sits Peter, who is making an aggressive gesture towards her with his left hand, as if to strike at her throat. This is because Peter was jealous of Jesus's love for Mary.

Art historians take a different view of the fresco's composition, however. While the figure sitting to Jesus's right is undoubtedly feminine looking, this is nothing unusual in Renaissance painting – and indeed Leonardo was very fond of painting beautiful, androgynous young men. In response to the suggestion that Peter is making as if to strike at the Magdalene/John figure, orthodox historians remind us that the moment depicted in the fresco is when Jesus has told his Disciples that one of them will soon betray him. Thus Peter is demanding to know the name of the betrayer, so that he can prevent him from doing so.

Was Leonardo in the habit of making coded references to the Priory of Sion and the holy bloodline of Jesus and Mary Magdalene?

If the Priory's mission was to maintain the secret, for fear that the Catholic Church would seek out and destroy the holy descendants, would it make sense for its Grand Master to leave clues that might be picked up by anyone with an eye for detail?

As for the Priory of Sion itself, it is not, as many fringe writers have maintained, an ancient secret society – far from it. And the only Grand Master it ever had was a man named Pierre Plantard (1920–2000), who invented it in 1956. It seems that Plantard was something of a fantasist with delusions of kingship, who claimed to have been elected as Grand Master of the Priory in 1981 and to be descended from the Merovingian King Dagobert II. He was the chief source of information for Baigent, Leigh and Lincoln when they were researching *The Holy Blood and the Holy Grail*, and many believe that it was Plantard who fabricated the now-famous *Dossiers Secrets*, documents deposited in the Bibliothèque Nationale in the 1950s and 1960s that include a list of the illustrious Grand Masters of the Priory.

Writing in the *Fortean Times*, issue 193, researcher Gordon Rutter notes that, in 1989, Plantard claimed a different set of origins for the group, dating from 1681, directly linking it to the Rennes-le-Château story. Plantard was still descended from Dagobert II, but only indirectly. This relaunched Priory also had a different list of Grand Masters, one of whom was Roger Patrice Pelat. This was to prove somewhat unfortunate, as Pelat was soon to be investigated for fraud, with Plantard called in to testify. He admitted, under oath, that the Priory was a complete tissue of lies. A severe reprimand followed, and Plantard never returned to the stories of the Priory again.

If the Priory of Sion is dismissed as an elaborate hoax, what of the claims regarding the intimate relationship between Jesus Christ and Mary Magdalene? Is there any evidence for this?

In December 1945, a young Arab peasant named Muhammad Ali al-Samman was digging for *sabakh*, a soft soil used for fertilising crops, near the town of Nag Hammadi in Upper Egypt, when he inadvertently made one of the most astonishing and significant archaeological discoveries of the twentieth century. Inside a buried earthenware jar he found 13 leather-bound papyrus books, containing what have come to be known as the Gnostic Gospels, or the Nag Hammadi library. These ancient texts contain information that differs radically from the accepted teachings of Christianity, including the claim that Jesus had a physical relationship with Mary Magdalene.

In her book *The Gnostic Gospels*, Princeton University professor of religion Elaine Pagels writes:

> About the dating of the manuscripts themselves there is little debate. Examination of the datable papyrus used to thicken the leather bindings, and of the Coptic script, place them c.AD 350–400. But scholars sharply disagree about the dating of the original texts. Some of them can hardly be later than c.AD 120–150, since Irenaeus, the Orthodox Bishop of Lyons, writing c.180, declares that heretics 'boast that they possess more gospels than there really are,' and complains that in his time such writings already have won wide circulation – from Gaul through Rome, Greece and Asia Minor.

One of these texts, the 'Gospel of Mary', describes the dialogue between the risen Jesus Christ and his Disciples, and also tells of a revelation given to Mary Magdalene by the Saviour. Unfortunately, four pages of the text are missing, so the major part of the revelation is lost, probably for ever; only the beginning and ending are extant.

When Mary tells the other Disciples what Christ has said to her, Peter asks if the Saviour really spoke with a woman without their knowledge. 'Are we to turn about and all listen to her?' he asks. 'Did he prefer her to us?'

Mary begins to weep, and says that she would not have made up such a lie, whereupon Levi says to Peter: 'I see you contending against the woman like the adversaries. But if the Saviour made her worthy, who are you indeed to reject her? Surely the Saviour knows her very well. That is why he loved her more than us.'

The idea that Mary Magdalene was considered 'worthy' by the Saviour is plausible, as is the assertion that the early Church Fathers tainted her memory with charges of prostitution in order to minimise her contribution to the earliest phases of Christianity. However, the idea that she was pregnant with Jesus's child at the time of the Crucifixion, that she escaped to what is now France, and that her daughter later married into the line of Merovingian kings (even though this line ended with the assassination of Dagobert II and was replaced with the Carolingian dynasty of Pepin the Short in AD 751) is elaborate speculation – if not outright invention.

The Mystery of Rosslyn Chapel

No examination of Grail legends would be complete without a (necessarily brief) look at Rosslyn Chapel, the exquisite fifteenth-century church in the village of Roslin, seven miles from Edinburgh. The chapel is famous not only for its astonishing carvings but in recent years has become inextricably linked to legends and speculations on the Knights Templar, the Holy Grail and the Freemasons.

The chapel was founded by Sir William St Clair, a Scottish nobleman and hereditary Grand Master of the Scottish Masons whose family, according to legend, was linked to the Knights Templar. Like the Cathars, the Templars are believed to have possessed the Holy Grail; indeed, it is said by some that the Templars discovered the Holy Grail during their time in Jerusalem in the twelfth century and later vouchsafed it to the Cathars.

The chapel's foundation stone was laid on St Matthew's Day, 21 September 1446. Sir William had intended the construction of a much larger church, and in fact Rosslyn Chapel merely forms the choir of the planned building; however, construction work ceased following his death in 1484.

While the chapel is impressive from the outside, it is only when one enters that the true majesty and mystery of the place becomes evident. The arched ceiling is festooned with small squares containing various motifs, including five-pointed stars and flowers; and there are numerous fleurs-de-lis scattered around the interior (those familiar with *The Da Vinci Code* will recall that this design is associated with the Virgin Mary as well as with royalty).

Some have described Rosslyn Chapel as 'the Bible writ in stone', since it contains depictions of so many biblical episodes, including Samson destroying the Philistines, Abraham regarding his son, and the Crucifixion. It has been claimed that the layout of Rosslyn is identical to that of the Temple of Solomon, although orthodox historians maintain that it is actually based upon the desert encampment of the Twelve Tribes of Israel.

One of the most striking features of the chapel's interior is the legendary Apprentice Pillar, with its beautifully carved vines that spiral up its length, issuing from the mouths of the eight dragons curled around the base. The Apprentice Pillar appears to have been inspired partly by the Norse legend of Yggdrasil, the great tree around which the Universe revolves, and at whose roots a great dragon incessantly gnaws. The pillar is named after the stonemason's apprentice who carved it while his master was away in Italy. So enraged was the stonemason when he returned to find that the job had been completed without him that he struck his apprentice on the head and killed him.

The huge number of coded symbols, drawn from many diverse religions and mythologies including Celtic, Norse, Judaic, Masonic and Christian, has resulted in Rosslyn being seen as a kind of 'Holy Grail' by countless maverick historians, occultists and conspiracy theorists (indeed, it has been nicknamed the 'Cathedral of Codes').

According to Dan Burstein, who edited what is perhaps the best of the many investigative and explanatory books that have been published in the wake of *The Da Vinci Code*:

Technology may, in the end, solve many of the chapel's mysteries. In January 2003, the grand herald of the local branch of the Scottish Knights Templar – the self-proclaimed successors to the warrior monks who fled to Scotland in the fourteenth century to avoid religious persecution – announced that the Knights were using new scanning technology 'capable of taking readings from the ground up to a mile deep'. They hope to discover ancient vaults beneath the chapel that contain the reputed Rosslyn treasure.

Whatever the true nature of the Holy Grail, and regardless of any further clues that may be discovered in the vaults of Rosslyn Chapel, Dan Brown's novel has certainly achieved what the author intended: to 'serve as a catalyst and a springboard for people to discuss the important topics of faith, religion, and history'. For better or worse, Brown has become, in fiction terms at least, the pre-eminent explorer of these questions.

10

DARK VIRGIN

The Mystery of the Black Madonnas

That more than 500 of the world's images of the Virgin Mary are either black or dark brown in colour is a little-known fact. Are they representations of ancient and powerful goddesses of sexuality and Earth-wisdom, the long-hidden alternative aspect of the Madonna's maidenhood? Do they personify the Holy Grail, the Ark of the Covenant or perhaps the ancient truth of feminine power and wisdom? Some historians speculate that the existence of the Black Madonnas points to the cult of Mary Magdalene and the heretical Gnostic-Christian tradition, which was followed in the West by the Cathars. What is the true meaning of the Black Madonnas?

As researcher Michael Duricy says, 'there are black Madonnas and Black Madonnas', by which he means that a differentiation should be made between images of Mary that have been created by African and African-American artists to 'convey a critical message inasmuch as they highlight the universal and thus trans-racial significance of the Christ event (including Mary)', and those images of Mary that were created in Europe during the medieval period and which are far more difficult to explain.

Among the most famous Black Madonnas are Our Lady of Hermits at Einsiedeln, Switzerland; Our Lady of Guadalupe in Mexico; Our Lady of Montserrat in Spain; and Our Lady of Altötting, Germany. There are also famous shrines at Chartres, Loreto, Zaragoza and Rocamadour.

The three pioneers of research into the origin of the Black Madonnas were Marie Durand-Lefèbvre, author of *Etude sur l'origine des Vierges Noires* (1937), Emile Saillens, who wrote *Nos Vierges Noires, leurs origines* (1945) and Jacques Huynen, author of *L'Enigme des Vierges Noires* (1972). However, these three books concentrate for the most part on images in France, with only a handful examined from further afield. Serious study of the Black Madonnas in the twentieth century had to proceed without the help of the Catholic Church. In his book *The Cult of the Black Virgin*, Ean Begg describes how the researcher Leonard W. Moss saw a Black Madonna in a church in Lucera in southern Italy in 1944 and asked the priest why she was black. The less-than-helpful response was: 'My son, she is black because she is black.'

Understandably dissatisfied with this 'explanation', Moss set about examining approximately 100 such statues from all over the world. He presented his conclusions in late December 1952 at a meeting of the American Association for the Advancement of Science. Moss had divided his sample into three groups:

> Madonnas with dark-brown or black skin matching that of the indigenous population.

> Madonnas that have been turned black as a result of various physical processes, such as the accumulation of dirt over the years, or smoke from votive candles, or the deterioration of lead-based pigments.

> An additional mysterious category with no easy explanation attached.

As Duricy notes in his article 'Black Madonnas', the processes described in the second group have been overused (particularly by those wishing to play down the mystery of the Black Madonnas) as an explanation for the Madonnas' existence. (In fact, there were several priests and nuns in Moss's audience, all of whom walked out of his presentation in disgust, displaying what Begg calls the Church's 'genuine lack of interest in and ignorance of the subject'.) However, it does seem to be the likeliest explanation for some of the images, for example that of Our Lady of Hermits at Einsiedeln, Switzerland, the story of which will serve as an example of the miraculous occurrences said to have occurred in the presence of the Madonnas.

Our Lady of Hermits is a four-foot-tall wooden statue, carrying a naked Christ Child on her left arm and a bird in her left hand. She is dressed sumptuously in robes of strawberry and gold, and is sometimes described as 'the best-dressed Madonna in the world'. Her shrine at Einsiedeln is visited by pilgrims from across the globe.

Our Lady of the Hermit takes her name from a monk named St Meinrad, who lived a solitary life on the Etzel peak near the Lake of Zürich. In 861, he was clubbed to death and, according to legend, two ravens which he had befriended revealed the identities of his murderers, thus ensuring that they were brought to justice (the researcher Ean Begg suggests that there is some connection between this legend and the Germanic god Wotan, who had two ravens, Hugin and Munin, as companions).

St Meinrad's head is now kept in a golden casket beneath the feet of the Virgin in the black marble Chapel of Grace in the Abbey founded by St Eberhard in 934, and is used every year for blessings. It is said that when St Conrad, the Bishop of Constance, came to consecrate the Chapel in 948, he 'witnessed a miraculous light and heard the singing of angels as Jesus and the four Evangelists offered the sacrifice of the Mass before the statue of Our Lady brought by St Meinrad'. As Conrad was about to begin the consecration, a voice said in Latin: 'Cease, cease, brother, the chapel has been divinely consecrated.'

Over the centuries, there have been several fires in the Abbey, all of which the Madonna survived. In 1799, when Napoleon's forces invaded the region, they were believed to be under orders to capture the statue and take it to Paris. However, a duplicate was constructed and taken instead, while the original was spirited away over the mountains in secrecy to the town of Bludenz in Austria, where it was whitened. When the danger had passed, and the Madonna was returned to the abbey, the decision was immediately taken to restore the statue to her original condition.

There are several theories to account for the existence of the Black Madonnas, perhaps the most striking of which is that they symbolise the appropriation of the ancient earth-goddess of the pagans by Christianity. Just as ancient shrines were chosen by the early fathers of the Church as sites for their own churches and cathedrals, so the dark-skinned goddesses of the pagans (hugely important in terms of their power over the seasons and the fertility of the land) were combined with the image of Mary as the Mother of God. The researcher Stephen Benko notes that many ancient goddesses, including Artemis, Isis and Ceres, were pictured as black and he points to Ceres, the Roman goddess of agriculture, as being particularly important. He reminds us that the darker the soil, the more fertile it is and the more suited to agriculture.

Duricy asks if these images were appropriated and reused in Christian worship, emphasising his question with the following quotation from a letter containing instructions to priests written by Pope Gregory the Great in 601:

> It is said that the men of this nation are accustomed to sacrificing oxen. It is necessary that this custom be converted into a Christian rite. On the day of the dedication of the temples thus changed into churches, and similarly for the

festivals of the saints, whose relics will be placed there, you should allow them, as in the past, to build structures of foliage around these same churches. They shall bring to the churches their animals, and kill them, no longer as offerings to the devil, but for Christian banquets in name and honour of God, to whom after satiating themselves, they will give thanks. Only thus, by preserving for men some of the worldly joys, will you lead them thus more easily to relish the joys of the spirit.

Benko extends his own analogy between the Black Madonnas and the earth-mother concept by noting that Mary the Mother of Jesus parallels the Earth as the 'mother' of humanity. In other words, Christ came from the Virgin Mary just as Adam came from the virgin earth of Eden. Leonard Moss cites a similar pronouncement from St Augustine, who 'noted that the Virgin Mary represents the earth and that Jesus is of the earth born'. Duricy cites a similar example from the Maronite Liturgy:

The Lord reigns clothed in majesty. Alleluia.
I am the bread of life, said Our Lord.
From on high I came to earth so all might live in me.
Pure word without flesh I was sent from the Father.
Mary's womb received me like *good earth* a grain of wheat.
Behold, the priest bears me aloft to the altar.
Alleluia. Accept our offering. [Emphasis Duricy's.]

It seems likely, therefore, that for a solution to the mystery of the Black Madonnas, we can look to certain pre-Christian traditions which the early Church Fathers appropriated and adapted for their own purposes, thus giving continuity to a strand of human thought that has its origins in the deep and mysterious past.

11

HOLY WOUNDS

The Mystery of Stigmata

On 14 September 1224, St Francis of Assisi was kneeling in prayer on Monte Alvernia, contemplating the suffering of Jesus on the Cross and praying to God that he might be allowed to share in that suffering. Looking up into the sky, he watched the descent of a winged seraph with the face of the Saviour. Following a long conversation with St Francis, the vision faded and St Francis saw that his hands, feet and side were bleeding – the wounds corresponding to those suffered by Jesus during the Crucifixion. St Francis was thought to be the first person to suffer the phenomenon of stigmata, but since that September day in 1224 many hundreds of others have experienced bleeding wounds on the hands, feet, head and side. No one knows what causes stigmata. The debate as to whether it is truly a miracle from Heaven or a state of mind continues.

In most cases of stigmata, the sufferer exhibits wounds on the hands and feet, mirroring those inflicted by the nails driven into the hands and feet of Christ on the Cross, and a gash in the side, corresponding to that inflicted upon the Saviour. Some, however, also experience bleeding from the forehead, as if an invisible crown of thorns had been placed there, while others exhibit corded marks on the wrists and whip marks on the back. A few also experience what is known as a stigmatic ring, a circular raised bump or an indentation around the ring finger of the left hand, symbolising, it is said, marriage to Christ. There have even been examples of painful swellings on the shoulder, just as Christ must have suffered when forced to carry the Cross to the Hill of Calvary.

Occasionally, nail-like protruberances develop in the wounds, as happened to St Francis, according to Thomas de Celano, who chronicled the event a mere four years after St Francis's death. According to Celano, they were not just the prints of nails but nails themselves that formed out of his flesh, 'retaining the blackness of iron'.

There are also cases (anecdotal, it must be said) of internal stigmatisation. For instance, Sister Maria Villani, a Dominican nun in seventeenth-century Naples, claimed that her heart was pierced by a flaming spear of love carried by an angel. When she died many years later, an autopsy was conducted on her body and, when her chest was opened, a stream of hot smoke apparently erupted from her heart. When the surgeon excised the organ, he found that it contained an old wound that looked like it had been made by a sharp implement. The same thing happened to St Teresa of Avila (1515–82), and her heart with its strange wound is now kept as a holy relic in Alba de Tormes, Spain.

The most famous stigmatic of recent years was the Capuchin monk Padre Pio (1887–1968). While praying on 20 September 1918, he experienced sudden stinging pains in his hands and soon developed the five stigmata in hands, feet and side. The wound on his side was so deep that doctors were afraid to measure it in case they damaged his internal organs while the wounds on his hands passed completely through the flesh. He was also credited with performing many miraculous cures and displayed both levitation and the phenomenon known as bilocation, or the ability to appear in two places at once.

Although it is widely accepted that Christ-like wounds are a genuine phenomenon, opinion is naturally divided on what the cause might be. Are they the psychosomatic results of intense and morbid brooding on the suffering of Christ?

There are certain cases on record that would seem to make this quite likely. In fact, if we return to the very first recorded instance of stigmatism, that of St Francis, we may note that his wounds appeared on Holy Cross day, during which he begged to share the suffering endured by Christ on the Cross. A stigmatic named Catherine Emmerich (1744–1824) exhibited a curious Y-shaped cross upon her chest, which closely resembled the unusual cross in the church at Coesfeld where she worshipped as a child. Gemma Galgani (1878–1903) displayed bleeding scourge marks which were identical to those depicted on a crucifix before which she prayed.

There is another intriguing facet to the mystery. Those suffering stigmatism display wounds in the palms of their hands, which correspond to visual depictions of Christ on the Cross. However, victims of crucifixion were nailed to crosses through their wrists, as the hands are not strong enough to support the weight of the body. If there were some supernatural connection between the stigmatic and the crucified Christ, one would expect the wounds to appear on the wrists rather than the palms. For this reason, it seems most likely that the important factor in these cases is the Christian iconography of the Crucifixion, rather than the event itself.

12

CHRIST'S BURIAL SHROUD?

The Mystery of the
Shroud of Turin

The Shroud of Turin is one of the most sacred relics of Catholicism. Authentic or otherwise, there is no doubt that it is an astonishing object. Measuring 14 feet three inches long by three feet seven inches wide, the sheet of linen bears the faint but unmistakable life-sized image of a man who bears the dreadful marks of crucifixion. For centuries Christians have wondered if this is the sindon – or burial shroud – of Jesus.

The Shroud's first confirmed appearance in history occurs in the mid-fourteenth century. Before then, there are only brief mentions of it, so it seems more a legend than a genuine historical artefact. It is said to have been seen in Jerusalem in AD 570, and again on the Scottish island of Iona a century later. Whether this really was the object we know as the Shroud of Turin is open to debate.

There is another legend of a cloth imprinted with the likeness of Jesus that dates from the sixth century. Known as the Mandylion, this artefact was said to have been placed over the Messiah's face immediately after the Crucifixion. Other legends suggest that the image of Jesus's face appeared miraculously on a piece of cloth and cured the leprosy of King Abgarus of Edessa when he requested an image of the Messiah.

In 1353, the Shroud makes its first confirmed appearance in history. In that year, it was displayed by a man named Geoffrey de Charny at Lirey, France. It is most likely that Geoffrey was related to a Templar Knight bearing the same name, who was executed nearly 40 years earlier during the great purge of the Knights Templar ordered by Philip IV of France.

In the years since their founding in the early twelfth century with the intention of offering protection to pilgrims travelling in the Holy Land, the Knights Templar had become the most powerful military order in the known world, with vast estates across Europe and a colossal amount of wealth. They are credited with inventing the international banking system: travellers could deposit money with Templars at home and would be issued with a promissory note (worthless to any brigands they might encounter along the way) that they could then exchange for money at their destination.

At the height of their power, they were answerable to no one but the Pope himself. Ultimately their wealth and power proved to be their downfall. Short of money, and eyeing the Knights Templar with fear and jealousy, Philip IV arranged for a series of trumped-up charges of heresy to be brought against them, and by 1314 the order had been exterminated.

It is possible that the Shroud of Turin was taken from the Holy Land by the Knights Templar and passed down secretly to Geoffrey de Charny. In 1453, it was sold to the Duke of Savoy, and after narrowly escaping destruction in a fire in the chapel where it was housed, it was moved to Turin Cathedral in 1578.

Modern interest in the Shroud only began in 1898 after a man named Secundo Pia was allowed to photograph it. Until then, the image had been very faint, but when viewed in photographic negatives, it became extremely vivid. Seen as a crucified man with wounds in the wrists and feet, and across the forehead, a gash in his side and whip marks across the back, it caused astonishment around the world.

According to the British researcher Ian Wilson, the Turin Shroud and the Mandylion are one and the same. He suggests that the Mandylion only appeared to show the face of Christ because it was folded into three sections when showed to the faithful in Constantinople. Following its removal from that city during the Crusades, it was displayed unfolded by Geoffrey de Charny at Lirey.

The scientific advances of the twentieth century inevitably led to requests for a forensic examination of the Shroud, and in 1988 the Vatican gave permission for several small pieces to be examined by three independent laboratories in Oxford, Tucson and Zurich.

The samples were dated by the carbon-14 method and the February 1989 edition of *Nature* contained the results. It was depressing news for those who believed that the Shroud carried the image of Jesus Christ. The results from each team closely corresponded and concluded that the Shroud had been manufactured some time between 1260 and 1390, thus explaining why there was so little verifiable evidence for its existence before the thirteenth century.

Those who believe in the Shroud's authenticity (Sindologists, after the Italian word for shroud, *sindone*) did not accept this conclusion. They pointed out (not without justification) that the Shroud had been damaged by fire in 1532 and had been handled countless times over the centuries; surely this would have resulted in severe contamination and invalidated the carbon-14 dating process?

They added that the figure's wounds, its three-dimensional accuracy (implying that it had been wrapped around a real human body) and the correspondence of its measurements to Syrian cubits all point towards its being genuine. As for the image itself, some Sindologists suggest that it might have been caused by a burst of radiation emanating from Jesus's body at the moment of his Resurrection. Dr Thomas Phillips of Harvard University's High Energy Physics Laboratory even suggested that the carbon-14 dating process might have been invalidated by a sudden burst of neutrons from Jesus's body.

Some researchers, such as Lynn Picknett and Clive Prince, have made the intriguing suggestion that the image on the Shroud of Turin was the result of an early experiment in photography conducted by Leonardo da Vinci. However appealing the notion, it is extremely unlikely, not least because he was born nearly a century *after* the first mention of the Shroud at Lirey.

Although Leonardo was almost certainly not the pioneer photographer, those who claim a non-divine origin for the Shroud suggest that someone did indeed project the image of a man onto sensitised cloth with a camera obscura, producing the image we all recognise today.

The story of the Turin Shroud – and the controversy surrounding this most enigmatic of religious icons – is not finished, and perhaps never will be.

13

OASES OF LIGHT

The Legends of Shambhala and Agartha

In 1933, James Hilton published his classic adventure tale *Lost Horizon*. In this enchanting novel Hugh Conway, a British consul, is taken with three others to the mysterious lamasery of Shangri-La, hidden somewhere in the mountains of Tibet. There they discover an apparent paradise-on-Earth, a utopian society dedicated to the pursuit of knowledge and spiritual enlightenment. After escaping from this monastery of sage lamas (in the mistaken belief that 'escape' is what he desires), Conway realises his error and the novel ends ambiguously with two of his acquaintances wondering whether he ever managed to find his way back to Shangri-La.

Lost Horizon is the perfect antidote for anyone fatigued by the modern, material world. The novel seized the public imagination on its publication, and many have wondered ever since if there could really be such a place hidden somewhere in the magnificent, desolate fastnesses of the Himalayas.

The answer to that question may be 'Yes', for Hilton based his tale of Shangri-La on a place that is of enormous spiritual significance to the people of Tibet. That place is known as Shambhala.

The Land of the Immortals

The writer and scholar of Tibetan mysticism Andrew Tomas spent many years studying the myths and legends of the Far East and his book *Shambhala: Oasis of Light* is an eloquent argument in favour of the realm's existence. Tomas cites ancient Chinese writings that refer to Nu and Kua, the 'Asiatic prototypes of Adam and Eve', and their birthplace in the Kun Lun Mountains of Central Asia. It is something of a mystery why such a desolate, forbidding place should serve as China's Garden of Eden rather than more hospitable regions such as the Yangtse Valley or the province of Shantung, and Tomas speculates that the Gobi Desert may at one time have been an inland sea with accompanying fertile land. As we shall see, the Gobi is a prime candidate as a site for one of the ancient and unknown civilising cultures whose wisdom has been passed down through the ages.

The Kun Lun Mountains hold a very important place in Chinese mythology, since it is in this range that the Immortals are believed to live, ruled by Hsi Wang Mu, the Queen Mother of the West. Hsi Wang Mu, who is also called Kuan Yin, the goddess of mercy, is said to live in a nine-storey palace of jade. Surrounding this palace is a vast garden in which grows the Peach Tree of Immortality. The wisest and most virtuous of human beings are permitted to visit the garden and eat the fruit, which appears only once every 6,000 years.

The Immortals who aid Hsi Wang Mu in her attempts to guide humanity towards wisdom and compassion possess perfect, ageless bodies and are said to be able to travel anywhere in the Universe and live on planets orbiting other stars. As Tomas notes, whether the ancient Chinese believed that the Immortals could travel through space in their physical bodies or by projecting their minds, this is still a remarkable concept since it is based on an acceptance of extraterrestrial existence.

Ancient Chinese texts are replete with legends of people

trying to cross the Gobi Desert to the Kun Lun Mountains. The most famous is surely that of the great philosopher Lao Tzu (c. 6th century BC), author of the book of Taoist teaching *Tao Te Ching*, who is said to have made the journey towards the end of his life. The Vatican Archives also contain many reports by Catholic missionaries concerning deputations from the emperors of China to the spiritual beings living in the mountains. These beings possess bodies that are visible but which are not made of flesh and blood: they are the 'mind-born' gods whose bodies are composed of elementary atomic matter that allows them to live anywhere in the Universe, even at the centres of stars.

Similarly, the people of India believe in a place of wisdom and spiritual perfection: they call it Kalapa or Katapa, which is reputedly in Tibet. According to Indian tradition, the Gobi Desert is the floor of what was once a great sea containing an island called Sweta-Dvipa (White Island). The great Yogis who once dwelled there are believed to still exist in its valleys and mountains. This island has been identified by Orientalists with the Isle of Shambhala of Puranic literature, which is said to stand at the centre of a lake of nectar.

In the seventeenth century, two Jesuit missionaries, Stephen Cacella and John Cabral, recorded the existence of Chang Shambhala, as described to them by the lamas of Shigatse, where Cacella lived for 23 years until his death in 1650. (Chang Shambhala means Northern Shambhala, to differentiate the abode of the spiritual adepts from the town called Shambhala which lies north of Benares, India.) Nearly 200 years later, a Hungarian philologist named Csoma de Körös, who lived in a Buddhist monastery in Tibet for four years, claimed that Chang Shambhala lies between 45 degrees and 50 degrees north latitude, beyond the River Syr Daria.

Legends of a hidden spiritual centre, a sacred zone whose inhabitants secretly guide the evolution of life on Earth, are widespread in the ancient cultures of the East. The writer and researcher Victoria Le Page describes this wondrous realm thus:

[S]omewhere beyond Tibet, among the icy peaks and secluded valleys of Central Asia, there lies an inaccessible paradise, a place of universal wisdom and ineffable peace called Shambhala . . . It is inhabited by adepts from every race and culture who form an inner circle of humanity secretly guiding its evolution. In that place, so the legends say, sages have existed since the beginning of human history in a valley of supreme beatitude that is sheltered from the icy . . . winds and where the climate is always warm and temperate, the sun always shines, the gentle airs are always beneficent and nature flowers luxuriantly.

Only the purest of heart are allowed to find this place (others, less idealistically motivated, who search for it risk finding only an icy grave) where want, evil, violence and injustice do not exist. The inhabitants possess both supernatural powers and an advanced technology; their bodies are perfect, and they devote their time to the study of the arts and sciences. The concept of the hidden spiritual centre of the world is to be found in Hinduism, Buddhism, Taoism, shamanism and other ancient traditions. In the Bön religion of pre-Buddhist Tibet, Shambhala is also called 'Olmolungring' and 'Dejong'. In Tibetan Buddhism, the Shambhalic tradition is enshrined within the Kalachakra texts, which are said to have been taught to the King of Shambhala by the Buddha himself.

As might be expected with such a marvellous, legend-haunted place, there has been a great deal of speculation as to the exact whereabouts of Shambhala (other than de Körös's vague map coordinates). While some esotericists believe that Shambhala is a real place with a concrete, physical presence at a secret location on Earth, others prefer to see it as existing on a higher spiritual plane. Alternatively, Shambhala might be considered a state of mind, comparable to the terms in which some view the Holy Grail (see Chapter 9). As with the Grail, Shambhala may be a state within ourselves, in which we may gain an insight into the higher spirituality inherent in the Universe, as distinct from the mundane world of base matter in which we normally exist.

The Blue Flower

In *Shambhala: Oasis of Light*, Tomas cites a curious episode described by the Orientalist Alexandra David-Neel, which took place in the town of Jyekundo in a remote district of eastern Tibet. She met a bard who had the strange reputation of occasionally disappearing into a snow-capped mountain region where no villages existed, where one could easily starve or freeze. Inevitably he would return saying he had seen 'gods' in the mountains. So one day Madame David-Neel asked the bard to present a small gift to the Ruler of the Mountains, a bunch of Chinese paper flowers.

After his next trip into the mountains, the Tibetan gave to David-Neel a beautiful blue flower, telling her it was a gift from the Guardian of the Mountains. The flower blooms in southern Tibet in July, while the region into which the Tibetan had travelled was in the grip of ice and snow; the temperature was 20 degrees below zero. David-Neel wondered whether there might be hidden warm valleys in the region.

The Roerich Expedition

Our knowledge of the Shambhalic tradition in the West has come mainly from Orientalist scholars such as Helena Blavatsky, René Guénon, Louis Jacolliot, Saint-Yves d'Alveydre and, perhaps most notably, Nicholas Roerich.

Roerich (1874–1947) was a poet, artist, mystic and humanist, and perhaps the most famous and respected of the esotericists who brought news of the fabulous realm of Shambhala to Westerners.

Born in St Petersburg, he came from a distinguished family whose ability to trace its origins to the Vikings of the tenth century inspired an early interest in archaeology which was coupled with a lifelong fascination with art. In the words of K.P. Tampy, who wrote a monograph on Roerich in 1935, he became 'possessed of a burning desire to get at the beautiful and make use of it for his brethren'. After attending the St Petersburg Academy of Fine Art, Roerich went to Paris to continue his studies. In 1906, he won a prize for his design of a new church and was also rewarded with the position of Director of the Academy for the Encouragement of Fine Arts in Russia. However, the Russian Revolution occurred while he was on a visit to the United States, and he was unable to return to his homeland.

Roerich's profound interest in Buddhist mysticism led to his proposing an expedition in 1923 that would explore India, Mongolia and Tibet. The Roerich Expedition of 1923–6 was made across the Gobi Desert to the Altai Mountains. It was during this expedition that Roerich's party had a most unusual experience. In the summer of 1926, Roerich had set up camp with his son, Dr George Roerich, and several Mongolian guides in the Shara-gol Valley near the Humboldt Mountains between Mongolia and Tibet. Roerich had just built a white *stupa* (or shrine), dedicated to Shambhala. The shrine was consecrated in August, with the ceremony witnessed by a number of invited holy men.

Two days later, the party watched as a large black bird wheeled through the sky above them. This, however, was not what astonished them, for far beyond the black bird, high up in the cloudless sky, they clearly saw a golden spherical object moving at tremendous speed from the Altai Mountains to the north. Veering sharply to the southwest, the golden sphere disappeared rapidly beyond the Humboldt Mountains. As the Mongolian guides shouted to one another in the utmost excitement, one of the lamas turned to Roerich and informed him that the fabulous golden orb was the sign of Shambhala, meaning that the lords of that realm approved of his mission of exploration.

Later, Roerich was asked by another lama if there had been a perfume on the air. When Roerich replied that there had been, the lama told him that he was guarded by the King of Shambhala, Rigden Jye-Po, that the black bird was his enemy but that he was protected by a 'Radiant form of Matter'. The lama added that anyone who saw the radiant sphere should follow the direction in which it flew, for in that direction lay Shambhala.

The Legend of the Chintamani Stone

The exact purpose of this expedition (aside from exploration) was never made entirely clear by Roerich, but many writers on esoteric subjects have claimed that he was on a mission to return a certain sacred object to the King's Tower at the centre of Shambhala. According to Andrew Tomas, the sacred object was a fragment of something called Chintamani in Sanskrit, and Norbu Rinpoch in Tibetan. The Chintamani Stone is said to have been brought to Earth by an extraterrestrial, and the great mass of it lies in the Tower.

According to tradition, a chest fell from the sky in AD 331 during the reign of King Tho-tho-ri Nyan-tsan; the chest contained four sacred objects, one of which was the Chintamani Stone. Many years after the casket was discovered, five strangers visited King Tho-tho-ri Nyan-tsan to explain the use of the sacred objects. The Chintamani Stone is said to have come from one of the star systems in the constellation of Orion, probably Sirius. The main body of the stone is always kept in the King's Tower in Shambhala, although small pieces are sometimes transferred to other parts of the world during times of great change.

According to Tibetan lore, the stone is carried on the back of a winged horse, called Lung-ta. For centuries, tales have been told of how Tibetan kings and sages flew enormous distances on Lung-ta, which is believed to be a messenger of the gods with the power to fly anywhere in the Universe. Andrew Tomas wonders if this winged horse is an allegory of a spaceship. 'Fantasy?' he asks. 'Yet should a nuclear holocaust destroy our civilisation, would the descendants of survivors believe in future ages that rocks from the moon were brought to earth by American astronauts? Myths alone will preserve this knowledge.'

The fragment of Chintamani which Roerich was returning to the Tower had allegedly been in the possession of the League of Nations, of which Roerich was a highly respected member. It is described as being about the size of a person's little finger and shaped like a heart. It is shiny and grey in colour, bearing four unknown hieroglyphics. According to Roerich, clouds gather when the stone turns dark, and when it feels heavy, blood is shed. When fire shoots up from it, the world will be in upheaval, but when a star shines above it, peace and prosperity will come.

The Caves beneath the Himalayas

The idea of a mysterious subterranean realm is common throughout the world's religions and mythologies. In his book *Shambhala*, published in 1930, Roerich described his attempts to understand the origins of underworld legends 'to discover what memories were being cherished in the folk-memory'. In commenting on the ubiquity of subterranean legends, he notes that the more one examines them, the greater the conviction that they are all 'but chapters from the one story'. An examination of the folklores of 'Tibet, Mongolia, China, Turkestan, Kashmir, Persia, Altai, Siberia, the Ural, Caucasia, the Russian steppes, Lithuania, Poland, Hungary, Germany, France' will yield tales of dwellers beneath the Earth. In many places, local people can even guide the curious traveller to cave entrances in isolated places, which are said to lead to the hidden world of the subterraneans.

The Altai Mountains are believed to be the home of a race called the Chud. In *Shambhala* Roerich states that the name 'Chud' in Russian has the same origin as the word for 'wonder'. His guide through the Altai Mountains told him that the Chud were originally a powerful but peaceful tribe that flourished in the area in the distant past. However, they fell prey to bands of marauding warriors and could only survive by leaving their fertile valley and departing into the Earth to continue their civilisation in the subterranean realms.

Roerich's guide said that at certain times the Chud could be heard singing in their underground temples. Elsewhere in the Altai Mountains, on the way to Khotan, Roerich reports that the hoofs of his expedition's horses sounded hollow upon the ground, as though they were riding over immense caves. Other members of the caravan called to him: 'Do you hear what hollow subterranean passages we are crossing? Through these passages, people who are familiar with them can reach far-off countries.' The caravaneers continued: 'Long ago people lived there; now they have gone inside; they have found a subterranean passage to the subterranean kingdom. Only rarely do some of them appear again on earth. At our bazaar such people come with strange, very ancient money, but nobody could even remember a time when such money was in usage here.'

When Roerich asked if he, too, could see such people, his companions replied: 'Yes, if your thoughts are similarly high and in contact with these holy people, because only sinners are upon Earth and the pure and courageous people pass on to something more beautiful.'

In the region of Nijni Novgorod there is a legend of a subterranean city called Kerjenetz that sank into a lake. In Roerich's time, local people still held processions through the area, during which they would listen for the bells of the sunken civilisation.

Roerich's party went on to discover four more groups of menhirs and several tombs, taking the form of a square outlined by large stones. To the people of the Himalayas, those who built these monuments, although now departed, are not to be found anywhere on the Earth's surface: 'all which has disappeared, has departed underground'.

Dr Ferdinand Ossendowski (1876–1945), whom we shall meet again in a little while, was told by the lamas of Mongolia of fabulous civilisations existing before recorded history. To Ossendowski's astonishment, the lamas claimed that when the homelands of these civilisations in the Atlantic and Pacific were destroyed by natural cataclysms, some of their inhabitants survived in previously prepared subterranean shelters, illuminated by artificial light. Andrew Tomas speculates that the Celtic legend of 'the Lordly Ones in the hollow hills' is a folk memory of the survivors of the destruction of the Atlantic continent.

In India, legends tell of a race of beings called the Nagas. Serpent-like and extremely intelligent, the Nagas live in vast caverns illuminated by precious stones. Although reptilian, the Nagas have human faces and are incredibly beautiful. Able to fly, they intermarried with kings and queens from the surface world, although they remain shy of surface dwellers and keep well away from all but the most spiritually advanced. Their capital city is called Bhogawati and is said to be covered with rubies, emeralds and diamonds.

Tomas writes that many Hindus and Tibetans have entered the caves of the Nagas, which stretch for hundreds of miles inside the mountains.

The inhabitants of this region speak of large lotus flowers floating on the surface of the Manasarawar Lake in the western part of the Tsang Po Valley. Radiant figures have also been seen near this extremely cold freshwater lake.

The Realm of Agartha

According to Louis Pauwels and Jacques Bergier in their fascinating, hugely popular (but far from reliable) book *The Morning of the Magicians* (1960):

> Thirty or forty centuries ago in the region of Gobi there was a highly developed civilisation. As the result of a catastrophe, possibly of an atomic nature, Gobi was transformed into a desert, and the survivors emigrated, some going to the extreme North of Europe, and others towards the Caucasus.

The Scandinavian god Thor is supposed to have been one of
the heroes of this migration.

After the cataclysm that destroyed the Gobi civilisation, the
survivors migrated to a vast cavern system beneath the Himalayas,
where they split into two groups, one of which followed the path
of spirituality, enlightenment and meditation, while the other
followed the path of violence and materialistic power. The spiritual
centre was called Shambhala, and the materialistic society was
called Agartha.

Despite its inclusion in many popular books on Eastern mysticism,
the name 'Agartha' is unknown in Asiatic mythology. In fact, one
of the many variations on the name, 'Asgaard', was first used by
the French writer Ernest Renan in the 1870s. Although clearly
inspired by Nordic mythology, Renan placed his Asgaard in Central
Asia, while another French writer, Louis Jacolliot (1837–90), was
writing at the same time about a city of Asgartha. A magistrate in
Chandernagore, India, Jacolliot wrote a number of books on the
relationship between Indian mythology and Christianity. He was
allegedly told the legend of Asgartha by a group of local Brahmins,
who allowed him to consult various sacred texts, such as the *Book of
Historical Zodiacs*.

According to Jacolliot, Asgartha was a prehistoric 'City of the
Sun', home of the Brahmatma, the visible manifestation of God on
Earth. Asgartha existed in India in 13,300 BC, where the Brahmatma
lived in an immense palace; he was invisible and only appeared to
his subjects once a year. Interestingly, Jacolliot stated that this high
prehistoric culture existed long before the Aryans, who conquered
Asgartha around 10,000 BC. The priests of Asgartha then formed
an alliance with the victorious Aryan Brahmins, which resulted in
the formation of the warrior caste of Kshatriyas. About 5,000 years
later, Asgartha was destroyed by the brothers Ioda and Skandah, who
came from the Himalayas. Eventually driven out by the Brahmins,

the brothers travelled north – and later gave their names to 'Odin' and 'Scandinavia'.

Ferdinand Ossendowski was another early writer on the legend of Agartha. Although born in Vitebsk, Poland, he spent most of his early life in Russia, where he attended the University of St Petersburg. For much of the 1890s, he travelled extensively in Mongolia and Siberia, developing his interest in and knowledge of Buddhist mysticism. He went to France in 1900 and gained a doctorate in Paris in 1903, before returning to Russia and working as a chemist for the Russian Army during the Russo-Japanese War of 1905. He then became president of the 'Revolutionary Government of the Russian Far East', before being taken prisoner by the Russian government for his anti-Tsarist activities.

After two years' imprisonment in Siberia, he taught physics and chemistry in the Siberian town of Omsk until the Bolshevik Revolution forced him to flee Russia with a small group of White Russians. Together they travelled across Siberia and into Mongolia, and he wrote of their adventures in his bestselling book *Beasts, Men and Gods* (1923). While in Mongolia, Ossendowski made the acquaintance of a fellow Russian, a priest named Tushegoun Lama who claimed to be a friend of the Dalai Lama. Tushegoun Lama told Ossendowski of the subterranean kingdom of Agartha, home of the King of the World. Intrigued, Ossendowski asked his new friend for further information, to which Tushegoun replied:

> Only one man knows his holy name. Only one man living was ever in Agartha. That is I. This is the reason why the Most Holy Dalai Lama has honoured me and why the Living Buddha in Urga fears me. But in vain, for I shall never sit on the Holy Throne of the highest priest in Lhasa nor reach that which has come down from Jenghis Khan to the Head of our Yellow Faith. I am no monk. I am a warrior and an avenger.

Several months later, while continuing across Mongolia with some guides left behind by Tushegoun Lama (who had since gone his own way), Ossendowski was startled when his companions suddenly halted and dismounted from their camels, which immediately lay down. The Mongols began to pray, chanting: 'Om! Mani padme Hung!' Ossendowski waited until they had finished praying before asking them what was happening. One of the Mongol guides replied thus:

> Did you not see how our camels moved their ears in fear? How the herd of horses on the plain stood fixed in attention and how the herds of sheep and cattle lay crouched close to the ground? Did you notice that the birds did not fly, the marmots did not run and the dogs did not bark? The air trembled softly and bore from afar the music of a song which penetrated to the hearts of men, animals and birds alike. Earth and sky ceased breathing. The wind did not blow and the sun did not move. At such a moment the wolf that is stealing up on the sheep arrests his stealthy crawl; the frightened herd of antelopes suddenly checks its wild course; the knife of the shepherd cutting the sheep's throat falls from his hand; the rapacious ermine ceases to stalk the unsuspecting salga. All living beings in fear are involuntarily thrown into prayer and waiting for their fate. So it was just now. Thus it has always been whenever the 'King of the World' in his subterranean palace prays and searches out the destiny of all peoples on the Earth.

Later, Ossendowski met an old Tibetan, Prince Chultun Beyli, who was living in exile in Mongolia and who furnished him with more details of the subterranean realm of Agartha and the King of the World. Agartha, he said, extends throughout all the subterranean passageways of the world. The inhabitants owe allegiance to the King of the World. They can cultivate crops due to a strange light that pervades the underground realm. Some of the inhabitants of these regions are extremely strange: one race has two tongues, enabling them to speak in two languages at the same time. There are also many fantastic animals, including tortoises with sixteen feet and one eye.

At this point, Ossendowski was approaching the Chinese border. It was his intention to take a train to Peking, from which he might find passage to the West. In the town of Urga he met an old lama, who provided him with yet more information about the mysterious King of the World. The King's influence on the activities of the world leaders was profound. If their plans were pleasing before God, then the King of the World would help them to realise them; but if they displeased God, then the King would surely destroy them. His power came from the mysterious science of Om, which was the name of an ancient Holyman who lived more than 300,000 years ago and was the first man to know God.

When Ossendowski asked him if anyone had ever seen the King of the World, the old lama replied that during the solemn holidays of the ancient Buddhism of Siam and India the King appeared five times in a 'splendid car drawn by white elephants'. He wore a white robe and a red tiara with strings of diamonds that hid his face. When he blessed the people with a golden apple surmounted by the figure of a lamb, the 'blind received their sight, the dumb spoke, the deaf heard, the crippled freely moved and the dead arose, wherever the eyes of the King of the World rested'.

Ossendowski then asked the lama how many people had been to Agartha. He replied that very many had but they never spoke about what they had seen there. He continued that, when the Olets destroyed Lhasa, one of their detachments found its way into the outskirts of Agartha, where they learned some of the lesser mysterious sciences. This is the reason for the magical skills of the Olets and Kalmucks, better known as gypsies. Another of Ossendowski's informants, a lama named Turgut, told him that the capital of Agartha is surrounded by the towns of the high priests and scientists, somewhat in the way that the Potala Palace of the Dalai Lama in Lhasa is surrounded by monasteries and temples. The throne on which the King of the World sits is itself surrounded by millions of incarnated gods, the Holy Panditas. The King's palace is surrounded by the palaces of the Goro, who possess fantastic power and who would easily be able to incinerate the entire surface of the Earth, should humankind be unwise enough to declare war on them.

The legend of Agartha was discussed at length by another writer, the self-educated Christian Hermeticist Saint-Yves d'Alveydre (1842–1909), whose marriage into money enabled him to indulge his yearning for mystical understanding. In 1885, he began to take lessons in Sanskrit from one Haji Sharif (1838–?), about whom very little is known save that he left India at the time of the Sepoy Revolt of 1857 and worked as a bird-seller in Le Havre. The manuscripts of d'Alveydre's lessons are preserved in the library of the Sorbonne in Paris. In them, Sharif refers to the 'Great Agarthian School' and the 'Holy Land of Agarttha' (one of several alternative spellings of the name).

Unable physically to visit Agartha, d'Alveydre found an ingenious alternative: through disengaging his astral body, he was allegedly able to visit the fabulous realm in spirit form. His astral adventures resulted in a series of books (*Mission des Souverains, Mission des Ouvriers, Mission des Juifs* and *Mission de l'Inde*), which he published at his own expense. Interestingly, he destroyed the entire edition of his last work for fear that he had revealed too many secrets of Agartha and might be made to pay for his transgression with his life. Only two copies survived: one that he kept himself and one that was hidden by the printer.

He might well have been concerned, for *Mission de l'Inde* contains a detailed account of Agartha, lying beneath the surface of the Earth somewhere in the East and ruled over by an Ethiopian 'Sovereign Pontiff' called the Brahmatma. The realm of Agartha was transferred underground at the beginning of the Kali-Yuga, about 3200 BC. The Agarthians possessed technology that was impressive in d'Alveydre's day, including railways and air travel. They know everything about the surface dwellers and occasionally send emissaries. Agartha contains many libraries in which all the knowledge of Earth is recorded on stone tablets in 'Vattanian' (the original language of humanity), including the means by which the living may communicate with the souls of the dead.

D'Alveydre states that, although many millions of students have tried to possess the secrets of Agartha, very few have ever succeeded in getting further than the outer circles of the realm. The Agarthians are superior in every respect – the true rulers of the world.

Darkness over Tibet

The legends and rumours surrounding the realms of Shambhala and Agartha are somewhat confusing and contradictory. As we have seen, some writers claim that they are physical places: vast cities lying miles underground with houses, streets, palaces and millions of inhabitants. Others maintain that they are altogether more rarefied places, existing on some other level of reality but apparently coterminous with our physical world.

Adding to this confusion is the frequently made assertion that the two 'power centres' are opposed to each other, with Shambhala following the right-hand path of goodness and light and Agartha following the left-hand path of evil and darkness (a dichotomy which is also expressed as spirituality versus materialism). There is also an opposing view that Shambhala is a place of evil and Agartha an abode of goodness.

Writers on fringe subjects have written about practitioners of black magic operating in Tibet who refer to themselves as the Shambhala or the Agarthi. Although apparently outlawed by Tibetan Buddhists, they are said to continue their activities in secret. One writer who claimed to have encountered them was a German named Theodore

Illion, who spent the mid-1930s travelling through Tibet. In his book *Darkness Over Tibet* (1937), he describes how he discovered a deep shaft in the countryside. Wishing to gauge its depth, he dropped several stones into it and waited for them to strike the bottom; he was rewarded only with silence. He was told by an initiate that the shaft was 'immeasurably deep' and that only the highest initiates knew where it ended. His companion added: 'Anyone who would find out where it leads to and what it is used for would have to die.'

Illion claimed to have gained access to a subterranean city inhabited by monks, whom he later found to be 'black yogis' planning to control the world through telepathy and astral projection. When he discovered that the food he was being given contained human flesh, he decided to make a break for it and fled across Tibet with several of the monks in pursuit. After several weeks on the run, he managed to escape from Tibet and returned to the West with his bizarre and frightening tale.

The mythology surrounding Shambhala is an example of how a genuine body of esoteric belief can be taken up enthusiastically by Western occultists and can lead to the development of additional and even spurious legends. As to whether Shambhala really exists, somewhere on Earth or in another realm, no one can say for sure. Perhaps that place of gentle enlightenment is potentially accessible to everyone, if they search within themselves.

14

A Beacon for the Gods?

The Nazca Lines

They have been called the largest work of art in the world – and are easily the most difficult to appreciate. The desert of Nazca, Peru, contains an astonishing collection of lines, striations and pictorial images which are so vast that they are only visible in their entirety from high in the air.

Although pottery fragments found in the area date the creation of the so-called 'Nazca lines' to sometime between 300 BC and AD 540, they were not discovered in modern times until 1926, when two members of a team of archaeologists digging on the Nazca Plain climbed a hill and noticed that the landscape was covered with strange markings. This discovery was confirmed more than a decade later when pilots of the Peruvian Air Force flew over the region and took photographs of the enormous network of lines and images.

The first in-depth investigation of the Nazca lines was undertaken by Dr Kosok, an agronomist from Long Island University. Along with other later observers, Kosok noted that the lines were virtually invisible at ground level, unless one stood astride them and viewed them lengthways. Kosok also noted their means of construction: a simple process of removing the thin, topmost layer of dark stones to reveal the yellowish-white soil beneath.

The true mystery of the Nazca lines does not lie in the physical process of 'drawing' them (which is quite straightforward), but in the scale and complexity of the designs. Some of the lines are eight kilometres long, and their straightness does not deviate by more than two metres in every kilometre.

The foremost investigator and authority on the Nazca lines is the German mathematician and archaeologist Maria Reiche, who took over from Dr Kosok in 1946 and who has spent her entire life examining them. Reiche's work supports Kosok's suggestion that the lines were perhaps some form of celestial calendar, marking the appearance of certain constellations and pointing to the location of sunrise and sunset on the horizon at the two equinoxes.

There have been a number of other theories on the purpose of the Nazca lines, one of the most famous (and least likely) being that they constitute a landing field and runways for alien spacecraft that visited Earth in the remote past and which were drawn to what the 'ancient astronaut' theorists describe as the 'ideal terrain'.

This theory was quickly and easily disposed of by Maria Reiche, who pointed out that, far from being ideal, the ground on the Nazca Plain is far too soft to support a working landing field, adding: 'I'm afraid the spacemen would have gotten stuck.' In addition, we might also note that the United States National Aeronautics and Space Administration (NASA) is currently attempting to develop a reusable vertical take-off and landing space vehicle, an attempt which will undoubtedly succeed within a few years. Why, therefore, would an advanced spacefaring civilisation untold centuries or millennia in advance of ourselves, capable of crossing many light years to reach Earth, need runways for their spacecraft to land?

There are many more plausible theories as to why the Nazca people created their colossal designs. The lines may have been markers and pathways pointing to sources of water (which have been discovered at the terminal points of some of them). They could have been symbols of ownership, with lines and symbols belonging to illustrious families. One of the most intriguing theories is that the lines and animal figures represent a map of the spirit world, the rationale behind this theory being that in shamanistic societies, holy men are believed to have the ability to fly while in their trance states. They would thus be in the ideal position to view and interpret the Nazca lines and animal symbols.

Maria Reiche concluded from her investigations that the Nazca people created their complex system of designs by means of small initial drawings, which were then reproduced on a grand scale on the Nazca Plain with lengths of rope and stone markers. She added, however, that the massive undertaking would have been easier to accomplish, and the geometrical perfection of the designs would have been easier to achieve, if the Nazca people had been able to fly.

In 1975, an American resident in Peru, Bill Spohrer, took this idea and ran with it – or rather, flew with it. Spohrer had noted the discovery of several pieces of Nazcan fabric which, when examined, were revealed to have a tighter and finer weave than parachute material or modern hot-air balloons. In addition, pottery fragments showed what looked like airborne objects, perhaps kites or even balloons.

Spohrer began to wonder whether the Nazca people were much more advanced than archaeologists realised – advanced enough, perhaps, to have developed non-powered flight hundreds of years before the Montgolfier brothers began ballooning in the eighteenth century. He investigated the idea further and in the course of his researches came across a legend of a young boy named Antarqui, who helped the Incas during a war by flying above the enemy and reporting their positions.

There were also the so-called 'burn pits' at various locations on the Nazca Plain. These large circular areas of blackened ground, some as much as ten metres in diameter, had been seized upon by the proponents of the extraterrestrial visitation theory who claimed that they had been caused by rocket exhausts (once again, one wonders why interstellar spacecraft would use such a primitive form of propulsion). The curious thing was that tests proved that these areas had indeed been exposed to intense heat, and Spohrer wondered whether it was here that the air for long-vanished balloons had been heated.

Towards the end of 1975, Spohrer was finally in the position to put his unusual theory to the test. Having constructed a hot-air balloon and reed gondola, using only materials that would have been available to the ancient Nazca people, he climbed into the gondola, and his colleagues lit the fires beneath the Condor I.

The balloon lifted off successfully and rose several hundred feet into the dry air above the Nazca Plain. Spohrer had proved his theory valid . . . however, it remained – and remains – only a theory, with little independent evidence to support it.

Did the ancient Nazca people really develop flight so many centuries before the Europeans? Spohrer and his colleagues proved that it is possible. Perhaps we will never know the answer and will have to content ourselves with admiring the vast, strange and weirdly beautiful relics the Nazcans left behind.

15

A FEMALE POPE?

The Legend of 'John Anglicus'

The year was AD 857 and Pope John VIII was two years into his reign. Romans were gripped by fear, for it seemed the end of the world was nigh. Southern Italy was in the grip of violent earthquakes; the Eternal City was plagued with locusts that swarmed through the streets in thick black clouds. Charlemagne had been crowned Emperor 50 years earlier, and many believed that this would bring about the End of Days.

In panic and terror, the people turned to Pope John VIII for reassurance. In the two years since his election, he had become loved and trusted. As he headed a procession from St Peter's Basilica to his residence in the Lateran Palace across the River Tiber, the papal party entered a narrow alley between the Colosseum and the Church of St Clement. Suddenly, Pope John stumbled and collapsed to the ground.

As the onlookers gathered around him, concerned faces became twisted with shock and abject horror as their beloved pontiff was revealed to be a woman – and not just a woman, but one in labour. Before their stunned eyes, she gave birth then and there in the street. The crowd's emotions were instantly transformed from shock to uncontrollable rage. They seized the woman and her newborn child, dragged them through the city gates and stoned them to death.

This is the outline story told in the twelfth century and it was repeated, with certain variations, throughout the following centuries. But is it true?

The tale of the female pope was first mentioned by the Dominican chronicler Jean de Mailly, and was elaborated upon in the writings of Anastasius the Librarian, Marianus Scotus and Sigebert de Gemblours, among others. Initially, the pope impersonator was not named. She was said to have been a talented and intelligent woman who, dressed as a man, became notary to the Curia (the administrative departments which assist the pontiff in the government of the Church), then a cardinal, and finally pope. She went out on horseback one day and gave birth to a son. When witnesses saw this, they tied her to the tail of her horse, dragged her around the city and finally stoned her to death. She was buried at the place where she died, a place which later popes always avoided during their processions.

A second version of the story appears in the 'Chronicle of the Popes and Emperors' by the Polish Dominican Martin of Troppau, which tells of the birth of a daughter, Joan, to English missionaries in the city of Mainz. The child was famed for her beauty and intellect. At the age of 12 she fell in love with a monk and together they fled from the city. Wearing boys' clothing, Joan offered herself as a novice at an unnamed monastery in order to be with her lover.

It was not long before the deception was discovered and once again the couple had to flee, this time disguised as pilgrims on their way to the Holy Land. In Athens, Joan's lover disappears from the story; alone, she made her way to Rome where, still disguised as a young man, 'Johannes Anglicus', she became a teacher of science. Her fame grew rapidly and she was greatly admired for her eloquence and erudition, both by her students and by philosophers, cardinals and papal courtiers.

When Pope Leo IV died in 855, Joan was unanimously elected as his successor and became Pope John VIII. Her true identity would have remained a secret but for one fatal mistake. Joan was as lonely as she was passionate and eventually succumbed to temptation by taking her valet as a lover, by whom she became pregnant. Following her awful punishment at the hands of the outraged mob, a new Pope, Benedict III, was quickly installed. In an attempt to expunge the female pope from history, Church historians placed the date of his accession to 855; and when another John became pope 15 years later, he was given the name John VIII, not John IX.

The story of Pope Joan was accepted as fact for hundreds of years, with believers pointing to the statue of a woman and child, which was discovered in a street between the Colosseum and the Church of St Clement, as evidence. More bizarrely, there was also the curious marble chair in the Lateran Palace known as the *sella stercoraria*, which had a hole in the seat. It was alleged that between the eleventh and fifteenth centuries newly elected popes were required to sit on it so that an examination could be performed by physicians to ensure that they were really men. When this examination had been completed, a deacon would shout to the crowd '*Habet!*' ('He has!'), and the crowd would rejoice, shouting '*Deo gratias!*' ('Thanks be to God!')

Although the story was accepted as historical fact, especially by Protestant writers who used it to bolster their attacks on the papacy, historians gradually came to question its veracity. However, it was a Calvinist writer, David Blondel, who mounted the first serious attack on the legend in his 1647 treatise *Familiar Enlightenment of the Question: Whether a Woman Had Been Seated on the Papal Throne in Rome.*

In fact, not one contemporary papal history mentions Pope Joan; nor is there any mention of her anywhere until the thirteenth century. Martin of Troppau places her between Leo IV and Benedict III, but Leo IV died on 17 July 855, and Benedict III was elected immediately afterwards, although he was not consecrated until 29 September, thanks to the activities of the antipope, Cardinal Anastasius.

Nevertheless, there was no interregnum between Leo and Benedict and therefore no room for the alleged papess. It seems that the legend is no more than a legacy of the medieval papacy, a relic of a time when popes were known much more for their corruption and hedonism than for their piety. At that time, people were more than willing to believe them capable of any outrage or strangeness – including being women in disguise.

And what of the strange marble throne with a hole in the seat in the Lateran Palace? It was merely a commode from one of ancient Rome's communal baths. The statue of the woman and child was discovered during the reign of Pope Sixtus V (1585–90) and, like the marble chair, was a relic of ancient Rome, with no obvious links to Joan and child.

16

DOOM SKULL

The Mystery of the Crystal Skulls

In 1927, Anna Mitchell-Hedges went to British Honduras (now Belize) with her adoptive father, Frederick Albert 'Mike' Mitchell-Hedges, to explore the ruins of the Mayan civilisation. Mitchell-Hedges could easily have been another inspiration for Indiana Jones: he was a flamboyant explorer who was fascinated by the fabulous hidden history of humanity and believed that clues to that history could be found in the ruins of ancient civilisations such as the Maya – potential descendants of the survivors of Atlantis.

It was in the ruined city of Lubaantum, amidst age-weathered, fallen masonry and the green chaos of encroaching jungle, that Anna made an astonishing discovery. Mitchell-Hedges's party were busy excavating a ruined temple, when Anna, who turned 17 that day, saw something shining in the rubble beneath an altar. Carefully removing the lumps of stone, she saw that the object was a carving of the upper part of a human skull, fashioned from quartz crystal. This was no crude representation: it was frighteningly realistic and exquisitely carved, with prismatic eye sockets that seemed to gather the light, so that the entire skull glowed with an unearthly luminescence. Not long afterwards, the skull's lower jaw was discovered a few metres away and, when the two were put together, it was found that they matched perfectly.

In spite of the significance of this find, Mitchell-Hedges felt that its rightful owners were the local people who had helped his party in their explorations and excavations, so he presented it to them. However, when they were about to return to England later in the year, the guides repaid the kindness that Mitchell-Hedges had shown to them by returning the crystal skull to him. They apparently added the warning that it was known as the 'skull of doom', since it possessed magical powers and could be used to will death upon another. They also told Mitchell-Hedges to treat the skull with respect, for misfortune had befallen those who treated it lightly.

That, at least, is the story of the crystal skull's discovery, as told by Anna Mitchell-Hedges. As we shall see, there are grounds for treating those claims with considerable caution – if not outright disbelief.

There is no doubt that the skull is a truly astonishing and sinisterly beautiful artefact – although questions of who made it, how and why are still open to debate. Mitchell-Hedges himself thought that the skull was at least 3,600 years old; however, such a date would place it well before the agreed date of the rise of Mayan civilisation and very far beyond the period from AD 700 to 900 which covers their great 'classic' period. This discrepancy did not concern Mitchell-Hedges overly, since he believed that the Mayans were descendants of the inhabitants of Atlantis, who migrated to the Americas following the destruction of their civilisation.

The truth about the skull of doom has been pieced together gradually by various investigators, not least the sceptical writer Joe Nickell, who says that rock crystal is not found in the Mayan area and that the nearest area bearing this type of stone is in southern Mexico. As we have mentioned, 'Mike' Mitchell-Hedges was an eccentric and flamboyant character with a mischievous sense of humour, and someone not averse to spinning tall tales about his exploits in the wild and unexplored parts of the world. He falsely claimed, for instance, to have fought alongside the Mexican revolutionary Pancho Villa.

More intriguingly, the first written mention of the Mitchell-Hedges skull occurs in 1936 in the journal *Man: A Monthly Record of Anthropological Science*, in which the anthropologist Dr G.M. Morant refers to it as the 'Burney skull'. The 'Burney' in question was Sidney Burney, a London art dealer who put the skull up for auction at Sotheby's in late 1943. However, the artefact did not reach its reserve price of £340 and Burney, who had been hoping for a good deal more, decided to withdraw it from auction and keep it. A year later, Burney apparently had second thoughts and sold it to Mitchell-Hedges for £400.

When Joe Nickell interviewed Anna and asked her to explain this curious discrepancy, she replied that her adoptive father had left the skull with Burney as security on a loan to finance one of Mitchell-Hedges's expeditions and that Burney had had no right to offer it for sale. By purchasing the artefact from Burney, Mitchell-Hedges was merely retrieving his own property.

Yet *Man: A Monthly Record of Anthropological Science* refers to the skull only as the 'Burney skull', making no reference at all to Mitchell-Hedges. Nor is there any paperwork to link Mitchell-Hedges to the skull. When we add to this the extreme unlikelihood that Anna Mitchell-Hedges was even in Lubaantum when the skull was allegedly discovered (there is certainly no record of her presence in the expedition's records), we are led to the conclusion that the story as told by the Mitchell-Hedges family is nothing more than a romantic yarn.

Nevertheless, we are still left with the mystery of the skull's origin. In 1963, Anna loaned the skull to the art restorer and crystal expert Frank Dorland, who took it to California and spent seven years studying it. In 1970, Dorland sent it to the Hewlett-Packard Laboratories in Santa Clara, one of the leading facilities for crystal research. The scientists came to some very intriguing conclusions.

They discovered, for instance, that the skull had been carved against the natural axis of the crystal – in other words, against the orientation of its molecular symmetry. Modern crystal sculptors are careful to carve along the axis or they risk shattering the crystal.

In addition, the scientists at Hewlett-Packard were unable to discern any markings on the skull that might have pointed to its having been fashioned with modern implements. They concluded that it had most probably been created in two stages, with the basic shape being hewn from the crystal with diamonds, and then the detail being achieved by a laborious process of rubbing with a mixture of fine sand and water. They calculated that the total number of man hours that would have been required added up to 300 years.

For his part, Dorland claimed that the skull possessed strange, mystical properties. Over the seven-year period during which he examined the artefact, he claimed to have heard the faint sound of distant, tinkling bells, and when he looked into its prismatic eyes, he saw images of other skulls and high mountains. Dorland suggests that these effects may be visual and auditory hallucinations caused somehow by the skull's crystalline structure – although precisely how this might work is open to conjecture.

There are several other crystal skulls besides the Mitchell-Hedges artefact. These include the Mayan amethyst skull, discovered in the early 1900s in Guatemala; the Texas skull, also from Guatemala; and the rose quartz crystal skull, discovered in Honduras. Many people with a 'New Age' outlook suggest that all these skulls are the work of an ancient and highly advanced civilisation (some suggest Atlantis while others favour Lemuria). There is also a legend that there is a total of 13 'master skulls', which contain the secrets of this vanished civilisation encoded within their crystalline structures and, that if they were ever to be brought together, those secrets would be revealed.

It's a wonderfully bizarre and romantic idea – worthy of Indiana Jones himself. However, the truth would appear to be rather more prosaic. In 1996, the BBC produced a programme in its *Everyman* documentary series in which several crystal skulls were examined with an electron microscope in an effort to determine, once and for all, their origin and age.

It was concluded that the skulls were not ancient and had, in fact, been carved some time during the last 150 years. Anna Mitchell-Hedges had been invited to submit her crystal skull for analysis, but she declined, stating that it had already been tested enough.

Whatever the truth about the crystal skulls, it is perhaps enough to marvel at their strange beauty – regardless of when and by whom they were made.

17

FROM A LAND WITH NO SUN

The Green Children of Woolpit

There are many tales of strange and inexplicable events to be found at the junction of history and folklore. Although many have been lost to oblivion, others survive in written records to delight us with their snapshots of a world that no longer exists.

One such tale is that of the green children of Woolpit, which has been kept alive in paranormal and Fortean literature even though it describes events that happened nearly 1,000 years ago. One reason for this (aside from its charm) is that it resonates with other perplexing mysteries, both of science and of the paranormal.

The tale was first told in two ancient texts, both from around the year 1200: the *Historia Rerum Anglicarum* by William of Newburgh and the *Chronicon Anglicanum* by Ralph of Coggeshall. The legend was next mentioned in *The Fairy Mythology* by Thomas Keightley, which was published more than 600 years later in 1850. These three books are the only source material for the legend of the green children of Woolpit, which has been repeated many times in the modern Fortean literature.

According to the legend, sometime between the years 1135 and 1154, several peasants were reaping the corn near the village of Woolpit in Suffolk when they heard the cries of children. They saw two youngsters, a boy and a girl, wandering across a nearby field, crying bitterly. They seemed to have come from the direction of the 'wolfpittes', ancient depressions that were once used to trap wolves and from which the nearby village took its name. The boy and girl were dressed in strange garments made of an 'unknown' material, but what really astonished the peasants who came upon them was that their skin possessed a strange green tinge.

The astonished peasants immediately seized the children and took them to the village, where many people came to gawp. Presently, the children were taken to the home of a wealthy landowner, Sir Richard de Calne. They would accept no food even though they were half starved and exhausted. According to William of Newburgh:

> [I]t happened that some beans were brought in from the field, which they immediately seized with avidity, and examined the stalk for the pulse, but not finding it in the hollow of the stalk, they wept bitterly. Upon this, one of the bystanders, taking the beans from the pods, offered them to the children, who seized them directly, and ate them with pleasure. By this food they were supported for many months, until they learned the use of bread. At length, by degrees, they changed their original colour, through the natural effect of our food, and became like ourselves, and also learned our language.

The children were baptised and, although the boy became ill and died not long after, the girl grew stronger and thrived. She later married a local man and went to live in the village of Lynne.

Although they initially spoke in an unknown tongue, both children quickly acquired the local dialect and were able to tell something of the place from which they had come. 'We are inhabitants of the land of St Martin,' they said, 'who is regarded with peculiar veneration in the country which gave us birth.'

When asked where their homeland was and how they had come to be here, the children replied:

We are ignorant of both those circumstances; we only remember this, that on a certain day when we were feeding our father's flocks in the fields, we heard a great sound, such as we are now accustomed to hear at St Edmund's, when the bells are chiming; and whilst listening to the sound in admiration, we became on a sudden, as it were, entranced, and found ourselves among you in the fields where you were reaping.

They confirmed that their people were Christians and that they worshipped in churches. However, they added:

The sun does not rise upon our countrymen; our land is little cheered by its beams; we are contented with that twilight, which, among you, precedes the sunrise, or follows the sunset. Moreover, a certain luminous country is seen, not far distant from ours, and divided from it by a very considerable river.

Ralph of Coggeshall offers a slightly different account of the children's arrival, as given by the girl:

[A]sked in what manner she had come from the land, aforesaid, with the boy, she replied that they were following sheep, and arrived at a certain cavern. On entering it they heard a certain delectable sound of bells and, trying to reach the sweet sound, they wandered for a very long time through the cavern until they came to its end. Thence, emerging, the excessive brightness of our sun and the unwonted, warm temperature of our air astonished and terrified them. And for a long time they lay upon the edge of the cave. When overcome with disquietude, they wished to flee, but they could not in the least find the entrance to the cavern, until they were seized by the people of the countryside.

Over the years, writers and researchers have put forward a number of theories to account for the children's sudden appearance. However, as the researcher Garth Haslam notes in his highly informative commentary on the legend, 'many of these make the mistake of trying to explain the unexplained with the unexplained', of invoking one paranormal event to explain another, which inevitably offers more confusion than enlightenment.

Haslam goes on to list the theories, the first of which is that the children came from another dimension of spacetime very similar to our own. It is intriguing (though rather unscientific) to note the girl's description of the twilight in which she and her countrymen lived, similar to that of our world just before dawn or just after sunset. Was that strange twilight actually caused by the light from our sun bleeding into the skies of an alien dimension? Almost certainly not, since one would expect another dimension to possess its own sun and stars.

The second theory is that the children were denizens of some unknown subterranean kingdom and that they inadvertently found their way to the Earth's surface while following the sound of bells. This idea, while possessing its own fantastical romance, is undermined not only by the girl's statement that her land had a dim sky but also by her statement that she and the boy followed the sound of bells, which led them to our world. If any sounds from the surface could find their way to the underground realm, that realm would have to be pretty close to the surface, and it's extremely unlikely that an entire nation of subterranean humans living beneath Suffolk could have remained undiscovered for so long.

The third theory, which has been suggested by several writers, is that the children were transported to the Earth from another planet. Harold Wilkins, for instance, in his book *Strange Mysteries of Time and Space*, speculates (without any justification whatsoever) that if there was a race of humanoid beings living in underground caverns on Mars, they might be of a blue or green colour. In addition, as with the theory that the children came from another dimension, no explanation is offered as to how they actually got here.

Of course, there is always the possibility of some kind of teleportation, the instant transfer of people of objects from one location or dimension to another. In his book *Supernatural Disappearances*, Rodney Davies has this to say on the subject:

> It may perhaps be . . . that St Martin really exists in another dimension of being and time altogether, one which mimics our own in many ways, yet differs from it in several important respects. Physicists have postulated that there are such parallel universes, which exist alongside, as it were, our own, but which are completely separate from it. If so, the green children were unfortunate enough to have been 'caught up in the spirit' in their world, from which they supernaturally disappeared, sent thereby across the divide which exists between their dimension and ours, and then rematerialized in a harvest-field outside Woolpit. And if that could happen to them, then there may well be a movement of people in the opposite direction, which suggests that some of those who supernaturally vanish from our world may be translocated to another dimension, one from which they can never return.

The fourth theory suggests that the children were the victims of some sadistic joke or experiment: that they were kept in total isolation and somehow 'brainwashed' into believing that they came from the mythical land of St Martin. While this could in principle be true, there is absolutely no evidence for it: no one ever claimed responsibility for it, and there is no mention of this idea in the near-contemporary accounts of William of Newburgh and Ralph of Coggeshall.

The fifth theory is that the children were not inhabitants of some other planet or dimension or subterranean kingdom, but rather were simply a couple of undernourished youngsters who became lost in the area around Woolpit. This idea was suggested by Paul Harris in an article in the always-dependable journal *Fortean Times*. In an effort to get to the bottom of the mystery, Harris visited Woolpit and interviewed many local people, who told him that the story is generally thought to derive from a legend concerning a medieval Norfolk earl who was guardian to two young children. The earl wished to take over the estate that would have passed to the children upon their reaching adulthood and tried to poison them with arsenic before abandoning them in Wayland Wood on the border between Norfolk and Suffolk. The earl assumed that the children would die out in the woods. However, they were discovered by the villagers of Woolpit, still alive but ill and disorientated. Harris notes that one of the symptoms of arsenic poisoning is chlorosis, in which the skin takes on a greenish tinge. Anaemia resulting from malnutrition can also turn the skin faintly green and this corresponds rather neatly with the accounts of the period, which state that the children's skin reverted to its normal colour once they had been given decent food to eat.

Harris offers potential clarification for another element in the mystery: the strange land of 'St Martin', from which the children claimed to have come. A few miles to the northwest of Woolpit there is a village called Fornham St Martin. In addition, if the children had been abandoned, half out of their minds with hunger and with a poison in their veins, in the midst of a wood, might not its dark interior be seen by them as a land of twilight?

Convincing as Harris's theory is, there is one more to consider: the notion that the mystery of the green children of Woolpit is nothing more than a charming folktale from the depths of English history. It should be remembered, for instance, that green is traditionally associated with the supernatural and that green beans are the food of the dead, according to Celtic lore. Does this strange tale of the sudden appearance of two green children, as if from nowhere, in fact describe the appearance of two denizens of the fabled land of Faerie?

18

THE WAY OF THE WITCH

The Female Practitioners
of the Hidden Arts

Talk of witches brings to mind hideous old hags with warts on their noses, broomsticks, conical hats and spine-chilling cackles. The first images likely to be conjured up by the word 'witch' are those of the wicked queen in Walt Disney's *Snow White*, the evil crone in *The Wizard of Oz*, or the three malicious hags dropping unspeakable ingredients into their bubbling cauldron in *Macbeth*. These representations are themselves the result of a long tradition of the depiction of witches in art stretching back to the thirteenth century. However, as the historian Jeffrey B. Russell observes, 'Probably no living person ever fitted this stereotype.'

In the mid-fifteenth century, witchcraft had become a heresy by papal decree, and demonologists produced writings describing the abominations witches were said to practise: how they took part in obscene rites, ate babies, destroyed crops and herds and killed their neighbours. During the time of the great persecutions in Europe and North America in the sixteenth and seventeenth centuries, the central tradition of witchcraft was invariably seen as Devil worship. While the persecutions in Europe began slowly and grew steadily worse, those in the American colonies began as a result of the hysterical behaviour of some children in Salem Village, Massachusetts, in 1692 that prompted adults to claim that they were victims of witchcraft. It ended with one of the most memorable and well-documented witchcraft trials in history.

The witch performed magical works in the service of the Devil. Her principal function was to worship the Devil, which involved the deliberate repudiation of God and the Christian faith. She constituted the dark side of Christian belief. Witches were seen as the emissaries of Hell, just as the Christian clergy were the human representatives of Heaven. Such were the beliefs of the time.

Most of those accused of practising witchcraft were innocent. A few may have been noted herbalists or pagans. The vast majority, however, had no connection whatsoever with the magical arts but were lonely women castigated for the possession of crossed eyes and a pet cat. To believe that battalions of witches were doing Devil's work is to give misplaced credence to a potent mix of politics and hysteria that swept Europe.

The Legend of Mother Shipton

One of the most famous witches was the legendary Mother Shipton. She was reputedly born in 1488 in a cave beside the River Nidd at Knaresborough, England. Close by was an ancient well whose water was said to turn any object to stone. The child was named Ursula Sontheil and, while little is known of her early life, it appears that her mother gave her into the care of a foster mother when she was about two years old.

Ursula was a bright, mischievous child. One of the first stories about her refers to the trouble she caused the woman who looked after her. Finding her front door open on returning from an errand, Ursula's foster mother feared that she had been burgled and called her neighbours to join her as she nervously entered the house. They had heard dreadful wailing noises but had been prevented by some invisible force from going into the kitchen. The child's cradle was empty. Ursula was discovered sitting naked on the iron bar in the chimney from which the cooking hooks were suspended. She was smiling happily, apparently very pleased with herself.

It quickly became apparent that she possessed remarkable gifts, most notably that of prophecy. By the time she was in her twenties, rumours of her abilities had spread throughout the country. She presented her prophecies in the form of riddles and verses. Not surprisingly, fear of her alleged powers quickly turned to hostility and some called her a child of the Devil. It seems that she had some form of physical affliction, perhaps a crooked spine or hunchback. At any rate, people who at first made fun of her stopped when misfortune began to plague them. Doubtless her physical appearance contributed to the rumours that she was possessed of infernal powers. She married a local carpenter named Toby Shipton when she was 24 – and some said she had used a diabolical charm on him.

According to tradition, Mother Shipton, as she came to be called, foretold many things that came to pass on dates she specified, including the defeat of the Spanish Armada in 1588, the Great Fire of London in 1666 and even her own death in 1561. Once a young nobleman asked her whether his father would die soon, for he was in need of money and was to inherit his father's estate. Mother Shipton would not answer him and presently the young man fell ill. His worried father visited Mother Shipton, begging for an assurance that he would recover. She answered him thus:

> Those who gape out for others' death,
> Their own, unlooked for, comes about.
> Earth he did seek; 'ere long he shall have
> Of earth his fill; within his grave.

When the young man died not long after, many came to believe that she had the power to punish the wicked.

After her death in 1561, Mother Shipton was buried in unconsecrated ground somewhere on the outskirts of York. Upon her headstone were carved the words:

> Here lies she who never lied,
> Whose skill so often has been tried.
> Her prophecies shall still survive
> And ever keep her name alive.

At some point, her headstone was removed and taken to a museum in York, and later disappeared. There is some debate as to whether Mother Shipton ever existed, but according to folk tradition a woman named Shipton who possessed remarkable occult powers did live in the fifteenth century. And her name and prophecies were remembered. For instance, when Charles I was beheaded and England ruled by Oliver Cromwell, many people recalled her words: 'The White King dead, the Wolf shall then With blood usurp the lion's den.'

When the Great Plague ravaged London in 1665, many more recalled Mother Shipton's words: 'Triumphant death rides London through.' And when the Great Fire swept through the city the following year, Samuel Pepys wrote in his *Diary*: 'See – Mother Shipton's word is out.'

The Witch of Berkeley

The practice of witchcraft also depends upon a belief in the spirit world, a supernatural realm filled with discarnate entities working either for or against humanity. In the earliest phases of human history, hunters attempted to evoke the spirits of the animals they intended to track, in the hope that communion with their spirits would form a bond between them that would make the animals easier to pursue.

This belief in the efficacy of communicating with spirits was undermined by Christianity, which taught that all such attempts could result in the unspeakable horrors of demonic possession in this life and eternal damnation in the next. The witch who served the Devil could expect him to come for her when she died, as is said to have happened to the famous Witch of Berkeley. Her story is told by the chronicler William of Malmesbury around 1142 and provides a vivid illustration of the perception of witches at that time:

> A woman living at Berkeley was a practitioner of sorcery and ancient divinations. She was a glutton and engaged in unbounded debaucheries, for she was not as yet an old woman. One day when she was feasting, a jackdaw, one of her favourites, set up a great commotion. When she heard his chattering, she dropped the knife from her hand, turned pale, and groaned: 'Today my plough has come to the end of its row; today I shall hear dreadful news.' She later heard of the death of her son and his family. Discouraged, she turned her face to the wall to die. Calling her other children to her, she told them that she had lost her soul by practising diabolical arts and pleaded with them for help. 'Although you cannot lift the sentence that has been passed on my soul, you may be able to save my body. Sew up my corpse in the skin of a stag, lay it on its back in a stone coffin; fasten the lid with lead and iron and lay upon it a stone bound round three times with a heavy chain; and let psalms be sung and masses said for fifty days. The children endeavoured to fulfil their dead mother's last wish, but so heavy was the woman's guilt and so terrible the Devil's violence that their work and their prayers were in vain. For on the first two nights, while the choir of priests was singing psalms around the body, a band of demons smashed the bolt and forced their way through the door of the church. On the third night, towards dawn, the whole monastery was shaken to its foundations by the noise of the approaching enemy. One demon, who was taller and more terrible than

the others, broke the gate to pieces. He called the woman up
from the coffin and dragged her out of the church, bearing
her off screaming on a black horse.

In the thirteenth century, tales of witches and witchcraft became
more lurid. In 1214, Gervaise of Tilbury gathered numerous stories
from alleged eyewitnesses to the witches' exploits. The people claimed
to have watched the witches fly overhead, and Gervaise added that
no witch would ever utter the name of Christ while in flight, for
to do so would result in her plummeting to the ground. In the
course of their nocturnal journeys, witches would sometimes enter
houses and sit on the sleeping inhabitants' chests, causing horrible
nightmares of suffocation and falling. They had sex with sleeping
men, sucked blood, stole infants from their beds and took the forms
of cats, wolves and other animals. The reason for the spreading of
these tales, often from the pulpit, was an attempt by the Church to
eradicate traditional folk beliefs.

The Persecution of Isobel Gowdie
In Scotland during the seventeenth century, the Presbyterian
Church persecuted alleged witches mercilessly. Once a person was
charged with being a witch, there was virtually no chance of their
being acquitted, as law courts colluded with the Church. Anyone
could be made a scapegoat in this way, from a lowly widow to people
of high social standing, the victims of the political machinations of
their enemies.

The most celebrated Scottish witch was Isobel Gowdie, whose
confession provides a detailed insight into the real or imagined
activities of the archetypal witch. The details were given by her in
four confessions, apparently obtained without the use of torture,
in the spring of 1662. It was partly from her statements that the
famous witchcraft historian Margaret Murray constructed her (now
discredited) theories of the witch cult in her book *Witch-Cult in
Western Europe*, published in 1921.

Isobel Gowdie lived in Auldearn, a small community to the east of Inverness in northwest Scotland. In her first confession, she claimed to have been rebaptised by the Devil, stating:

> As I was going betwixt the towns of Drumdewin and the Heads, I met with the Devil, and there covenanted in a manner with him; and I promised to meet him, in the night-time, in the kirk of Auldearn; which I did. And the first thing I did there that night, I denied my baptism, and did put the one of my hands to the crown of my head and the other to the sole of my feet, and there renounced all betwixt my two hands over to the Devil . . . He marked me on the shoulder, and sucked out my blood at that mark, and spouted it in his hand, and sprinkling it on my head, said, 'I baptise thee, in my own name.'

She also told how she and other witches travelled on flying horses, crying: 'Horse and Hattock in the Devil's name!' Any people who saw them and did not immediately bless themselves would be shot dead with the dreaded 'elf-shot', the prehistoric flint arrowheads that are found in abundance around Auldearn. Their souls would go to Heaven, while their bodies remained with the witches.

In her second confession, Gowdie described how the witches made a clay image to kill the sons of the local laird:

> John Taylor brought home the clay in his plaid; his wife brake it very small, like meal, and sifted it with a sieve, and poured in water among it, in the Devil's name, and wrought it very soft, and made of it a picture of the Laird's sons. It had all the parts and marks of a child, such as head, eyes, nose, hands, feet, mouth, and little lips. It wanted no mark of a child; and the hands of it folded down by its sides. We laid the face of it to the fire till it shrivelled; and a clear fire round about it till it was red like a coal. After that we would

roast it now and then; each other day there would be a piece of it well roasten. The Laird's male children will be made to suffer by it, if it not be found and broken . . . Till it be broken, it will be the death of all the male children the Laird of Park will ever get. Cast it over a kirk, it will not break till it be broken with an axe, or some such like thing, held in a man's hands. If it be not broken, it will last 100 years.

The witch also described less harmful activities, such as taking milk from a cow by magical means, stealing crops and tying knots in thread from a local dye-house, so that the vats could dye no colour but black, the Devil's colour.

In her third confession, Gowdie gave the names of fifteen people killed with elf-shot, as well as numerous magical spells including that for changing into a hare:

> I shall go into a hare,
> With sorrow and such and mickle care;
> And I shall go in the Devil's name
> Until I come home again.

At her fourth and last appearance before the court, her examiners asked her to go through parts of her story again, which she did without contradicting herself. She also displayed a self-destructive urge in her statement: 'Alas, I deserve not to be sitting here, for I have done so many evil deeds, especially killing men. I deserve to be writhing on iron spikes, and worse, if it could be devised.'

Isobel Gowdie's fate is not recorded, but after such revelations it is hard to believe she could have escaped execution. It is probable that she believed every word of her confessions. As Jeffrey B. Russell notes, 'Her case is one of the clearest indications that people of unstable mind could under the influence of prevailing beliefs come to believe themselves diabolical witches.'

The Voodoo Queen of New Orleans

Witches could wield incredible power and thrive in the most hostile environments. Marie Laveau (c.1801–81), the legendary Voodoo Queen of New Orleans, was both revered and feared throughout nineteenth-century Louisiana. Her influence stretched from the lowest levels of society to the highest, astonishing for a 'free woman of colour' in the era of slavery. She gained her unique position through a mixture of the ancient rites of Voodoo fused with Catholicism and a healthy dose of down-to-earth shrewdness. In public, she often appeared with a snake draped around her. Incantations and herb mixes appeared to bring forth desired magical outcomes. But many of her successes were due as much to information she discovered through her work as a hairdresser and brothel keeper or connections she made in high places as by that elicited through charms and spells. Further confusion was inspired by Marie and her lookalike daughter, for whom she was often mistaken. Marie Laveau made a return to her Catholic roots as she got older. Evidently, this was unacceptable to her followers and in 1869, at a meeting held near Maison Blanche on the shores of Lake Pontchartrain, Marie was voted out and replaced as Voodoo Queen by a woman named Malvina Latour. Marie spent the rest of her life as a devout Catholic and devoted much time and effort to visiting prisoners in the local jail, even helping them to build prayer altars in their cells.

Malvina Latour could not, however, maintain cohesion within the Voodoo community around New Orleans and soon she was challenged by rival Voodoo queens and doctors, none of whom could offer the inspiration or control required to unify the Voodoo faith. As a result, Voodoo in New Orleans began an irreversible decline.

Marie Laveau lives on in New Orleans legend. Her grave is visited all year round by devotees of the Voodoo religion and those possessed of macabre curiosity. Many place small offerings on the tomb, such as pieces of food and various Voodoo items. It is believed that Marie's spirit rises from the tomb on St John's Eve, 23 June, and holds court at a spectacular Voodoo ritual. Many, of course, deny the existence of Marie's ghost, but one thing cannot be denied: of all the practitioners of Voodoo in New Orleans, no one was more renowned, influential or powerful than the down-to-earth Marie Laveau.

Sex and Witchcraft

During the great persecutions, witches were branded as heretics because, it was generally thought, they consorted with the Devil, making a conscious and willing pact with him and committing themselves, body and soul, before and after death, to the Devil's work. These pacts were thought to take the form of a ceremonial entry into a kind of secret society devoted to evil.

The novice witch would be taken to a Witches' Sabbath and there presented to the Devil, who was believed to preside at such meetings. The ceremony of initiation varied from place to place but always included sacrilegious and obscene elements. Accounts have traditionally been vivid, lurid and erotic. One ritual was described by a seventeenth-century Italian demonologist, Francesco-Maria Guazzo, who listed eleven separate stages:

1. A spoken denial of the Christian faith.

2. Rebaptism in the Devil's name, after which the novice was given a new name in place of his or her Christian one.

3. Symbolic removal of the baptismal chrism (consecrated oil mixed with balm) by the Devil's touch.

4. Denial of godparents and the gaining of new sponsors.

5. The gift of a piece of clothing to the Devil as a token of submission.

6. An oath of allegiance made to the Devil while standing in a magic circle.

7. Inclusion of the initiate's name in the *Book of Death*.

8. A promise to sacrifice children to the Devil.

9. A promise to pay an annual tribute to the Devil of black-coloured gifts.

10. Marking the initiate with the Devil's mark – a strangely shaped area of the skin that became insensitive (a mole or birthmark of any shape would do).

11. Various vows of special service to the Devil, including the destruction of holy relics and keeping the secrets of the Sabbat.

The witches' celebrations frequently included a sexual element. Female witches regularly received the attentions of their infernal master, as a reaffirmation of the evil bond between them. It was said that sexual intercourse with the Devil was extremely painful and that his penis was as cold as ice. More pleasurable was sex with certain demons, the male being known as an incubus and the female as a succubus. Some witches confessed they had been visited by their demon lovers regularly for many years.

It was also believed that incubi and succubi visited people who were not witches, in order to lead them into sexual sin and thus snare their souls for the Devil. Incubi outnumbered succubi nine to one, possibly because chastity was considered more important in women or maybe because women were considered by the Christian Church to be more licentious than men.

The idea of incubi and succubi was the product of the highly charged erotic imaginations of both the prosecutors and those under investigation. Sex is, of course, a perennial human obsession but it was especially so in the repressed Middle Ages. The witch-hunters insisted that sexual malpractices be a main feature of an accused witch's confession and also insisted upon discovering every detail of such activities.

Sex has always played an important part in the activities of witches, their rituals, celebrations and initiations. In the 1960s, the photographer Serge Kordiev and his wife Anne became members of a witches' coven. Kordiev had written an article in a Sunday newspaper describing his interest in the occult. A few days later, he received a telephone call from a man who asked whether he would be interested in joining a coven. Intrigued, Kordiev replied that he would.

The Kordievs were picked up in an expensive car and driven to a large old house. After being given drinks, they were instructed to take off their clothes and put on small black satin aprons. They were then taken into a large room with a black door and red carpets hanging on the walls. Half a dozen hooded figures stood in front of an altar, before which appeared a naked man, his body covered with oil. On either side of him stood two black-robed girls. The Kordievs were then ordered to kneel before the altar, to swear perpetual homage to Satan and to sign their oaths in blood. They were given magical names and the naked man placed his hand on their genitals, causing a strange tingling sensation. What caused this sensation is unclear; but the use of lotions containing a variety of strange and exotic ingredients is quite common in such rituals, and the man's hands may have been coated with such a lotion.

After several meetings, the Kordievs began to grow apprehensive at the coven's unpleasant activities. On one occasion a girl was accused of betraying the group's secrets. She was made to serve as a human altar while a Black Mass was said over her, after which she was ravished by the Master. The Kordievs then discovered that they still had to go through a 'confirmation ceremony' in which they would be required to have sex with both the Master and a High Priestess. At that point, they decided it was high time they left the coven.

Almost immediately, strange things began to happen. On one

occasion, they heard sounds of insane laughter and smashing glass coming from Serge's studio. When they investigated, they found that the studio had been completely wrecked. The doors, however, were still locked, and the windows had apparently been smashed from the inside, with the glass scattered outside on the lawn.

19

ALIENS AND FAIRIES

Strange Correspondences

One might think that the subject of leprechauns, pixies, fauns and other fairy spirits has no place in our modern secular, scientific world view. Surely such creatures belong to the folklore of vanished ages, the products of the same naivety that held the world to be flat, or to reside at the centre of the Universe? And yet there are striking and unsettling parallels between the appearance and behaviour of those creatures of folklore and the creatures of what many suggest is a modern form of folklore: UFOs and extraterrestrial entities.

In the centuries of the Common Era, the relationship between the human and non-human underwent two profound alterations. The first was the demonising of pagan polytheism by Christianity. In his fascinating book *Daimonic Reality: A Field Guide to the Otherworld*, Patrick Harpur illustrates this with a quote from the epistles of St Paul: 'The things which the gentiles sacrifice, they sacrifice to the devils, and not to God.' Harpur goes on to remind us that the complex realm of non-human intelligence revered by pagan peoples across the world was assimilated into the Christian world view, becoming part of the angelic realm, or, more precisely, the realm of fallen angels, cast out of Heaven along with Satan.

And yet, in spite of this attempt to organise the realm of the supernatural into sharply demarcated regions of good and evil, of angels and demons, there remained an intermediate realm whose denizens were not content to be so ignominiously pigeonholed. These entities are, of course, the fauns, satyrs, leprechauns, pixies and nymphs – the Good People, the Gentry, the fairies.

The second profound alteration in the relationship between the human and non-human involved not assimilation but exclusion, at the hands of the seventeenth-century rationalists. Thinkers such as Descartes and Spinoza were scientific and secular, relying upon the exercise of reason, rather than empiricism, as the only valid source of knowledge. Thus the world of the supernatural was simply not recognised: supernatural events could not exist within the contemporary rationalist world view, and therefore they did not exist.

René Descartes (1596–1650) founded his influential philosophy upon the one premise he held to be indisputable, his existence as a thinking subject ('I think, therefore I am'). Thereafter the result was the separation of the world into subjective consciousness and the objective, external world. To attempt this total denial of the mythical and supernatural (what today we call the paranormal) was not only unhealthy and dangerous but doomed to failure. In denying even the subjective reality of non-human intelligence, the rationalists tried to deny the very processes that had driven human civilisation onward from Neolithic times, through the founding of the first cities, on to the architectural triumphs of the ancient Egyptians, the civilisations of Greece and Rome, and ultimately to their own invention of rationalism. For it was through myth that the great civilisations came to know themselves and their place in the cosmos, giving rise to their phenomenal success in the fields of art, philosophy and science.

Jacques Vallée has done more than any other ufologist to promote the idea that there are profound connections between modern reports of encounters with UFOs and their occupants and reports from previous centuries regarding the entities commonly called 'fairies'. Before citing particular cases, it is worth looking at the 16 conclusions arrived at by Reverend Robert Kirk, who lived in Aberfoyle, Scotland, in the seventeenth century. Reverend Kirk spent much of his life pondering the nature of the numerous entities that were believed to interact with human beings in remote regions of Europe. Here is Jacques Vallée's summary of Kirk's conclusions:

They have a nature that is intermediate between man and the angels.

Physically, they have very light and fluid bodies, which are comparable to a condensed cloud. They are particularly visible at dusk. They can appear and vanish at will.

Intellectually, they are intelligent and curious.

They have the power to carry away anything they like.

They live inside the earth in caves, which they can reach through any crevice or opening where air passes.

When men did not inhabit most of the world, the creatures used to live there and had their own agriculture. Their civilisation has left traces on the high mountains; it was flourishing at a time when the whole countryside was nothing but woods and forests.

At the beginning of each three-month period, they change quarters because they are unable to stay in one place. Besides, they like to travel. It is then that men have terrible encounters with them, even on the great highways.

Their chameleon-like bodies allow them to swim through the air with all their household.

They are divided into tribes. Like us, they have children, nurses, marriages, burials, etc., unless they just do this to mock our own customs or to predict terrestrial events.

Their houses are said to be wonderfully large and beautiful, but under most circumstances they are invisible to human eyes. Kirk compares them to enchanted islands. The houses are equipped with lamps that burn forever and fires that need no fuel.

They speak very little. When they do talk among themselves, their language is a kind of whistling sound.

Their habits and their language when they talk to humans are similar to those of local people.

Their philosophical system is based on the following ideas: nothing dies; all things evolve cyclically in such a way that at every cycle they are renewed and improved. Motion is the universal law.

They are said to have a hierarchy of leaders, but they have no visible devotion to God, no religion.

They have many pleasant and light books, but also serious and complex books dealing with abstract matters.

They can be made to appear at will before us through magic.

The parallels between the two orders of being (fairy and alien) are so striking that I shall make my way through all 16 conclusions, illustrating each one with examples of our current information regarding alleged alien visitors.

1. The gradual secularisation of twentieth-century society is both undeniable and understandable, in view of the huge advances made in science and in our comprehension of the Universe. Alien visitors, therefore, fulfil a profound need on our part for an order of being that is both vastly superior to us and acceptable within the current secular context. Like the 'Good People' of past

centuries, they occupy an intermediate position between mortal, fallible humanity and an immortal, omniscient Creator. Taken in isolation, this would seem to militate in favour of a purely mythological origin for non-human entities; however, viewed in a wider context, the nature of aliens is exactly parallel to that of the fairies of folklore.

2. The majority of reports suggest a certain physical type for aliens. They are frequently described as being thin and frail looking, though are apparently strong. This is especially true of the so-called 'Greys', whose spindly limbs and large, featureless eyes are reminiscent of insects. Ufologists who subscribe to the extra-terrestrial hypothesis for the origin of these beings suggest that this physical structure might enable the aliens to withstand the enormous pressures resulting from the spectacular performance of their vehicles. These craft have also been reported on numerous occasions to appear and vanish without a trace, as if suddenly becoming invisible, or simply winking out of existence.

3. The aliens are also, of course, highly intelligent and profoundly curious: two qualities which would seem to be necessary for the exploration of other worlds.

4. If reported alien abductions are to be believed as representing objective reality, aliens certainly have the power to carry away anything (and anyone) they like. And, like our ancestors' encounters with the Good People, these meetings are sometimes quite enjoyable, sometimes terrifying.

5. The interior of the Earth has been put forward increasingly in recent years as the main centre of operations – if not, in some cases, the ultimate origin – of the various alien groups present on Earth.

6. With the idea that the aliens were around 'when men did not inhabit most of the world', we find ourselves on shaky ground as far as parallels with modern encounters go, mainly because the idea refers to their history, rather than their direct attributes. However,

the belief that the Good People have a long history, one that might pre-date humanity, would seem to support the assertion, made by Vallée and others, that what we now call 'UFO' and 'alien' encounters have occurred throughout recorded history.

7. If the ultimate origin of the non-humans is somewhere other than Earth, the very fact that they are here proves their liking for travel, whether for reasons of exploration, research or whatever. However, here we once again enter the territory of mythology, of our own psychological and cultural history. It seems the non-humans' liking for highways is significant. Just as travellers of previous centuries frequently encountered members of the fairy race (with varying consequences) on lonely highways, contemporary sightings often occur on isolated stretches of road. The anthropologist Victor Turner called such locations 'liminal zones'. They are places of transition, of travel in terms of both space and time. Highways, crossroads, bridges and shores are liminal zones; the hours of dawn and dusk – the boundaries between day and night – are liminal times; so is the turn of the year. Patrick Harpur notes that caravan sites and trailer parks are often haunted by strange creatures and flying objects, perhaps because, as he says, they are 'liminally situated between town and country, habitat and wilderness'. It is easy to understand why such locations were (and are) regarded as places where strange things could happen. Like the forest, the roads spanning the open country between the safety of habitats were seen as harbouring a host of potential dangers, both natural and supernatural. In these places, the traveller of centuries past kept a wary eye open for both robbers and vampires, sinister vagabonds as well as werewolves and other creatures. It is an apprehensiveness that has been carried through to contemporary urban life, which prompts me to lock the doors whenever I am in a car, day or night. So it was common sense for our ancestors to regard their highways with caution. It may be, as Harpur thinks, that this is the reason for the high incidence of strange encounters in liminal zones, where

'the laws of time and space, matter and causality seem attenuated; and we glimpse for an instant an unseen order of things'. Perhaps our heightened sense of our surroundings – the modern versions of predator-haunted forests – at these times forces a subtle alteration in our consciousness, making us more amenable to interaction with a hitherto invisible non-human intelligence. After all, they do like to travel.

8. In the majority of alleged alien encounters, and especially the modern abductions, the entities are described as moving in a variety of abnormal ways. Some shuffle their feet awkwardly; others move without any walking motion whatsoever, gliding gracefully across the floor; while more still are downright ludicrous, such as the entities encountered in Brazil in 1977 by Antonio la Rubia, who described creatures having a single leg, like a pogo stick. One of the most striking motifs of the modern alien abduction experience is the way in which the aliens move, particularly at the beginning and end of the episode. They are described as floating into the victim's home through windows or even walls, subduing their targets and then floating them up through the air, out of the room and into the UFO. This strange mode of locomotion subtly echoes the chameleon-bodied fairies described by Reverend Kirk.

9. Just as the fairies are divided into tribes, so it seems are our current alien guests. The aliens allegedly visiting us now can be divided into a number of groups, including Greys (of which there are several subgroups); humanoid Nordics (again, in several subgroups); reptilians and monsters (which include Bigfoot-type creatures and the so-called 'bellicose hairy dwarfs'); and others.

10. Fairy houses are said to be wonderfully large and beautiful enchanted places from which there is occasionally no return. This imagery of beauty, light and wonderful, sometimes colossal, architecture is frequently encountered in descriptions of UFO interiors. Indeed, the lamps that burn forever and the fires that

need no fuel have their counterparts in the soft, ubiquitous light with no obvious source which is often noticed by UFO abductees.

11. In common with the fairies of past centuries, the Greys speak very little, at least verbally, preferring to communicate with their unwilling guests via telepathy. Frequently, witnesses describe aliens' native language as resembling whistles or chirps, like the 'whistling sound' of the fairy language.

12. One of the most intriguing attributes of the Greys, which has led many researchers to suggest that they have spent considerable time eavesdropping on our culture, perhaps by monitoring our radio and television broadcasts, is their apparent mastery of our language structures and idioms. They are reported to use phrases such as 'don't worry', 'we're not going to hurt you' and 'everything's going to be all right'. Again, we can see a connection between this behaviour and that of the fairies, in view of Kirk's claim that the fairies' habits and their language when they talk to humans are similar to those of local people.

13. One of the defining characteristics of the contactee cases of the 1950s and 1960s was the aliens' propensity to ramble on about their system of ethics and philosophy. They constantly reiterated their concern regarding humanity's irresponsible use of nuclear energy, saying that we were disrupting the balance of the Universe and threatening the safety of the other inhabited planets. This concern with balance, harmony and the cyclic nature of time echoes the philosophy of the Good People, who believe that nothing dies, and that all things evolve cyclically. An example of alien interest in the concept of time is described by researcher John Keel in his book *UFOs: Operation Trojan Horse*. In November 1966, two Minnesota women had an encounter with a strange flying object. During the encounter, one of the women fell to her knees in a trance-like state. A strange, metallic voice issued from her lips, asking: 'What . . . is . . . your . . . time . . . cycle? What

... constitutes ... a ... day ... and ... what ... constitutes ... a ... night?'

'A day is approximately twelve hours long and a night is twelve hours long,' replied the other woman. After a few more questions, the woman came out of her trance and the object departed.

14. Extraterrestrial attitude to God has also, on occasion, featured in encounter reports. Like the Good People, they often seem to lack any devotion to a Creator. In 1952, a Peruvian man, known simply as C.A.V., met UFO entities described as looking like mummies with joined legs or one double leg. They wanted to speak to his 'chief' about (once again) the danger to the Universe posed by our nuclear weapons tests. C.A.V. said:

> I asked them who their God was and I noticed a sort of mockery. 'God?' they said. 'What God?'
>
> 'Well, the Supreme Creator,' I said, 'who made the Universe.'
>
> 'Well, we are like gods,' they said.
>
> 'How can you be gods?' I asked. And they said we were very backward.

15. The fairies have pleasant and light books, and also serious, complex books. Likewise the aliens: there are many reports of communication taking the form of strange writings passed on to contactees. The most famous contactee, George Adamski, met a 'Venusian' in November 1952 in the California desert. The spaceman asked for one of Adamski's photographic plates, which he took away. The following month, the plate was returned to Adamski, who discovered some strange writing on it.

In March 1965, John Reeves, who lived near Weeki Wachee Springs, Florida, apparently encountered a Martian spacecraft and occupants while he was walking in some woods. After taking a photograph of Reeves, the entity returned to its craft and departed. Reeves discovered two pieces of folded paper at the landing site, which bore strange symbols like 'oriental writing or shorthand writing'. The message was later deciphered (precisely how was never made clear). It read: 'Planet Mars – Are you coming home soon – We miss you very much – Why did you stay away too long.'

During the abduction of Barney and Betty Hill in New Hampshire in 1961, Betty asked the leader of the group of entities if she could take something from their craft, as proof of her experience. He gave her a 'book' containing strange writing but then changed his mind, evidently having decided that it would be better if she had no proof.

16. It is difficult to see how any parallel can be drawn between the fairies' appearance through the use of magic and modern aliens. However, a tenuous link can perhaps be identified if we look at the problem in terms of culture and imagination. Magic, as defined by Aleister Crowley, is the alteration of natural processes in accordance with human will; and this extends to the processes governing the activities of the Good People, who could be forced to appear before a sufficiently powerful magician. However, it could be claimed that modern humanity possesses its own form of powerful magic, its own method of altering natural processes (at fundamental levels) in accordance with its will.

Nuclear physics fits the bill rather neatly, and the reader will probably be aware that what is called the modern era of ufology began in the 1940s, when nuclear weapons were first tested (and used). Ufologists are keen to remind us that strange objects are frequently sighted in the vicinity of military bases and nuclear power stations, probably because they are the places where our latest technology is developed and tested. It could thus be argued that our manipulation of the atom is the 'magical process' that summons the technological equivalent of the non-human entities of folklore.

In listing the connections between fairies and ufonauts, I have referred to the accounts of contactees as well as abductees. This will cause serious problems for many ufologists, who look upon the claims of the contactees with something approaching outright contempt. In order to understand why, we must remind ourselves of the differences between a contactee and an abductee.

These differences can be described in terms of time and motive. As mentioned above, the wave of contactee reports occurred mainly in the 1950s and 1960s. Their claims centred on the arrival on Earth of gentle, human-looking beings, usually from planets within our own solar system, who dispensed pearls of cosmic wisdom and made polite requests that humanity cease its nuclear tests forthwith.

This is entirely at odds with the more recent wave of alien abductions, which centre on the activities of an altogether more unpleasant bunch of entities, the Greys. This group are fond of taking people into their craft against their will and performing hideous physical and psychological experiments upon them. The abduction scenario is treated with a good deal more respect by ufologists than the contactee scenario, probably because it fits more neatly with modern ideas about the nature of highly advanced beings, because their motives (selfish, materialistic, geared towards their own well-being at the expense of ours), seem eminently understandable and plausible to a humanity that is capable of the same arrogance and disregard for others. (A Grey is reported to have asked one victim why she was so indignant at her treatment when human beings behave in the same way towards animals and even other humans.)

Whatever the relative merits of abductee and contactee scenarios, for our immediate purposes we must place them side by side, since they are elements in a coherent progression from the supernatural beings of traditional folklore through to the present. This can be seen from the parallels between the attributes of folkloric beings and those of the non-humans reported throughout the latter half of the twentieth century.

There are grounds for suggesting that we are witnessing the activities of a genuine non-human intelligence that is constantly reshaping itself in order to correspond to the prevailing world view in any particular period. They have appeared to human eyes as angels and demons, as fairies, as brilliant scientific inventors, and as the pilots of extraterrestrial space vehicles. They are the harbingers of a reinvented mythology, a psychic process by which we may bridge the gap between a dangerous and uncertain present and the boundless potential of our future.

20

A City Made of Gold?

The Legend of El Dorado

When Hernán Cortés subdued the Aztec Empire in Mexico in 1521, and Francisco Pizarro overran the Inca Empire in Peru in 1533, it became clear to European eyes that the vast, unexplored lands of Central and South America were a source of great wealth where vast fortunes and prestige could be gained. The dangers were great but the rewards, it seemed, were more than worth the initial hardships of exploration.

In the arrogant eyes of the Conquistadors, the indigenous peoples of the region were poor savages living in pagan darkness and it was their duty to bring word of the Christian God so that their souls might be saved (and their lands and wealth might be transferred to European ownership).

One such adventurer was Gonzalo Jiménez de Quesada, a 36-year-old lawyer from Granada who was deputy governor of the settlement of Santa Marta on the northwest coast of Colombia. In April 1536, Quesada took command of an expedition of about 900 Europeans, which set off along the Magdalena River, following it to its source with the intention of discovering a new route across the Andes Mountains to Peru. It was also his hope to discover another native empire, whose lands and riches could be taken with as little effort as possible.

The journey was long and arduous, littered with swamps and jungle vegetation. When they ran out of food, they were forced to subsist on frogs and lizards – while alligators and jaguars looked at them as prey. Their plight was not relieved by the natives who flitted ghostlike amongst the trees and fired poisoned arrows. Whether felled by poisoned arrows, wild animals or hunger and fever, more than 600 of Quesada's party had died by the time the great Cundinamarca Plateau came into view. The bedraggled survivors gazed in astonishment at the signs of orderly human activity and habitation that unfolded before them. There were fields of crops, including corn and potatoes, and small villages whose obvious neatness and cleanliness hinted strongly at a peaceful and prosperous society.

When the explorers entered the nearest village, they discovered that doorways to the dwellings were decorated with objects like tinkling wind chimes that were fashioned from thin sheets of pure gold. The Europeans looked at each other with satisfaction for it seemed that their terrible journey had not been in vain. They were within a hair's breadth of reaping rich rewards.

The inhabitants of the villages, the Chibcha people, were at first profoundly shocked by the sight of the strange newcomers and many were so afraid that they fled into the fields. Others, however, were curious and quickly came to believe that they were being visited by gods from the sky. Anxious to please the 'gods', the Chibchas offered them food and shelter. And when it became obvious (although perplexing) that the visitors seemed deeply interested in golden ornaments, the Chibchas gathered together as much gold as they could and offered it to them.

The Europeans demanded more gold. Nor did they stand on ceremony but instead raided homes and shrines, taking whatever they pleased. When the Chibchas finally realised that the new arrivals were not gods and that they had come to plunder their lands and villages, they turned on the Europeans. However, like the Aztecs and Incas to the north, they quickly discovered their weapons were no match for those of the newcomers. Within a short time, Quesada and his men had conquered the Cundinamarca Plateau and the entire Chibcha nation.

Having violently consolidated their position, Quesada and his men decided that their next priority was to discover the source of the Chibcha gold. The Chibchas didn't gather it themselves, but bartered it with other tribes for emeralds and salt. Somewhere out in the dense jungle, there had to be more gold and perhaps many other riches besides. Now the Europeans demanded that the Chibchas tell them exactly where to find it.

Presently, they were given some apparently useful information by an old man (it is possible that they tortured him in order to get it). At any rate, the old native told them of the 'Golden Man' – El Dorado. There was a tribe, he said, living to the east in the mountainous lands around a deep lake. This tribe had an annual ritual in which their chief had his entire body covered with gold dust, then sailed out to the centre of the lake on a raft laden with gold and emeralds. As a sign of thanks to their gods, the chief threw the gold and emeralds into the lake, and then dived in after them. As the waters washed the gold dust from him, the gods would receive their tribute, and would look kindly upon the tribe.

This was a strange story but such was the Europeans' greed for gold and other riches that they eagerly believed every word. Had they been less consumed by their insatiable hunger for wealth, Quesada and his men might have paused to wonder whether their informant, a member of a frightened and defeated nation, had simply spun this tale in a desperate attempt to persuade them to move on, to leave the Chibchas in peace and harass someone else.

Quesada renamed the land of the Chibchas New Granada, and was about to leave for Santa Marta to confirm his governorship, when word reached him of another group of Europeans that was fast approaching from the northeast. Sure enough, about 160 men arrived in Quesada's capital, Santa Fé de Bogotá, not long after. They were led by a German named Nikolaus Federmann who, like Quesada and his men, was anxious to repeat the successes of Cortés and Pizarro.

The new arrivals were a sorry sight – just as Quesada's group had been when they finally gained the Cundinamarca Plateau. Virtually naked and half starved, they were given food and clothing, while Quesada made plans to recruit them for his forthcoming assault on 'El Dorado'.

Before long, Quesada learned that yet another expedition was approaching Santa Fé de Bogotá from the southwest. This one was led by a deputy of Pizarro's, Sebastián de Belalcázar, who had recently founded Quito in Ecuador. Having heard legends of fabulous riches to be found in the interior, Belalcázar started out from Quito at about the same time that Quesada's expedition left Santa Marta.

As might have been expected, the three commanders couldn't agree on who should have priority in the anticipated conquest of El Dorado, and so they all left the New World for Spain, with the intention of presenting their cases at court. However, none of them was destined to discover the hidden land of gold, nor even to conduct a search for it. Federmann's employers, the commercial firm of Welser in Augsburg, lost their influence in Venezuela and he was unable to return to the New World. Belalcázar was given the governorship of one of the cities he had founded in Colombia and made no further attempt to discover El Dorado. Quesada was granted the honorary title of Marshal of New Granada, and although he never ceased dreaming of the fabled land of gold, he ended his days in relative obscurity.

However, the legend of El Dorado did not die. Quesada's brother, Hernán, found the lake of which the old Chibcha man had spoken, Lake Guatavita, and he and his men attempted to empty it by hand with gourds so that they might retrieve the gold and jewels that were believed to have been thrown in. This ambitious but Sisyphean project succeeded in lowering the water level by no more than about ten feet, and yielded a mere handful of trinkets.

A much more comprehensive attempt to drain the lake was made in 1580 by a merchant from Bogotá, who employed several thousand natives to dig a trench in one of the walls forming the extinct volcanic caldera which formed Lake Guatavita. This succeeded in lowering the water level by some 60 feet, and yielded a good deal of gold and jewels – although the hoard was nothing like impressive enough to justify the enormous labour involved.

Down the centuries since then, several other attempts were made to drain Lake Guatavita in the belief that a colossal hoard of treasure would be found at the bottom (some estimates put the total value at more than $300 million). The final attempt was made by a British party who succeeded in draining most of the water from the lake in 1912; however, the mud and silt at the bottom quickly set as hard as concrete, making further exploration impossible.

In 1965, the Colombian government declared Lake Guatavita a national historic site and forbade all further searches for the legendary gold of El Dorado. Nevertheless, the name has entered both legend and common parlance, denoting an unreachable goal. The irony is that this fascinating and seductive legend may well have begun life as no more than a desperate lie told by a Chibcha native to persuade a group of greedy Europeans to leave him and his people alone.

21

MAGUS OR CHARLATAN?

The Extraordinary Life of Count Cagliostro

The world of the occult has had its own luminaries and superstars, people whose fame has transcended the normally shadowy realm in which they operate and extended into the imagination of the wider public. The best-known example of this was Aleister Crowley, who was dubbed 'the wickedest man in the world' by an outraged press.

Another figure, no less controversial than Crowley, was Count Alessandro Cagliostro – a man whose very name conjures images of strange and mysterious magic. Thomas Carlyle (1795–1881) called him the 'Prince of Quacks', while later historians came to re-evaluate him and suggested that he may not have been quite such a charlatan after all. Indeed, the occult historian Lewis Spence called him 'one of the greatest occult figures of all time'. Meanwhile, the British writer on the supernatural, Peter Underwood, stated that 'while he seems to have been party to a number of disgraceful intrigues and forgeries, he was nevertheless a true wizard'.

Early Life

Cagliostro was born Giuseppe Balsamo in 1743 in Sicily. His father, Peter Balsamo, died while Cagliostro was still a child and his mother, unable to support him, looked to her brother for assistance. Despites his uncle's efforts, the boy proved to be all but unmanageable, demonstrating little interest in formal education and absconding several times from the religious seminary at Palermo in which he was placed. He was sent next to a Benedictine order, where the Father Superior discovered the boy's natural aptitude for chemistry and arranged for him to become the assistant of an apothecary attached to the convent. Here he received a reasonably thorough grounding in the principles of chemistry and medicine, although he was invariably more interested in pursuing his own researches than in paying attention to his teacher.

But it was not long before Giuseppe grew bored and again he escaped, making straight for Palermo and finding a new home among the criminal fraternity there. Aged just 14, he is said to have been involved in numerous crimes, including murder. Later, as Spence has it, 'becoming tired of lesser villainies he resolved upon a grand stroke, upon which lay the foundations of his fortunes'.

At 17 he chose for his dupe a stupid, greedy and superstitious goldsmith named Marano. Posing as an expert on the occult, alchemy and the supernatural, Giuseppe cultivated a friendship with Marano, who strongly believed in the power and efficacy of magic. The goldsmith was told that there lay a considerable treasure in a field near Palermo, which he could locate with certain magical ceremonies.

There was a catch, however. Giuseppe would need certain ceremonial items to exact the treasure, including 60 ounces of gold – a small fortune. When Marano said this would not be possible, Giuseppe replied that he would enjoy the treasure alone. Eventually the avaricious goldsmith agreed to supply Giuseppe with everything he needed.

They entered the field at midnight and Giuseppe began to recite his bogus incantation while Marano, convinced that infernal powers were about to manifest themselves, threw himself on the ground in terror. At that moment, malignant forces did indeed reveal themselves – although they were far from supernatural. Giuseppe's accomplices appeared and beat Marano mercilessly before making off with his gold.

News of this crime spread quickly through Palermo and Guiseppe left hurriedly. He made for Messina, where he adopted the unwarranted title of 'Count' and changed his name to Alessandro Cagliostro.

Althotas

Some time after his arrival in Messina, he encountered an enigmatic character dressed in an Oriental caftan and accompanied by an Albanian greyhound. Struck by his unusual appearance, Cagliostro introduced himself. The man, who was about 50 years old, responded politely and offered to tell Cagliostro the story of his highly eventful life. The stranger pointed out his house and invited Cagliostro to visit just before midnight. If he knocked twice and then three times more slowly, he would be admitted.

That night, Cagliostro did so and was led into a narrow, dimly lit passageway leading to a large, candlelit room containing numerous items of alchemical equipment. The host, who had introduced himself as Althotas, discussed his theories of magic. According to Spence, Althotas 'expressed himself as a believer in the mutability of physical law rather than of magic, which he regarded as a science, having fixed laws discoverable and reducible to reason'. Althotas said he was planning to travel to Egypt, and wondered if Cagliostro would accompany him. Cagliostro readily agreed.

Althotas said that he had no money with him, but that this would not be a problem, since he possessed the secret of manufacturing gold. He also said that he was far older than he looked, possessing as he did another secret: that of eternal youth.

The two bought passage on a Genoese ship bound for Alexandria. During the voyage Althotas volunteered a little more information about himself. He claimed to know nothing of his place of birth or his parents, adding that he had spent his early years near Tunis, where he had been the slave of a wealthy Muslim pirate. At 12 he was fluent in Arabic, studied botany and read the Koran to his master, who died when Althotas was 16.

Following their travels through Egypt, they journeyed south and east, visiting kingdoms in Africa and Asia, and finally establishing a base on Rhodes, where they pursued their alchemical researches. From there they travelled to Malta, where Althotas apparently died.

Cagliostro then travelled to Naples, where he became acquainted with a Sicilian prince who so enjoyed his company that he invited Cagliostro to his castle near Palermo. With trepidation, he returned to the haunts of his youth where he had committed so many crimes, few of which had been forgotten. On a trip to Messina, he ran into an old friend, one of the thugs who had turned over the goldsmith, Marano. His friend confirmed that it was indeed dangerous for him to stay in Messina or even Palermo and suggested that Cagliostro join him in a new venture: a casino in Naples in which wealthy foreigners might be relieved of their cash.

The casino was a success, so much so that it attracted the attention of the Neapolitan authorities, who took a dim view of their activities. It was time to move on again, this time to the Papal States. Accounts of Cagliostro's life offer few details as to how he passed his time here, aside from confirming that he parted company with his colleague, and continued to prey on the naive and stupid.

Lorenza

Not long after, Cagliostro established himself as an apothecary in Rome, offering remedies for all manner of ailments and making a great deal of money. It was here that he met a beautiful young woman named Lorenza Feliciani, with whom he immediately fell in love and proposed marriage. Her father's consent was a mere formality, such was Cagliostro's apparent wealth. Lorenza was, by all accounts, a delightful young woman, charming, honest, endearingly modest and completely devoted to her new husband.

Cagliostro's biographers are unanimous that her marriage to him signalled the beginning of Lorenza's moral decline. While it is certainly true that his shady character made him a less than suitable match for her, the exact nature of their relationship is open to debate. According to Lewis Spence:

> The most dreadful accusations have been made concerning the manner in which Cagliostro treated his wife, and it has been alleged that he thoroughly ruined her character and corrupted her mind. But . . . this account has been coloured by the unscrupulous imagination of the Jesuitical writers of the Roman Inquisition. All biographers agree that Cagliostro hastened his wife's ruin, but it is difficult to know how they came by their data; and in any case they disagree substantially in their details.

It is known, however, that the couple's household quickly became the headquarters of various conmen and other ne'er-do-wells. Following a disagreement, Cagliostro and Lorenza were forced to flee Rome in the company of a character called the Marquis D'Agriata. For the next few years they wandered through southern Europe, finally ending up in Barcelona, where they stayed for six months before moving on to Madrid and then Lisbon. They then set sail for England and moved into an apartment in Whitcomb Street, London, where Cagliostro continued to dupe foreigners while continuing his studies in chemistry and physics.

In 1772, Cagliostro and Lorenza left for France, taking with them an acquaintance named Duplaisir. Soon after their arrival, Duplaisir eloped with Lorenza. Cagliostro pursued them and had his wife arrested. She spent several months in a penitentiary; however, upon her release she and Cagliostro were apparently reconciled.

The Comte de Saint Germain

It seems that Cagliostro's alchemical researches met with some success in France, which drew him to the attention of Parisian society. Such was the taste for mysticism in Europe at the time that he became a great favourite among the aristocracy. Nevertheless, once again he went too far with his claims and he was forced to flee with Lorenza, first to Brussels and then back to Palermo.

News of his return spread rapidly and reached the ears of the goldsmith Marano, who promptly had him arrested. Luck, however, was once again on Cagliostro's side. A Sicilian nobleman stepped in and arranged for Cagliostro's release and, with Lorenza, he recommenced his meandering travels, first to Malta, then Naples, Marseilles and Barcelona. Here, Cagliostro cheated a certain alchemist out of 100,000 crowns and so, yet again, the couple had to flee, this time back to England.

In London, Cagliostro became a Mason, having seen the possibility of financial benefits. He set about visiting the various London Lodges, making friends among rich and powerful members. While browsing in a bookstall one day, Cagliostro came across an odd manuscript, which apparently had belonged to one George Gaston, about whom nothing is known. The manuscript was essentially a treatise on Egyptian Masonry and contained a great deal of information on magic and mysticism. According to his biographers, it was this document that inspired Cagliostro to delve yet deeper into the arcane mysteries of the occult.

Following yet another peripatetic trip through Holland, Italy and Germany, Cagliostro visited another legendary occult figure, the Comte de Saint Germain. In a bizarre episode, the Comte agreed to receive Cagliostro and Lorenza at two o'clock in the morning, at which time they arrived at his 'Temple of Mystery' dressed in white robes. A drawbridge was lowered and they were greeted by an exceptionally tall man who led them to a dimly lit room, where folded doors sprang open to reveal a temple illuminated by hundreds of candles. The Comte de Saint Germain sat upon the altar; at his feet sat two acolytes who swung golden censers.

The Comte wore a diamond-studded pentagram upon his chest. On the steps leading to the altar stood a statue holding a vase bearing the inscription 'Elixir of Immortality'. An enormous mirror hung on one wall, above which were the words 'Store House of Wandering Souls'. The silence in the room was broken by the Comte, who asked the couple who they were, where they came from, and what they wanted. Cagliostro and Lorenza prostrated themselves before the Comte and Cagliostro declared: 'I come to invoke the God of the faithful, the Son of Nature, the Sire of Truth. I come to demand of him one of the fourteen thousand seven hundred secrets which are treasured in his breast, I come to proclaim myself his slave, his apostle, his martyr.'

After a long pause, the Comte asked what Lorenza wanted, to which she replied: 'To obey and to serve.'

A man dressed in a long mantle appeared, telling them that the ultimate goal of the Comte and his followers was the government of humanity. The Comte proceeded to tell them how he had long ago grown disillusioned with all the affairs with which humanity concerned itself. Politics, science, theology, philosophy and history were all the ridiculous amusements of a dullard race. It was only through the discovery of magic that the Comte perceived the true vastness and majesty of the Universe.

The encounter ended with a sumptuous feast, during which the couple were entreated to avoid so-called men of learning, and to spread the teachings of the Comte among the rest of humanity.

'The Divine Cagliostro'

Following his establishment of several Masonic Lodges (and the acceptance of the gifts and money that came with such establishments), Cagliostro travelled to St Petersburg, where he quickly made a reputation for himself as an effective physician. Spence notes that there has been a great deal of controversy concerning the large number of cures that were attributed to Cagliostro, adding that the likeliest explanation is 'a species of mesmeric influence', or hypnotism. It has been said that he trusted simply to the laying on of hands; that he charged nothing for his services; that most of his time was occupied in treating the poor, among whom he distributed vast amounts of money.

When he returned to Germany, Cagliostro found himself greatly admired as a benefactor of humanity, although some suspected that his cures were the result of sorcery rather than miracles. Cagliostro himself invariably claimed that they were performed with the assistance of God.

Cagliostro remained at Strasbourg for three years, during which he cultivated a close friendship with the Cardinal-Archbishop Louis de Rohan. De Rohan belonged to one of the most important and illustrious families in France. Greedy, arrogant and debauched, he enjoyed a lifestyle that was scandalous by any standards. He was also an extremely gullible man who was obsessed with alchemy and was thus a prime target for Cagliostro. It is said that he succeeded in transmuting base metal into gold under the rapt gaze of de Rohan, who was impressed enough to shower him with money. Nor had he any doubt that Cagliostro possessed the secret of eternal youth, the Elixir of Immortality, and built a house in which he intended to receive it.

When he had relieved de Rohan of the vast majority of his funds, Cagliostro decided it was once again time to be on his way and so he set off first for Bordeaux, then to Lyons, where he established a

Masonic headquarters, and then to Paris. Here he became known as a 'master of practical magic', with the power to invoke phantoms, which appeared in vases of water or mirrors. Of course, it was probably trickery, although some historians of the occult, including A.E. Waite, believe that the visions were similar to those of crystal-gazing and that Cagliostro himself was astonished at his success in the invocation of spirits. In any event, he became famous throughout Paris as 'the Divine Cagliostro' and was even introduced to the court of Louis XVI.

Cagliostro and Lorenza took full advantage of the air of mystery surrounding them. They lived in an isolated house surrounded by huge gardens. While Cagliostro conducted various magical and alchemical experiments in his laboratory, Lorenza maintained an intense privacy and only appeared very occasionally before groups of carefully selected admirers. She hosted magical suppers to which the Parisian elite waited breathlessly to be invited and at which séances would be conducted with the intention of communicating with the illustrious dead.

However, the evocation of the dead without doubt took second place to the spreading of Cagliostro's rite of Egyptian Masonry. His Lodges admitted women as well as men, with the former being instructed by Lorenza, the Grand Mistress of the Order. Cagliostro himself took the title of Grand Copt. It hardly need be said that membership of the Order came at a price and Cagliostro's coffers swelled enormously, courtesy of the powerful and wealthy who flocked to join. A confidence trickster of great skill he may have been but, as noted above, he did not keep his vast wealth entirely to himself. He gave away huge sums to the poor and needy, and did his best to ensure care for the sick.

Naturally, much mystery surrounds the Masonic rites that were practised at the headquarters in the Faubourg Saint Honoré. In his *Encyclopaedia of Occultism*, Lewis Spence offers some information on the nature of the female initiations. The initiates were required to take off their clothes and put on white robes. They were then taken into a temple containing 36 armchairs covered with black satin. Here they found Lorenza, clothed in white, seated upon a throne, on either side of which stood a tall figure dressed in such a manner that their sex could not be determined. As the light was gradually lowered, Lorenza commanded the initiates to uncover their left legs up to the thigh and to raise their right arms, to rest them on neighbouring pillars. Two young women then entered carrying swords and bound the initiates together with silk ropes.

After a lengthy silence, Lorenza gave an impassioned speech about the emancipation of women from the bonds that had been imposed upon them throughout history, symbolised by the silk ropes binding the initiates. When the speech was over, the women were freed from their bindings and were led to separate rooms, then out into the garden. Some were pursued by men who harangued them with unthinkably lewd solicitations, while others experienced the altogether more pleasant attentions of men who threw themselves sighing at their feet.

When these rites were over, the initiates returned to the temple and were congratulated by Lorenza. At this point, a skylight in the roof opened and Cagliostro descended into the room, perched upon a golden sphere with a serpent in his hand and a star upon his head. Lorenza introduced him to the initiates as the genius of truth, the Divine Cagliostro, the repository of all knowledge. He then commanded the women to disrobe, for if they were to receive truth, they should be as naked as truth itself. Lorenza also let her robes fall to the ground and watched as Cagliostro proceeded to dispense his wisdom. The magical arts, he said, were the secret of humanity's salvation and ultimate happiness. Such was the completeness of this happiness that it was not confined solely to the spiritual but applied to the material also.

When he had finished his speech, Cagliostro seated himself once more upon the golden sphere and disappeared through the ceiling.

The completion of the proceedings was marked with a ball – a rather bizarre conclusion but perhaps one that was in keeping with the extravagant theatrics of the rite itself.

The Affair of the Diamond Necklace

It is perhaps fitting (and certainly unsurprising) that a man such as Cagliostro should have become implicated in one of history's most preposterous and famous scandals.

It began when royal jewellers Boehmer and Bassenge created what was probably the most elaborate and valuable piece of jewellery in the world, a golden necklace containing no fewer than 647 diamonds. It had been intended for the notoriously ostentatious Madame du Barry, the mistress of King Louis XV of France. In today's currency, the necklace would have cost between five and ten million pounds.

Unfortunately for Boehmer and Bassenge, Louis XV died of smallpox before payment for the necklace was made. The jewellers had tied up their entire assets in its production and feared that, if another buyer could not be found, they would be ruined. Fortunately, Marie Antoinette, the wife of Louis XVI, was fully the equal of Madame du Barry when it came to extravagance and so Boehmer tried desperately to sell her the necklace. However, she declined, saying the necklace should be broken up and the diamonds sold separately.

Then enters the seductive and unscrupulous adventuress Jeanne de Valois. Having heard of Cardinal de Rohan's disgracefully hedonistic lifestyle, Jeanne managed to get herself invited to one of his castles and soon he fell prey to her charms. Jeanne's husband, a dashing gendarme named Nicolas de Lamotte, was heavily in debt; she had de Rohan pay off his debtors and promote him to captain. In one of her most daring scams, she went to Versailles and pretended to faint in a reception room. Nicolas explained to the concerned courtiers that she was of royal blood yet was suffering from malnutrition. This incredible audacity was rewarded with a large annual pension.

For Jeanne, who by now had started calling herself the Comtesse de Lamotte-Valois, the success of each escapade spurred her on to acts of ever greater trickery and mischief. It was at this time that she met Cagliostro, who told her of Cardinal de Rohan's desire to gain acceptance at the court of Versailles and despair of ever doing so owing to the queen's intense dislike of him.

It is unclear how Cagliostro and Jeanne met, or even why he told her of de Rohan's desire for royal recognition, a weakness she exploited. Perhaps he simply recognised a kindred spirit, and happily supplied her with this information about the contemptible cardinal.

Never one to miss an opportunity, Jeanne began to drop hints to de Rohan that she and the queen were great friends, promising him that at the next court event Marie Antoinette would nod to him, which he perceived she duly did. With the help of her secretary and love Retaux de Villette, Jeanne forged notes on gilded paper with the royal fleur-de-lis, to convince de Rohan that the queen had changed her mind about him.

De Rohan was falling further under Jeanne's spell and, in possession of Cagliostro's information, she searched for a scheme that would ensnare him completely. Eventually, she arranged a secret meeting between de Rohan and the 'queen' near the Grove of Venus in Marie Antoinette's private gardens.

A Parisienne prostitute called Nicole, who bore a resemblance to the queen, was dressed in a white gown, a replica of one worn by Marie Antoinette in a well-known portrait, and coached on her lines. Although she could not pull off a convincing impersonation of Marie Antoinette, Nicole's role was fleeting for the secret rendezvous. The greedy and gullible de Rohan entered the queen's private gardens and when he saw the 'queen', he emerged from his cover, approached her and bowed deeply.

Struggling to remember her words, the dim-witted Nicole whispered: 'You may hope that the past will be forgotten.' Before de

Rohan could breathe a word, a manservant in palace livery rushed up to the couple and begged the 'queen' to return to the palace immediately. As he did so, he made certain that de Rohan saw his face.

Soon afterwards Boehmer and Bassenge decided to try once more to sell their ridiculously extravagant diamond necklace to the queen. To Jeanne, this had the potential to be her most lucrative scam so far, so she immediately contacted de Rohan, telling him that the queen wished him to provide security for the purchase of the necklace. When she added that the queen had agreed to pay 1,600,000 livres in four half-yearly instalments, the cardinal's blood drained from his face. Nevertheless, he added his signature to the agreement. The necklace was duly delivered to de Rohan's house and shortly afterwards a manservant presented himself, informing the cardinal that, by order of the queen, he was to take the necklace to the palace. This was the same man seen by de Rohan on the evening he met the fake queen.

With the necklace now in her possession, Jeanne lost no time in doing what Marie Antoinette herself had advised. She broke it up, prying the diamonds from their settings with an old knife and selling them separately.

When the date of the first instalment of 400,000 livres became due, Boehmer went to see de Rohan, who was unable to pay. Noting the cardinal's anxiety and sharing his belief that Marie Antoinette possessed the necklace, Boehmer went to Versailles where he met one of the queen's ladies-in-waiting. When he mentioned the diamond necklace, the lady asked him what he was talking about: the queen had certainly not purchased any such necklace.

Knowing now that something was terribly wrong, Boehmer went to see Jeanne, who laughed in his face and told him that the affair had nothing to do with her. He would be best advised, she said, to go back to de Rohan and get the money from him. His head filled with awful visions of financial ruin, Boehmer went instead directly to King Louis XVI, who listened to his story in amazement. Marie Antoinette was also present, and when he turned to ask her if she knew anything of this affair, she shouted indignantly that Boehmer had been pestering her to buy the necklace but she had refused. What angered her more than anything, however, was that the detested de Rohan should be connected with the scandal. She demanded that he be arrested, along with all the other suspects, including Cagliostro and Lorenza, whom Jeanne accused of stealing the necklace.

Jeanne made all manner of claims against Cagliostro, including that he was a confidence trickster and a false prophet. It did not take him long, however, to prove his innocence on theft charges and at his trial he provided the galvanised public with what Lewis Spence calls 'one of the most romantic and fanciful, if manifestly absurd, life stories in the history of autobiography'. His outrageously bloated and embellished account of his life, delivered in court, illustrated his delightfully fertile and self-aggrandising imagination.

Everyone in the court thought his life story hilarious, including the judges. Although he was acquitted of any wrongdoing, his very innocence made him yet more enemies in high places. Nevertheless, he was a hero to the people, who remembered the kindness and generosity with which he had treated them.

Jeanne de Valois did not fare so well. Both Retaux de Villette and the prostitute Nicole told everything they knew about her (Nicolas de Lamotte had already fled the country and was never seen again). The punishment suffered by Jeanne further damaged the already tarnished reputation of Marie Antoinette. Jeanne was sentenced to be flogged, branded with a 'V' for *voleuse* (thief) and then imprisoned for life.

News of these dreadful events quickly spread, arousing near-universal sympathy for Jeanne. Huge numbers of people went to the Bastille to visit her, including the highest of Parisian society. A few weeks later, Jeanne managed to escape from prison disguised as a boy and fled to England, where she took her own life by jumping from the window of a brothel in 1791. Cardinal de Rohan was acquitted but was banished from court and forced to spend the rest of his life in anonymity in the countryside far from Versailles.

Cagliostro and Lorenza were released and shortly afterwards went to London, where he wrote an open letter to the French people. The letter, which was circulated widely, predicted the French Revolution, the destruction of the Bastille and the downfall of the monarchy – events that were perhaps hastened by the affair of the diamond necklace.

Decline

Not long after Cagliostro's arrival in London, an exposé of his life was printed in *Courier de l'Europe*, a French newspaper published there. His reputation was irreparably damaged, prompting further wanderings through Switzerland, Austria and finally Italy. In Rome, he found himself welcomed at first; he continued his studies in medicine and lived quietly with Lorenza. His intention had been to establish a Masonic Lodge in the Eternal City itself, which of course inspired the wrath of the Catholic Church. On 27 September 1789, Cagliostro was arrested by order of the Holy Inquisition and imprisoned in the Castle of Saint Angelo.

Following an interrogation that lasted fully 18 months, he was sentenced to death on 7 April 1791. This sentence was commuted to life imprisonment by order of the Pope, the sentence to be served in the castle in which he had been interrogated. He made a desperate attempt to escape on one occasion. Requesting the presence of a confessor, he attacked the priest sent to him, intending to strangle him and take his habit as a disguise in which to slip from the castle. The priest, however, was too strong and it was Cagliostro who was overpowered.

Cagliostro was transferred to the remote Castle of San Leo near Montefeltro. The castle's galleries, which had been cut from solid rock, were divided into cells. Cagliostro was imprisoned in one of the old dried-up cisterns that had been converted to serve as dungeons for the worst criminals. Although the sentence of death that the Inquisition had passed on him had been commuted to life imprisonment by the Holy Tribunal, it was stipulated that the commutation should be equivalent to a death sentence. Cagliostro was kept in complete isolation: his only sight of another human being was when the jailers opened the trapdoor in the ceiling of his dungeon and dropped food down to him. For three years, he languished in this dreadful hole, until the prison governor took pity on him and had him moved to a cell on ground level.

His time in the dungeon proved too much for him, however, and Cagliostro died of a stroke in 1795. Lorenza had suffered a similar fate. Sentenced by the Inquisition to imprisonment for life, she was incarcerated in the Convent of Saint Appolonia, a women's prison in Rome, where she died in 1794.

Although most historians agree that Cagliostro was Giuseppe Balsamo, others, such as W.R.H. Trowbridge, maintain that this is not the case, and that the identification of Cagliostro with Balsamo is the result of the exposé by the editor of *Courier de l'Europe*, 'a person of the lowest and most profligate habits', according to Lewis Spence. Whatever his true identity, whether he possessed genuine magical ability or whether his true talent lay simply in separating the gullible from their money, Cagliostro was without doubt one of the most charismatic figures in the history of Western occultism.

22

THE MAN WHO BUILT GOD

The Strange Life
of John Murray Spear

Since Mary Shelley's gothic masterpiece *Frankenstein* spawned the icon of the irresponsible scientist seeking to unlock the secrets of life, we have been both appalled and fascinated by the concept. Through human cloning and the development of computers with human-level intelligence, the ghost of Victor Frankenstein casts a frightening shadow across the laboratories of the genetic engineer and the computer scientist, evoking fears about what the future will bring.

However, this desire to control the creation of life is the exclusive province neither of modern technology, nor the world of gothic horror. In 1854, an experiment far stranger than that described in Shelley's novel, and more disturbing than anything in the high-tech laboratories of today, was conducted by a New England clergyman. The man's name was John Murray Spear (1804–87), and the experiment he conducted was nothing less than the construction of a living god.

The experiment reached a bizarre climax on a hilltop in Lynn, Massachusetts, in October 1854. Although Spear's experiment remains largely unknown to the general public, being merely an obscure footnote in the history of the paranormal, it resonates powerfully with the modern world, with our own hubristic ambitions and the fears and uncertainties that they are generating.

Born in Boston, Massachusetts, John Murray Spear was baptised by his namesake, John Murray, the founder of the North American branch of the Universalist Church. Spear grew up to be a widely respected man, noted for his gentleness and kindness, as well as a keen and restlessly enquiring mind.

In some ways, Spear was well ahead of his time, and his abolitionist views did not sit well with the congregation of his church at Barnstable, Massachusetts, which he acquired at 26, even though Universalism teaches that humanity is a unified whole, that all souls are destined to be saved and accepted into Heaven, and that Creation is moving inexorably towards a final state of universal holiness and love.

Nevertheless, Spear's flock became more and more hostile towards him, and eventually he lost his ministry in Barnstable. Although he briefly preached at churches in New Bedford and Weymouth, he rapidly found himself unwelcome there also. In 1844, that anger turned to violence, and Spear was badly beaten by a mob following a speech against slavery that he delivered in Portland, Maine. It took him several months to recover. Undaunted, he worked for the 'Underground Railroad' in Boston, a secret group dedicated to helping runaway slaves head north towards Canada, and freedom. He also worked tirelessly to improve the conditions in penitentiaries and to abolish the death penalty, for which he acquired the nickname 'the Prisoners' Friend'.

While Spear was in Boston, nobly but secretly following his humanitarian principles, other events were occurring in upstate New York – events that would come to divert the course of his life and beliefs, forcing them into strange and unknown territory.

The Fox family, who had recently moved into a farmhouse in Hydesville, New York, began to be disturbed by strange and inexplicable noises in their new home, including raps, sharp knocks and the sounds of furniture being moved. These noises seemed to be concentrated in the bedroom of ten-year-old Maggie Fox and her sister Kate, aged seven. The girls thought of a name for the unseen cause of the mysterious noises: they called it 'Mr Splitfoot'.

One day in March 1848, Kate Fox clapped her hands loudly several times, crying: 'Mr Splitfoot, do as I do!' At once, to the family's astonishment, the same number of knocks came back. Thus the family established contact with whatever was causing the sounds, and through a simple 'yes and no' code of knocks the Fox family discovered that their farmhouse was being haunted by the ghost of a peddler named Charles Rosma, who had been murdered five years earlier in one of the bedrooms.

Word of these bizarre events spread rapidly, and before long the Fox sisters had become famous throughout the country. With the introduction of an alphabet code, more complex messages began to be received. Soon, other spirits seemed to join that of Charles Rosma, one of which gave this cryptic message:

> Dear friends, you must proclaim this truth to the world. This
> is the dawning of a new era; you must not try to conceal it
> any longer. When you do your duty God will protect you and
> the spirits will watch over you.

The Spiritualist movement was born amongst the whisperings of the dead at the Fox family home in Hydesville. Maggie and Kate gave countless demonstrations to the public, and thousands of ordinary people seized on the idea that communication with the spirit world was potentially open to anyone. Séances were conducted in homes across the country and Spiritualism became the hot topic of conversation everywhere. Everyone seemed fascinated with the possibilities it offered, especially reformers like Spear, who realised that the world of the spirit, contact with which had hitherto been mediated by priests and preachers, was in reality open to all.

Spear decided that in Spiritualism his own true path lay. He left the Universalist Church in 1851 and, with the encouragement of his daughter Sophronia, began to work as a trance medium. As with so many who have followed this calling, Spear quickly managed to make contact with the spirits of a number of famous historical personages, including the great mystic Emanuel Swedenborg and Benjamin Franklin.

A few months later, Spear was contacted by the spirit of John Murray, the founder of the Universalist Church, who gave him 12 messages. He published these under the title *Messages from the Superior State* and then gave a series of public demonstrations in which he entered a trance state and allowed the 'spirits' to speak through him. His audiences, however, were less than impressed: it looked to them suspiciously like Spear himself, rather than the denizens of the beyond, was speaking.

While the Fox sisters enjoyed national fame and other Spiritualists were drawing great public attention, Spear continued to struggle in obscurity, and would probably have continued to do so, had he not travelled to Rochester, New York, at the suggestion of his 'spirit advisers'. There, in 1853, the special mission for which he had been chosen was revealed to him.

The group of spirits with which he was in contact identified themselves as the 'Association of Beneficence'. They declared themselves to be a benign fraternity dedicated to elevating humanity to a higher spiritual state through the (perhaps paradoxical) use of advanced technology. The Association of Beneficence was composed of a number of subgroups with bizarre and rather clumsy names such as Electricizers, Healthfulizers, Educationalizers, Agriculturalizers, Elementizers and Governmentizers.

Spear was entrusted with the first and most important task in the programme of human spiritual elevation: the construction of the 'New Messiah', which would bring new life and vitality to all things on Earth, both living and inanimate. The Electricizers instructed

Spear to begin construction of the Messiah on High Rock, a wild and lonely hill overlooking the town of Lynn, Massachusetts. Like many places in New England, Lynn's history was steeped in witchcraft and the strange struggle between light and darkness. In his article on Spear in *Fortean Times* (Issue 158), Damon Schneck notes that the town 'is now poor and unemployment is high, but it was once well known for shoe manufacturing and has a history that is pure Lovecraft, full of witchcraft, sea serpents, spontaneous human combustion and rioting Quakers'.

It is perhaps unsurprising that such a place would not be entirely unsympathetic to the rise of Spiritualism and its vast popularity. In fact, High Rock and the nearby cottage which took its name were owned by the Hutchinsons, enthusiastic Spiritualists and reformers who had hosted a number of séances and known to Spear during his time as a minister in Boston.

The Hutchinsons readily agreed to contribute to Spear's (or the spirits') plan, and gave him their woodshed in which to construct what would later come to be known as 'the God machine'. In effect, a small woodshed on the side of a hill in Massachusetts would be the modern corollary of the manger in Bethlehem in which another Messiah was born 2,000 years ago.

The construction of the Messiah would be achieved in four phases, the first of which involved Spear entering a trance state and receiving plans or blueprints from the Electricizers. During the nine-month-long phase of construction-proper, he received some 200 messages containing instructions on which materials to use and how to put them together.

When the contraption was finally completed following its nine-month 'gestation', it was placed on the Hutchinsons' dining-room table. It was like nothing anyone had ever seen or imagined. Schneck quotes a description of the New Messiah thus:

From the centre of the table rose two metallic uprights connected at the top by a revolving steel shaft. The shaft supported a transverse steel arm from whose extremities were suspended two large steel spheres enclosing magnets. Beneath the spheres there appeared . . . a very curiously constructed fixture, a sort of oval platform, formed of a peculiar combination of magnets and metals. Directly above this were suspended a number of zinc and copper plates, alternately arranged, and said to correspond with the brain as an electric reservoir. These were supplied with lofty metallic conductors, or attractors, reaching upward to an elevated stratum of atmosphere said to draw power directly from the atmosphere. In combination with these principal parts were adjusted various metallic bars, plates, wires, magnets, insulating substances, peculiar chemical compounds, etc. . . . At certain points around the circumference of these structures, and connected with the centre, small steel balls enclosing magnets were suspended. A metallic connection with the earth, both positive and negative, corresponding with the two lower limbs, right and left, of the body, was also provided.

Impressive as this device must have appeared, the Electricizers informed Spear that it was merely a working model, a kind of practice run for the real Messiah, which would be much larger and would cost ten times as much to construct. Since this model had cost $2,000, Spear and his colleagues must have wondered where on earth they were going to get the money for the project.

The next phase involved the charging of the machine with an electric current, after which several carefully selected men and women were brought into its direct vicinity, presumably to charge it with an energy of an altogether subtler kind.

The final phase in the construction of this working model of the

New Messiah involved a woman (whose identity remains unknown) who was called 'the Mary of the New Dispensation'. She arrived at High Rock Cottage on 29 June 1854 and lay on the floor in front of the machine. For two hours she writhed on the floor, apparently in labour, although it does not seem that she was actually pregnant. Presently, she stood up and touched the machine, and, according to Spear and the others, for a few moments the machine became alive.

Shortly afterwards, the Spiritualist journal *New Era*, which was edited by one of the participants in the experiment, proclaimed: 'The time of deliverance has come at last, and henceforward the career of humanity is upward and onward – a mighty noble and godlike career.'

Spear himself was even more effusive, describing the machine as 'the New Motive Power, the Physical Savior, Heaven's Last Gift to Man, New Creation, Great Spiritual Revelation of the Age, Philosopher's Stone, Art of all Arts, Science of all Sciences, the New Messiah'.

One feels sorry for Spear for several reasons, not least because he was so clearly and profoundly delusional – a fact made all the more poignant by the undeniable goodness and nobility of his heart. He was without doubt a brave and enlightened man: the severe beating he received at the hands of the mob in Portland did not discourage him from his anti-slavery cause and his pronouncements on the rights of women and the moral bankruptcy of the death penalty command the greatest admiration and respect.

Another cause for sympathy is the less than enthusiastic reception his machine received even from ardent Spiritualists. A letter to the *Spiritual Telegraph* from one man who was invited to view the machine remarked that the contraption did not seem animate in the slightest. While there was some very small movement in some of the hanging spheres, this was hardly evidence of life! One wonders whether Spear himself was dismayed at the fruit of his labours; at any rate, he quickly responded by saying that this feebleness was only to be expected in a newborn infant.

The famous medium and healer Andrew Jackson Davis, who was known as the 'Seer of Poughkeepsie', wrote at length on Spear's strange experiment. While he accepted the essential goodness and nobility of Spear's intentions, Davis did wonder whether the spirits had been entirely truthful with him when making their claims for the 'New Messiah' (he also wondered whether Spear had been in touch with spirits at all, or merely with his own mind).

It seems, however, that the spirits were also rather concerned at the machine's patent lack of animation, and the Electricizers suggested that perhaps it should be moved to another location. Spear promptly complied, and the New Messiah was taken from High Rock to the town of Randolph, New York, and placed in a temporary enclosure.

Unfortunately, the townspeople got wind of what had been brought into their midst, and a mob broke into the shed to smash the New Messiah to pieces. That, at least, is what Spear himself claimed; however, as Schneck notes, there is no mention in contemporary sources of any such event having occurred in Randolph, and Schneck speculates that the machine may simply have been 'discreetly sunk into a pond or buried in the woods'.

In his article, Schneck provides a cogent assessment of the story of the New Messiah, noting that it was 'characteristic of the period'. Spear believed that in technology lay the most promising route to humanity's salvation: it was through technology, 'the most powerful force of the era', that men and women would ultimately come to know God. It is a belief whose significance today can only increase, as we uncover ever greater and more profound mysteries of the Universe.

23

A Superhuman Villain?

The Weird Exploits of Spring-heeled Jack

At 8.45 on the evening of 20 February 1838, the bell of the Alsop family cottage rang suddenly and loudly. The cottage near the village of Old Ford, to the east of London, was isolated and visitors or even passers-by were few and far between. The family was perplexed at the thought that someone was paying them a visit at this late hour on a cold winter night.

When the bell rang again, more loudly this time and for longer, 18-year-old Jane Alsop volunteered to see who it was. She opened the front door and hurried to the gate, peering into the ink-darkness at the tall cloaked figure. Jane could just about make out some kind of helmet on the figure's head, an impression that seemed to be confirmed when the dark figure cried out: 'I am a policeman! For God's sake, bring me a light, for we have caught Spring-heeled Jack here in the lane!'

Jane gasped at the mention of the name, for in only a few months the demonic villain known as Spring-heeled Jack had become notorious throughout London. Nobody knew who or what he was, save that sometimes he appeared as a ghost clad in clanking armour, sometimes as a monkey, sometimes as a bear – and sometimes as the Devil himself.

Without uttering a word, Jane ran back to the cottage to do as the policeman had ordered. She returned with a lighted candle, which she held out to him, expecting him to take it and make off towards his fiendish quarry.

Instead, he threw back his cloak and held the candle to his chest, so that its flickering flame illuminated his face.

And it was a face of such hideousness that Jane Allsop could do nothing but scream in shock and terror. The man's eyes were the colour of burning coals and shone as brightly in the chill winter darkness. His head was indeed crowned with a helmet, but it was not a policeman's helmet, as Jane had at first supposed, nor was it like any helmet she had ever seen. The man's features were pinched and unnaturally tight, as if he wore some kind of horrible flesh-fashioned mask, and he was dressed in a tight-fitting suit that shone in the candlelight. A strange, box-like object, resembling a lamp, was strapped to his chest.

As if galvanised to dreadful action by her scream, Spring-heeled Jack lunged forward and belched a stream of blue fire into her face. He grabbed her with fingers that seemed like long, sharp metal talons, which tore at her face and clothes.

Screaming again, Jane managed to tear herself free of his grip and fled towards the front door of the cottage. But Jack would not be denied his prey, and he sprang after her up the short garden path, catching her on the doorstep where he resumed his attack, ripping her clothes and tearing chunks of hair from her head.

Alerted by the commotion, Jane's younger sister Mary appeared at the door. But so shocked was she by the sight which greeted her that she could do nothing but stand and stare in terror and dismay. Fortunately for Jane, her elder sister, Mrs Sarah Harrison, also appeared. She managed to wrestle her sibling from the monster's grip and slammed the door in his face.

Jack was not so easily thwarted, however, and he remained at the front door, banging loudly upon it, until the Alsop family retreated to an upstairs room, flung open the window and screamed at the tops of their lungs for the police. It would seem to have been a forlorn hope, given the cottage's lonely location, and yet it had the desired effect, for presently Spring-heeled Jack departed into the enveloping darkness from which he had emerged.

The history of the paranormal is filled with tales of strange beings who appear suddenly and without warning in the world of 'normality', to frighten, torment or even to offer assistance to the perplexed humans who encounter them. In the years since his first appearance, the legend of Spring-heeled Jack has grown and transformed, given our changing attitudes in the wake of alleged visits from extraterrestrials. That something strange visited England on several occasions in the nineteenth and early twentieth centuries is beyond doubt. However, whether it was a real person or entity or simply an outbreak of mass hysteria is still open to conjecture.

The Alsop family were not the only ones to suffer Jack's attentions in the month of February 1838. Two days earlier, Lucy Scales and her sister were returning home from a visit to their brother. They were walking along Green Dragon Alley in the Limehouse area of London's docklands when they became aware of a tall, thin figure lurking in the alley's shadows. As they approached the figure, it turned and spat a stream of blue fire at Lucy, who collapsed to the ground in terror. As she rushed to her aid, Lucy's sister caught a glimpse of the figure bounding off into the darkness, a strange lamp-like device strapped to his chest.

A few days later, an attack very similar to the one committed at the Alsop residence was reported. A stranger rapped loudly upon the door of a Mr Ashworth's house in Turner Street, and when the servant boy answered, the figure threw back its cloak, revealing the bizarre, tight-fitting costume reportedly worn by Spring-heeled Jack. One glance at the strange pinched features of Jack's hideous face was enough to bring forth a high scream from the boy. Apparently mindful of possible pursuit, the apparition made off immediately – but not before the boy noticed that upon the hem of Jack's cloak there was an embroidered letter W . . .

By this time, the exploits of Spring-heeled Jack were spoken of throughout London. It seems he had appeared dozens of times to attack and terrify unwary night-time travellers across the metropolis. His modus operandi was always the same: he would skulk in the shadows of dark streets and alleyways, and then would leap out upon his victims, breathing blue fire into their faces and tearing at them with his fearsome metal talons. His method of escape was as outrageous and inexplicable as his appearance and actions: he was capable of making extraordinarily long leaps, bounding like some monstrous frog across the rooftops of the surrounding buildings, leaving the screams of his victims far behind.

Nor were his attacks confined to the capital: reports of his nefarious activities came from across the Home Counties, where he would hide in remote lanes and then leap upon travellers, frightening them senseless before bounding off into the night. Between 1840 and 1870, he widened his circle of terror, visiting counties from Warwickshire in the north to Devon in the south. Although his chief targets were women, he would also, on occasion, attack men, especially coachmen, whom he would leap upon without warning as they made their way along lonely roads after dark.

Most of the time, Jack seemed content with frightening people and ripping at their clothes, but in November 1845 his legend took an altogether darker and more horrible turn. It happened in Jacob's Island, Bermondsey, an area of filthy slums, ramshackle houses and rotting tenements surrounded by fetid marshes and stinking open sewers. On that dreadful night, a 13-year-old prostitute named Maria Davis was walking across a rickety wooden bridge that precariously spanned one particularly foul marsh-sewer called Folly Ditch.

Without warning, Jack appeared and bounded onto the bridge.

In full view of several terrified and appalled onlookers, he breathed his blue fire into the girl's face, lifted her above his head and cast her down into the filthy slime of Folly Ditch. The hapless child stood no chance of escape, for the filth-clogged sewer was like quicksand. She struggled briefly and then vanished into its depths. Before any of the onlookers could act, Jake bounded away into the night, a murderer.

In the spring of 1877, Jack apparently decided to take on the British Army, which led many to suppose that he must either be an out-and-out lunatic or possess genuinely superhuman powers. The Aldershot barracks in Hampshire were home to 10,000 troops at any given time and were of course well guarded by armed sentries. It became a habit of Jack to leap up onto the roofs of sentry boxes and reach down to grab the sentries' faces with his ice-cold taloned hands before bounding off with impossibly long strides across the surrounding countryside. On several occasions, sentries were able to shake off their fear and surprise quickly enough to loose a few rounds after him. They never managed to hit him . . . or if they did, his rapidly retreating figure showed no signs of having been injured.

A few months later, having left the combined might of the British Army shaken and nonplussed, Jack travelled north to Lincoln, where he appeared dressed in an outlandish sheepskin costume, bounding over rooftops and prancing upon the ancient Roman monument known as Newport Arch. Having taunted the inhabitants of Lincoln, he once again made his leaping escape across the countryside.

For the next 30 years, little was heard of Spring-heeled Jack, and in 1904 he made what would be his last appearance – at least in England. For several nights, he terrorised the residents of William Henry Street in Liverpool, leaping from the street to the rooftops and back down again, and flinging terrified witnesses to the ground.

His very last appearance was in broad daylight. After running up and down William Henry Street, he made an astonishing 25-foot leap onto the rooftops, cast a contemptuous glance at the witnesses and, with a loud, mocking laugh, disappeared into the shadowy realms of myth from which he had come.

Mike Dash, one of the most sober and critical of researchers into the paranormal, has conducted an exhaustive examination of contemporary newspaper reports in an effort to get to the bottom of the mystery of Spring-heeled Jack. He notes that most newspapers conceded that something must have caused the widespread panic that gripped London at the time and that several, including *The Times* and the *Morning Chronicle*, reported the rumour that a gang of bored noblemen was causing the frightful mischief as part of a wager. Apparently, the gang was made up of 'rascals connected with high families and that bets to the amount of £5,000 are at stake upon the success or failure of the abominable proceedings'. The 'proceedings' were, it was claimed, 'to destroy the lives of not less than 30 human beings! viz. eight old bachelors, ten old maids, and six ladies' maids, and as many servant girls as they can, by depriving them of their reason, and otherwise accelerating their deaths'.

To some members of the public, this seemed a plausible explanation. According to one unnamed individual, in a letter to the Lord Mayor of London:

> [S]ome individuals (of, as the writer believes, the higher ranks of life) have laid a wager with a mysterious and foolhardy companion (name as yet unknown), that he durst not take upon himself the task of visiting many of the villages near London in three disguises – a ghost, a bear and a devil; and, moreover, that he will not dare to enter gentlemen's gardens for the purpose of alarming the inmates of the house. The wager has, however, been accepted, and the unmanly villain has succeeded in depriving seven ladies of their senses. At one house he rung the bell, and on the servant coming to open the door, this worse than brute stood in a no less dreadful

figure than a spectre clad most perfectly. The consequence was that the poor girl immediately swooned, and has never from that moment been in her senses, but, on seeing any man, screams out most violently, 'Take him away!' There are two ladies (which your lordship will regret to hear) who have husbands and children, and who are not expected to recover, but likely to become a burden on their families.

The attack upon Jane Alsop was reported to Lambeth Street Police Office and was investigated by the famous detective James Lea, who had solved the infamous Red Barn murder case in 1827, and who was regarded as the best detective in London at the time.

Lea lost no time in going to work, and within a day had drawn up a report, which was described in the *Morning Herald* of 23 February 1838:

[Lea] stated that from what they had learned he had no doubt that the person by whom the outrage had been committed had been in the neighbourhood for nearly a month past, frightening men as well as women, and had, on one occasion, narrowly escaped apprehension. A person, answering precisely his size and figure, had been frequently observed walking about the lanes and lonely places, enveloped in a large Spanish cloak, and was sometimes in the habit of carrying a small lantern about with him. On one occasion he partially exhibited his masquerade in Bow-fair fields, and was closely pursued by a number of men in the employment of Mr Giles, a coach-master at Bow, but, by the most extraordinary agility and apparently a thorough knowledge of the locality of the place, he got clear off. The officer added he was perfectly satisfied of the truth of the statement of Miss Alsop as to the violence inflicted upon her by the person she described; indeed the whole family, all of whom had seen him, agreed precisely in this description; but he differed in opinion with Mr Alsop that there was more than one person concerned in the outrage. The situation of Mr Alsop's house being at a considerable distance from any other, and in a very lonely spot, afforded ample opportunity for the ghost, as he was called, to play off his pranks with impunity; but besides this, it was quite evident that the family were not strangers to him, as he was well acquainted with the name of Mr Alsop. After the outrage was committed, it appeared, the family threw up the windows, and called out loudly for the police and assistance, and their cries being heard at the John Bull public house, some distance off, three persons set out from thence in the direction of Mr Alsop's and on their way thither they met a tall person wrapped up in a large cloak, who said as they came up that a policeman was wanted at Mr Alsop's, and they took no further notice of him. This person, he felt convinced, was no other than the perpetrator of the outrage himself.

Lea's investigation revealed several (entirely human) suspects, but no one was ever convicted of Spring-heeled Jack's crimes. The most promising contender would, at first sight, appear to have been Henry, Marquis of Waterford. Henry was notorious for his sadistic sense of humour, and his title would seem to fit neatly with the embroidered 'W' seen on Jack's cloak. However, Waterford died in 1859, and Jack's exploits continued, on and off, for nearly 50 years afterwards. Moreover, Mike Dash was unable to find even a single mention of the embroidered 'W' in his exhaustive search through the newspaper reports of the period and concludes that it is almost certainly one of the many rumours and embellishments of the Spring-heeled Jack legend that appeared at the time and in the many years since.

Also of dubious authenticity is the most lurid and frightful of Jack's exploits, the horrible murder of Maria Davis, allegedly hurled from a bridge by the monster to drown in an open sewer.

Dash searched contemporary newspapers and coroners' records but could find no mention of a Maria Davis or her dreadful end. There is a contemporary woodcut showing two men in a punt, apparently looking for something in the surrounding waters. The illustration accompanied the article on Spring-heeled Jack that appeared in the partwork *The Unexplained* in 1981 and was credited to what is now the Hulton Getty Picture Collection. Dash contacted the Collection, where a librarian informed him that the woodcut had nothing whatsoever to do with the murder of Maria Davis. The librarian sent him a large copy of the print, which shows the figures in the punt gathering water in a pan, not searching for a dead body. It would seem that the dreadful fate of Maria Davis was merely one of the many legends associated with Spring-heeled Jack's reign of terror.

24

THE MOST MYSTERIOUS MANUSCRIPT IN THE WORLD

The Enigma of the
Voynich Manuscript

When Wilfred M. Voynich found himself in the library of the Jesuit college at Villa Mondragone in Frascati, near Rome, he could scarcely have guessed at the unique puzzle he was about to discover – a puzzle which remains unsolved to this day.

The year was 1912, and Voynich, an unprepossessing antique book dealer and collector, had been accepted by the Jesuits as buyer of part of their manuscript collection, numbering more than 1,000 volumes. The sale was an unfortunate necessity for the college, which needed to fund restorations for the villa. Voynich was chosen as buyer over one other, from Padua, apparently the only other competitor for the right to buy the Mondragone manuscripts.

Here in the rarefied atmosphere of a theological college Wilfred Voynich stumbled upon the fantastic enigma that would one day be named after him. Having inspected a number of extremely valuable manuscripts, Voynich picked up a drab volume with a limp vellum cover. It measured six inches by nine and contained over 200 pages. The pages were made of soft, light-brown calfskin and were uneven at the edges. The volume was held together by three leather thongs and was wrapped in more vellum that had been folded in around the edges to make a cover. When asked about its origin, the priests could only inform Voynich that the book had been discovered in an old chest in the college.

As he carefully leafed through the book, Voynich grew more and more puzzled by its contents. The bizarre illustrations of unknown plants and human figures encased in vessels connected to each other by complex systems of pipes led the collector to suspect that the strange book might hold some profound significance in the history of science. Scanning the text in the not-unreasonable hope that it would reveal something of the book's nature, Voynich was quickly disappointed, for it was written entirely in a beautifully ornate but utterly indecipherable script. The only elements that bore any relation to recognisable reality were the illustrations, yet even these posed more questions than they answered. What were the strange vessels containing the human figures? Why were they connected to each other by such intricate piping? Were the figures homunculi, artificially created beings and, if so, did this imply some long-lost treatise on alchemy? Perhaps most disturbingly, why did the book contain carefully drawn illustrations of plants that did not exist and objects that looked like galaxies?

His curiosity thoroughly piqued, Voynich bought the book, along with 30 or so other manuscripts, from the Jesuits and returned to America, where he immediately began to devote himself to deciphering the mysterious text. He had a number of intriguing clues to guide his investigations. There was a letter attached to the book's first page, dated 19 August 1666, by the scientist and Rector of Prague University, Johannes Marcus Marci, presenting the book to the Jesuit scholar Athanasius Kircher (famous for trying and failing to decipher Egyptian hieroglyphics and for having lowered himself into the crater of Mount Vesuvius to observe the actions of subterranean forces) along with a faded signature on the first page, indicating that the book had once belonged to one Jacobus de Tepenec. Finally, there was also the fact that the collection housed in the Villa Mondragone had once been part of the private library of P. Petrus Beckx SJ, 22nd General of the Society of Jesus.

Voynich lost no time in pursuing the first of these clues, the letter from Marci to Kircher, which stated that Marci had received the book from a close friend and had decided that no one would be able to understand it except Kircher. Voynich noted that the book had once belonged to the Holy Roman Emperor Rudolph II of Bohemia, who had paid 600 ducats for it. This was a sizeable amount, equal to about $13,000 in Voynich's time. The collector wondered who had presented the book to Rudolph (the letter referred to him only as 'the bearer'), and so he consulted the biographies of many of the known visitors to the Emperor's court. Eventually he decided that the most promising candidate was the famous occultist Dr John Dee. Voynich was convinced that the book itself was the work of Roger Bacon, the English scientist, encyclopaedist, philosopher, alchemist and Franciscan monk, who was known as Doctor Mirabilis (Admirable Doctor) in recognition of his vast range of skills. Dee was a great admirer of Bacon and was known to have taken a number of the latter's works with him on his European travels.

Voynich decided that the best way to proceed would be to make photostat copies of the book and circulate them among various scholars whom he assumed would have little trouble deciphering the text. These included palaeographers, medieval historians, cryptographers, linguists, philologists, even astronomers and botanists. Although he had high hopes for a speedy resolution to the enigma, the numerous experts whose help he sought were unable to offer any satisfactory answers.

However, there was plenty of work to be done on the provenance of the manuscript, and Voynich established that sometime after 1608 it was passed to Jacobus de Tepenec, the director of the Emperor's botanical gardens (whose signature was on the first page). When de Tepenec died in 1622, the manuscript passed to an unidentified individual, who subsequently left it to Marci in his will. It is not entirely clear what happened to the manuscript between 1666 and 1912, when Voynich acquired it, although it is known that it resided for some time in the private library of Petrus Beckx, who removed it and a number of other manuscripts from the Collegio Romano (now called the Pontificia Università Gregoriana), the main centre of Jesuit learning in Rome, in 1870.

The Pontificia Università Gregoriana is also the repository of the letters received by Athanasius Kircher (a collection known as the *carteggio kircheriano*). Certain material in this collection (not to mention the cryptic letter attached to the manuscript) suggests that the unnamed individual who left the manuscript to Johannes Marcus Marci sent several transcribed portions to Kircher; however, there is no record in the *carteggio* of Kircher's response to this material. Intriguingly, there is some evidence that Marci inherited the manuscript along with the alchemical library of one George Barschius, who is unknown to historians of alchemy, in spite of there being a letter from him in the *carteggio kircheriano*.

The *Voynich Manuscript* has become something of a cause célèbre in both occult circles and the field of cryptanalysis, by virtue of its utter impenetrability. The cipher in which it is written has defied all attempts at decryption. At first sight, it looks like an ordinary medieval 'herbal', or treatise on the medicinal uses of various plants. This would also explain the astronomical and astrological diagrams. As the British writer on occultism Colin Wilson reminds us: 'One would expect astronomical or astrological diagrams in a herbal, because the plants were often supposed to be gathered by the full moon, or when the stars and planets were in a certain position.' The only problem is that most of the plants illustrated do not exist. One of the exceptions is a drawing of what looks like a sunflower, which indicates that this part of the book had to have been written after 1492, when Columbus voyaged to America.

The possibility that the manuscript was a hoax perpetrated upon the Emperor Rudolph has prompted researchers to consider having it radio-carbon dated. However, this is unlikely to be of much help, since an accurate dating of the vellum of the pages would tell us nothing of the date at which the ink was applied to those pages.

All of this notwithstanding, Wilfred Voynich had little doubt that the manuscript would yield its secrets once twentieth-century decryption techniques had been applied to it, and so he distributed copies to various interested parties. Unfortunately, the experts who examined the manuscript could not even figure out which language it had been written in prior to encoding. (It could be a natural language, such as English, German, Spanish, Greek, Hebrew; or an invented language such as the Enochian of John Dee, the lingua ignota of Hildegarde von Bingen, Beck's 'Universal Character', or Johnston's 'Synthetic Language'.)

While the secrets of the *Voynich Manuscript* remain intact, there have been a number of 'false dawns' over the years, notably the work of William Romaine Newbold, a professor of philosophy at the University of Pennsylvania who in 1921 claimed to have cracked the manuscript's code. According to Newbold, the text had originally been written by Roger Bacon in Latin anagrams, which, once unravelled, revealed that the thirteenth-century philosopher and Franciscan monk possessed an intellect far surpassing those of even Galileo or Isaac Newton. Newbold claimed that the tadpole-like drawings in the manuscript's margins were actually spermatozoa seen through the microscope Bacon had invented. In addition, Bacon had also invented the telescope four centuries before Galileo, through which he had observed the great spiral galaxy M31 in Andromeda (at 4.2 million light years, the closest spiral galaxy to our own Milky Way).

In 1931, however, Newbold's conclusions were disproved by the philologist Dr John M. Manly of the University of Chicago, who showed that Newbold's anagramming process could not be counted on to produce accurate results. In addition, Newbold had integrated certain unusual manuscript symbols, similar to shorthand, into his interpretative system; but when Manly examined these symbols more closely, he realised that they had been made to look like shorthand by the ink peeling off the vellum in certain places.

The *Voynich Manuscript* interests cryptanalysts chiefly as an intriguing intellectual puzzle, while occultists are fascinated by the arcane knowledge it might reveal, if only it could be decoded. Indeed, in 1960 an antiquarian bookseller named Hans Kraus bought the manuscript from Voynich's widow for no less than $160,000, suggesting that it might well contain astonishing information on the history of humanity. He even maintained that a fair asking price for such information (decoded or not) would be a million dollars. When no one showed any interest in paying this sum, he donated it to Yale University in 1969, where it remains in the Beinecke Rare Book Library, its secrets intact.

The *Voynich Manuscript* is one of those fascinating historical puzzles which, by their very impenetrability, provide us with the perfect template on which to project our most outlandish fears and desires. For some it is nothing more than a book on medicinal herbs, a quaint relic of medieval times; while for others the strange diagrams and non-existent plants hint at far more sinister information. Some have suggested that, should the *Voynich Manuscript* ever be deciphered, it will reveal itself to be none other than the frightful *Necronomicon*, the forbidden book of ancient lore described by H.P. Lovecraft in his wonderfully weird and macabre stories (Colin Wilson wrote a story called 'The Return of the Lloigor' in which this is proved to be the case). If those who hold such sinister suspicions about the *Voynich Manuscript* are to be believed, then the day of its decipherment may spell the beginning of the end for humanity on Earth.

25

THE LADY IN THE LIGHT

The Visions at Fatima

People had been gathering all morning, a steady murmuring stream flowing over hills that looked like the shoulders of prone giants beneath a blue marble sky. Lucia realised that they were not just coming from her village of Fatima but from many other villages scattered across the surrounding countryside. Lucia wondered how many villages there were in Portugal and how many more there were in the world; she wondered if one day people might come from all of them to watch her speak with the vision who had come from beyond the clouds.

She knew it was naughty to think like that, but no one had ever really paid her any attention before – except her family, of course – but now . . . now there were hundreds of people watching her, perhaps thousands! It felt good to be in everyone's thoughts like this. She knew that some people didn't believe her and had told her parents that she was only claiming to have seen what the Catholic Church knows as Our Lady to get attention. Why, they asked, would the Holy Virgin appear to a ten-year-old girl and her two cousins? It was ridiculous, they said, adding that Lucia, Jacinta and Francisco should be punished for the sins they were committing in telling such lies.

But Lucia and her cousins were not lying. As she watched people arriving at the ancient hollow in the hillside called the Cova da Iria, Lucia thought again of the first time Our Lady had appeared, exactly two months previously. The children had been out tending the family's flock of sheep. As the eldest, Lucia had been given the responsibility of being in charge; she had been angry with Francisco for wanting to play all the time, instead of doing what he had been told.

When the bright flash of light came from amongst the clouds to the east, Lucia thought a thunderstorm was on its way. Calling out to Jacinta and Francisco, she began to gather the flock, preparing to return home. But no thunder followed the flash and no rain fell. This surprised Lucia: thunder always followed lightning. She remembered how her father had taught her to count the seconds between the flash and the roar; by doing that, you would always know how far away the storm was. She counted and counted . . . and still no sound came from the sky.

Instead, a second flash came and now Lucia grew afraid, for it did not come from the sky but from the gnarled and ancient oak tree in the hollow of the Cova da Iria. She had heard stories of people who had been struck by lightning; her mother said it was one of the ways in which God punished sinners, ending their lives in a single moment. That's why it was so important to be good at all times, because God could do that: He could reach down from Heaven whenever He chose and take you out of the world and there was nothing more you could do until the Day of Judgement, when everyone would have their souls weighed and the decision would be made – the final, terrible decision . . .

As she gazed uncertainly at the oak tree, Lucia wondered whether God was angry enough at Francisco to take him out of the world. Her fear grew, for she loved her cousin and did not want him to be harmed, no matter how naughty he was. With a trembling hand, she took the Rosary from her pocket and began to pray. Francisco and Jacinta ran up to her, full of questions, all thoughts of play forgotten, their faces drawn in lines of confusion.

Yet another flash appeared over the oak tree; only this time the light remained, a cloud of illumination in the dull midday air. Although the light hurt their eyes at first, they quickly became accustomed to it: to Lucia it was like going from a dark room into bright sunlight. A figure appeared within the bright cloud of light: a woman more beautiful than any she had ever seen. She was dressed completely in white, radiating brightness like a glass of clear water held up to the rays of the sun. 'Do not be afraid,' she said. 'I will do you no harm.'

Jacinta and Francisco were struck dumb with astonishment. Lucia stepped forward and asked: 'Where is Your Grace from?'

'I am from Heaven.'

'What does Your Grace want of me?' asked Lucia. She had completely forgotten the Rosary she still held in her hand.

'I have come to ask you to come here for six months in succession, on the thirteenth day, at this same hour. Later on, I will tell you who I am and what I want. Afterwards, I will return here yet a seventh time.'

'Will I go to Heaven?' asked Lucia. She surprised herself with the question: it had leaped unbidden to her mind; and yet, now that she had asked it, it seemed the correct one, the only one.

'Yes,' the Lady replied, 'you will.'

'And Jacinta?'

'Also.'

'And . . . ' Lucia hesitated. 'Francisco?'

'Also, but he will have to say many Rosaries.'

Suddenly, Lucia remembered two friends of hers who had died recently. They used to visit her family often, to learn weaving from her eldest sister. 'Is Maria das Neves in Heaven?'

'Yes, she is,' the Lady replied.

'And Amelia?'

'She will be in Purgatory until the end of the world.'

Lucia didn't know why this was, and she felt tears well up in her eyes; her heart suddenly ached with sadness and a longing for something she could not describe.

'Are you willing to offer yourselves to God to bear all the sufferings He wants to send you, as an act of reparation for the sins by which He is offended, and for the conversion of sinners?'

Lucia wiped the tears from her eyes. 'Yes, we are willing.'

'You are then going to have much to suffer, but the grace of God will be your comfort.'

As she said these words, Our Lady opened her hands, and within them the children saw a light that was yet more intense than the radiance surrounding her. The light penetrated their eyes and filled their beings to the very depths of their souls; and in the light they saw themselves in the presence of God; and their reflections were clearer than ever they had seen them in the cleanest mirror.

'Recite the Rosary every day,' the Lady said, 'in order to obtain peace for the world and the end of the war.'

'Will the war last a long time? Will it end soon?' Lucia asked.

'I cannot tell you yet, for I have not yet told you what I want.'

The Lady had then risen into the air, moving towards the east, in the direction from which the first flash had come.

Lucia held on tightly to her father's hand and looked again at the people who had now gathered amongst the olive trees. They looked like blades of grass, she thought; with eyes that watched her without blinking: full of hope, full of joy and sadness and love and anger. She remembered asking Francisco what he had seen in the light the Lady had held in her hands. 'Sadness,' he replied. 'I saw the sadness of God. I thought I was going to die.' She had felt the same way, as if she could not live for long in the Divine Presence.

The first two 'secrets' revealed to them referred to the end of the First World War and the beginning of the Second World War and a warning regarding the danger presented to the world by the Soviet Union. Lucia passed on the so-called Third Secret to Pope Paul VI in

1967. It is said that when he heard the final secret, he turned white and recoiled from her. The successive popes who led the Catholic Church during the latter years of the twentieth century considered the Third Secret of Fatima to be too frightening, too dreadful, to be made known to humanity, and so they kept it hidden in the Papal Secret Archives of the Vatican.

It was finally revealed to the world in 2000 by Pope John Paul II. According to Vatican sources, the vision experienced by the three Portuguese children described a bishop in white, agonisingly making his way to the Cross through a place littered with the corpses of murdered Christian martyrs, only to fall in a rain of bullets.

Together with this information, Vatican officials offered an interpretation which applied in part but which failed to address completely the other elements of the prophecy. The Vatican officials concluded that the Third Secret of Fatima referred to the attempted assassination of John Paul II in St Peter's Square in 1981.

The attack on the Pope was committed by a Turkish gunman named Mehmet Ali Agca. During his 1985 trial, Agca claimed that his assassination attempt was 'connected to the Third Secret of the Madonna of Fatima'. Agca made his assassination attempt on 13 May 1981; the apparitions at Fatima first occurred on 13 May 1917, 64 years earlier.

The Vatican, and especially Pope John Paul II, found the coincidence of dates compelling, but what really seized their attention was Agca's reference to Fatima at his trial, since no one knew the contents of the prophecy and the nature of the Third Secret except the Pope himself and a very few of the highest Papal Cardinals. The implication is that Agca must have been influenced by supernatural means – that the Holy Spirit had used the gunman to verify the truth of the Fatima prophecy.

Although John Paul II believed that the prophecy contained within the Third Secret referred to his attempted assassination, there are elements that do not sit well with this interpretation. For instance, there are the corpses of the Christian martyrs that surround him as he is gunned down. The 'bishop in white' dies in a place where an awful massacre has occurred – not in St Peter's Square, but somewhere else . . .

It is therefore possible that the vision experienced by the children at Fatima does not refer to the attack on John Paul II but to another event, something far more momentous – something that has yet to happen. Perhaps it refers to Daniel's vision of the defining moment when the world passes from Christian rule and reverts to the reign of Satan. Maybe it refers to something else entirely. The Third Secret of Fatima and its recent revelation to the world by John Paul II imply that this event is now close at hand.

26

THE MUSIC OF MADNESS

The Strange Tale of 'Gloomy Sunday'

Few people would deny that music affects the emotions. It can be uplifting and create a sense of sheer joy . . . or flood the mind and imagination with sadness. That songs and tunes possess a strange power to alter our state of mind is beyond doubt, but is it possible that a piece of music can unhinge the mind to the extent that the person hearing it commits suicide? Such an idea is a staple of horror fiction, especially the weird fiction of writers such as H.P. Lovecraft, whose protagonists are frequently driven to the edge of madness and beyond by their experiences. But can such things really happen in real life?

Such a claim is made regarding an immensely sad and darkly beautiful song called 'Gloomy Sunday'. According to the legend that grew around it, 'Gloomy Sunday' was written one miserable, rainy Sunday in 1932 in Paris by the Hungarian composer Reszö Seress. His girlfriend had ended their engagement the day before and Seress was sitting in his apartment, consumed with despair and loneliness. As he sat there listening to the incessant rain in the profound inner night of his depression, a strange and melancholy tune began to drift through his mind.

So powerful was the tune, so completely did it express his dark mood, that he wrote it down and added lyrics which described the thoughts of a man whose lover had died and who was contemplating suicide so that he might cast off the bonds of his lonely life and be reunited with her again.

He called the song 'Gloomy Sunday' and took it to several music publishers, none of whom would touch it. Legend has it that one publisher, after listening to the song, said: 'It is not that the song is sad; there is a sort of terrible compelling despair about it. I don't think it would do anyone any good to hear a song like that.'

This is the central problem of the strange tale of 'Gloomy Sunday': it has taken on the characteristics of an urban legend, and it has become very difficult to separate fact from fiction, verifiable truth from darkly romantic myth.

Seress eventually found a publisher for his song and it became a huge hit in Europe. It was not long, however, before clouds of dark legend and notoriety began to cling to it. Several people, it was said, had been driven to take their own lives by the feelings of terrible and irresistible sadness that the song inspired.

The first known victim was a young man who was sitting in a Budapest café and asked the band to play 'Gloomy Sunday'. After listening to the song, he went home and put a gun to his head.

The song's original lyrics were replaced with slightly less bitter and hopeless – but still darkly melancholic – lyrics by the Hungarian poet László Jávor, and its success spread beyond continental Europe. Sam Lewis and Desmond Carter translated the song into English, and it was recorded in 1935 by the great American singer Paul Robeson.

With its international success came further tales of the awful effect it had on some listeners. In one case, the residents of a block of flats in London were perplexed by the strains of the song that were issuing endlessly from one of the apartments. When they could stand it no more, they knocked on their neighbour's door. When there was no reply, they broke in and discovered the owner, a young woman, dead. Evidently, she had set her gramophone to repeat the record over and over and had taken an overdose.

The song also became a hit in America in 1936, largely due to a publicity campaign which actually played up its sinister reputation. Before long, 'Gloomy Sunday' became known as 'the Hungarian suicide song', and many major artists recorded versions of it, including Billie Holiday, Artie Shaw, Hal Kemp, Mel Tormé, Sarah Vaughan and Ray Charles.

The sinister legend associated with the song continued to grow, and several researchers of mysteries and the paranormal have breathlessly quoted examples of people who were driven to suicide after hearing it. One victim was the young woman who had ended her relationship with Seress. Encouraged by the success of his song, he had contacted her, hoping for a reconciliation, only to discover that she had poisoned herself. Her body had been discovered beside a sheet of paper on which she had written the words 'Gloomy Sunday'.

In all, some 200 deaths were linked to the song. In Berlin, a young shopkeeper hanged herself; beneath her feet lay a copy of the song's sheet music. In New York, a typist gassed herself, leaving behind a note requesting that 'Gloomy Sunday' be played at her funeral. In Rome, a boy heard a beggar humming the tune; he walked over to the beggar, gave him all his money and drowned himself in the Tiber.

As the 1930s drew to a close, the Hungarian government, which had been growing increasingly uneasy, began to discourage public performances of the song. In his book *The Unexplained*, Karl Shuker wryly notes that many musicians were grateful for this, since they had begun to fear for their own mental well-being. This unease was shared in other countries: the BBC considered banning it from the airwaves and several US radio stations allegedly refused to play it.

Shuker goes on to quote the reminiscences of a pilot named Gordon Beck, who served with 76 Squadron at RAF Yeravda in

Poona, India. Beck recalled how in 1946 one of the squadron's pilots became visibly upset whenever he heard 'Gloomy Sunday', claiming that it made him feel suicidal. The version in question was recorded by the Artie Shaw Orchestra:

> Beck thought little of this until he began flying, too, and discovered to his alarm that he could not get the song's haunting melody out of his head; it penetrated his mind even above the noise of the aeroplane's engines. Never again did Beck play 'Gloomy Sunday'.

Although the tale of 'Gloomy Sunday' makes for an intriguing and spine-tingling read on a stormy night, there is little if any documentary evidence to back up the claims made concerning this eerily beautiful song. The suicides and radio bans, for instance, would seem to be the results more of rumour than real events. Some commentators claimed that the BBC banned the song and that the ban remains in place to this day. However, it has recently been heard on the BBC Radio 4 programme *Desert Island Discs*, which puts paid to that particular legend!

However, that a shadow of sadness clings to the song and its history is beyond doubt. In 1968, the song's composer and original lyricist, Reszö Seress, jumped to his death from his apartment. His obituary in the *New York Times* reads:

> Budapest, January 13. Reszö Seress, whose dirge-like song hit, 'Gloomy Sunday' was blamed for touching off a wave of suicides during the nineteen-thirties, has ended his own life as a suicide it was learned today. Authorities disclosed today that Mr Seress jumped from a window of his small apartment here last Sunday, shortly after his 69th birthday. The decade of the nineteen-thirties was marked by severe economic depression and the political upheaval that was to lead to World War II. The melancholy song written by

Mr Seress, with words by his friend László Jávor, declares at its climax, 'My heart and I have decided to end it all.' It was blamed for a sharp increase in suicides, and Hungarian officials finally prohibited it . . . Mr Seress complained that the success of 'Gloomy Sunday' actually increased his unhappiness, because he knew he would never be able to write a second hit.

27
∞∞∞

A DREAMER ON THE NIGHTSIDE

The Strange Visions of H.P. Lovecraft

It is one of literature's great ironies that a writer who was virtually unknown in his lifetime, never saw his work published in book form and died in near poverty, should have profoundly influenced not only the genres of science fiction and dark fantasy but also the wider realm of popular culture through which the power of his innovative imagination has seeped like one of his own unspeakable creations. Stranger still, this writer had nothing but contempt for occultists and considered them either weak-minded fools or out-and-out charlatans. And yet H.P. Lovecraft (1890–1937) was one of the greatest (some would say the greatest) horror writers of the twentieth century, not to mention one of the pioneers of cosmological science fiction that was the inspiration for an entire branch of occult thought and practice.

Lovecraft had no time for spirituality in any form: he believed that humanity had no significance whatsoever in the Universe, which was at best indifferent to our presence and at worst actively hostile towards it. The belief of both religionists and scientists, that humanity occupies the pinnacle of creation, was little more than risible wishful thinking to Lovecraft, whose stories expressed his incredibly bleak personal philosophy that came to be termed 'cosmicism' or 'mechanistic materialism'. In Lovecraft's belief system (perhaps one should call it an anti-belief system) there is no benign god watching over us, and hence no possibility of salvation.

That is not to say that by his account we are alone in the Universe – far from it. Both this dimension and countless others are teeming with strange life, but the denizens of these unknown realms are not 'gods', 'angels' or 'demons' in the traditional sense, rather extraterrestrials of immense power and incomprehensible intelligence. Since Lovecraft was an atheist, he considered the traditional and hackneyed tropes of horror fiction to be inadequate to describe the structure of an indifferent or inimical Universe: vampires and ghosts didn't interest him; werewolves and demons were merely fodder for the nightmares of children. How to inspire terror in sophisticated adults, who had no belief in such things?

The answer, as he saw it, was to invoke the unspeakable grandeur of the Universe and our own utter insignificance in the face of vast tracts of time and limitless reaches of space. The essence of Lovecraft's fiction is perhaps best expressed in the opening lines of 'The Call of Cthulhu', one of his finest tales:

> The most merciful thing in the world, I think, is the inability of the human mind to correlate all its contents. We live on a placid island of ignorance in the midst of black seas of infinity, and it was not meant that we should voyage far.

The statement is, in effect, a warning to humanity that the Universe is not merely something 'out there', a realm far removed from our comfortable little world with its humdrum joys and tribulations. The Universe is here and now: we are in it, a part of it; we are corks tossed on the surface of a bottomless ocean of space and time, and there are things lurking in the depths of which most of us are blissfully unaware.

Lovecraft gave a name to his pantheon of nameless horrors: he called them the Great Old Ones, although he never had an overall plan or scheme for their creation and development. He merely added to his 'anti-mythology' as and when he saw fit, as each new tale demanded. Among the terrible beings and forces from this and other universes that haunt his pages are Azathoth, the 'monstrous nuclear chaos' that 'blasphemes and bubbles' at the centre of infinity, beyond the realms of angled space. There's Yog Sothoth, the 'All-in-One and One-in-All', coterminous with all space and time, appearing to those unfortunate enough to encounter him as a 'congeries of iridescent globes'. He is the gate through which the Great Old Ones will one day re-enter our Universe to wreak their havoc. Shub Niggurath is the 'black goat of the woods with a thousand young', Hastur the Unspeakable is 'Him Who is not to be Named' and, perhaps most memorable of all, the vast, tentacle-headed Cthulhu, the living abnormality that came from the stars when the Earth was young and who now lies 'not dead, but dreaming' within the horrible sunken city of R'lyeh, built millions of years before the coming of humanity. Cthulhu's nature is expressed in the strange couplet from the *Necronomicon*, Lovecraft's invented book of primal and forbidden lore: 'That is not dead which can eternal lie/ And with strange aeons even death may die.'

Occasionally in Lovecraft's stories, a phrase in the language of R'lyeh is presented and is deeply unsettling, in spite of (or perhaps because of) the virtual impossibility of correct pronunciation. The most well known of these snippets of an ancient alien tongue is: '*Ph'nglui mglw'nafh Cthulhu R'lyeh wgah'nagl fhtagn*', which translates roughly as 'In his house at R'lyeh, dead Cthulhu waits dreaming'. When these beings erupt into our Universe, as they are wont to do from time to time as a result of the activities of their cultists and worshippers (and those unwise enough to conduct occult research with forbidden books such as the *Necronomicon*), the consequences are invariably dire, for to be in their presence is to know madness and death.

The *Necronomicon* might be termed 'the most famous book never written'. Its title has been translated variously as 'The Book of Dead Names', 'Book of the Dead', or 'Book Concerning the Law of the Dead'. To sate the curiosity of interested correspondents, Lovecraft created an elaborate pseudo-history for his frightful tome, which was originally penned in the eighth century AD by the 'mad Arab' Abdul Alhazred, which is the name Lovecraft invented for himself as a child, having been enchanted by the *Arabian Nights*.

Early Life

Lovecraft was born on 20 August 1890 in his maternal grandfather's home at 454 Angell Street in Providence, Rhode Island. A few months after his birth, Lovecraft's parents returned to their rented home in Dorchester, Massachusetts. His father, Winfield Scott Lovecraft, was a commercial traveller based in the Boston area for Gorham & Co., Silversmiths. In the summer of 1892, the family spent a holiday in Dudley, Massachusetts, and later moved for a while into the Auburndale home of the poet Louise Imogen Guiney, who was a friend of Lovecraft's mother, Sarah Susan Phillips.

It seems that the Lovecraft family would have moved permanently to Massachusetts had it not been for the sudden deterioration of Winfield's health. He suffered a seizure in a Chicago hotel in April 1893 and was brought home in a straitjacket. On 25 April, he was admitted to the Butler Hospital, an asylum in Providence. According to S.T. Joshi, the foremost scholar of Lovecraft's life and work, in his book *A Subtler Magick*: 'The subsequent diagnosis was "paresis", at that time a catch-all term for a variety of neurological diseases, but it is now virtually certain that Winfield had syphilis.'

Winfield's illness forced Lovecraft and his mother to return to the family home in Providence. It was located on the exclusive East Side of the city, where the wealthiest and most respected families lived. In Lovecraft's youth, Providence (and the rest of New England) was largely untouched by the modernity that was encroaching elsewhere. This environment heavily influenced his outlook and opinions: he often stated that he felt like a stranger in his time and wished that he had been born in the eighteenth century.

His great intelligence was evident from his earliest years: he could speak at the age of one and was learning Latin by eight. At that time, it was not mandatory for children to attend public school, and so Lovecraft was allowed to explore the large family library in solitude. Here he discovered Grimm's *Fairy Tales* and the *Arabian Nights*, which contributed to his growing love of the exotic and fantastic. The worlds of classical antiquity fascinated him and broadened his intellectual development considerably, as did the works of the great eighteenth-century poets and essayists.

His devotion to fantasy and romance was, however, tempered by his discovery around the age of ten of chemistry, geography and especially astronomy. The resulting sense of scientific rationalism that characterised his intellect led him not only to be contemptuous of professional occultism but also enabled him to add convincing detail to his later stories, thus heightening their power to unsettle. This can be seen most strikingly in the short novel 'At the Mountains of Madness' (1931), in which a research expedition to Antarctica discovers a vast derelict city hidden behind a chain of mountains. The protagonists explore the city and realise that it was constructed by alien beings tens of millions of years before the rise of humanity. The inclusion of detailed geographical and palaeontological information adds an eerie plausibility to an already splendidly macabre science-fiction tale.

In 1898, Lovecraft discovered one of his greatest literary influences, Edgar Allan Poe. As he later wrote: 'Then I struck EDGAR ALLAN POE!! It was my downfall, and at the age of eight I saw the blue firmament of Argos and Sicily darkened by the miasmal exhalations of the tomb!' Along with such writers as

Arthur Machen, Algernon Blackwood and Lord Dunsany, Poe was to cast a literary shadow over the rest of Lovecraft's short life, but of perhaps greater importance in shaping his philosophy and the concerns he addressed in his later weird fiction was the science of astronomy.

In *A Subtler Magick*, Joshi notes that by 1904, 'much had happened in Lovecraft's personal life'. Following his father's illness, his maternal grandmother died in 1896, and the boy became extremely frightened by the mourning clothes of the women in his family. It was at this time that Lovecraft's 'career as a great dreamer' began, for he was plagued by terrifying nightmares in which horrific beings which he called 'night-gaunts' seized him and carried him off on bizarre cosmic voyages. He would later incorporate this idea into his weird fiction: the night-gaunts became among the strangest and most sinister of his creations, carrying their victims to the dreadful Vale of Pnath, where an unimaginable fate awaited them. In fact, many of his stories were inspired by the nightmares he suffered throughout his life.

This curious fact is of extreme importance to the many occultists who are fascinated by his work, for they claim that it was through his nightmares that Lovecraft made unwitting contact with the realms of the Outer Darkness, the vast gulfs stretching beyond the sane and ordered Universe of space and time. The only way he could give voice to the shuddersome information he obtained during sleep was through the writing of his macabre and outré stories.

With his father in a mental asylum, the role of intellectual mentor to the young Lovecraft was assumed by his maternal grandfather, Whipple Van Buren Phillips, a wealthy industrialist who offered constant encouragement to Lovecraft in his writing.

During his high-school period, Lovecraft wrote two stories, 'The Beast in the Cave' (1905) and 'The Alchemist' (1908) but then abandoned fiction in favour of scientific writing and poetry. Although many mistakenly believe him to have been a lifelong recluse, in the period following high school Lovecraft did indeed withdraw completely from society, reading voraciously in diverse fields, including the cheap pulp literature of the time.

The trite love stories of a writer named Fred Jackson prompted Lovecraft to write a scathing letter, which was published in the September 1913 issue of *Argosy*. This elicited an equally angry response from Jackson's supporters, including a John Russell, who criticised Lovecraft in a poem. Lovecraft responded with his own satirical verse, and the literary spat continued for several months, until finally the editor of *Argosy* decided enough was enough and asked Lovecraft and Russell to abandon their hostilities. This they did and metaphorically shook hands by composing a poem together, which was published in the October 1914 issue.

What seemed initially like a minor controversy among the devotees of popular literature was to have profound and positive consequences for Lovecraft as a writer. The Jackson correspondence came to the attention of Edward F. Daas, official editor of the United Amateur Press Association (UAPA), who invited both Lovecraft and Russell to join. Lovecraft did so in April 1914, Russell a year later.

The amateur press turned out to be the perfect outlet for Lovecraft, who was able to shake off his reclusiveness and ultimately find an enthusiastic audience for his literary endeavours.

So taken was he with the amateur press that Lovecraft even allowed his two early tales, 'The Beast in the Cave' and 'The Alchemist', to be published in amateur journals. Pleasantly surprised by the enthusiastic response, he decided to begin writing fiction again, the first results being 'The Tomb' and 'Dagon', both written in the summer of 1917. However, it was not until two years later, when he discovered the work of the great fantasist Lord Dunsany, that Lovecraft finally threw himself headlong into fiction writing.

New York and Providence

On 24 May 1921, Lovecraft's mother died, having spent the last two years of her life at Butler Hospital following a nervous breakdown.

Joshi suggests that this event, while obviously tragic, was also a 'liberating influence' for Lovecraft. Given her ambivalent feelings towards her son, with whom she had shared the house on Angell Street from 1904 to 1919, this is not as harsh a statement as it sounds. Susan Lovecraft's worsening mental illness caused her to become disorientated in public and to believe that she could see strange creatures watching the family home. She also informed acquaintances that her son did not like to leave the house because of his 'hideous' face. (Although no matinee idol, Lovecraft was far from 'hideous'.) It is likely that horror and embarrassment at the awful manner of her husband's death was the cause of this odd attitude to her son, in addition to vehement disapproval of his association with the amateur press.

Although initially devastated by his mother's death, Lovecraft recovered quickly, and his physical and mental health improved dramatically after the age of 30. It was at this time that he began to travel throughout New England, frequently with friends who were amazed at his new-found energy and vitality.

While attending the UAPA's national convention in Boston in July 1921, Lovecraft met Sonia Haft Greene, a Russian Jewish widow who was ten years his senior. Although profoundly racially prejudiced, Lovecraft was nevertheless captivated by her charm and intelligence. After a three-year courtship, they married and settled in Sonia's large apartment in Brooklyn, New York. However, financial misfortune befell them almost immediately. The hat shop Sonia managed went bankrupt, cutting off all income for the household. Lovecraft searched for work diligently but without success. This is unsurprising: not only was this the era of the Great Depression but the 31-year-old Lovecraft had the additional disadvantage of never having been employed. With no work experience, and the country in financial turmoil, he had no conceivable hope of finding a regular job, a predicament that weighed heavily upon him.

Another serious problem was that he was singularly unsuited to

New York life, and his failure to bring in money for himself and Sonia only exacerbated the trauma. The couple's financial pressures took their toll on Sonia, whose health began to suffer. Eventually, she found a job at a department store in Cleveland, Ohio. This, of course, meant that she had to relocate there, while Lovecraft stayed in New York.

They could not afford to keep the apartment in Brooklyn, so on New Year's Eve 1924, Lovecraft moved into a decrepit one-room flat on Clinton Street in Brooklyn Heights, a less than salubrious neighbourhood. A few months after he moved in, his flat was burgled and he was left only with the clothes on his back. Although he had a number of friends and acquaintances in New York through his activities in the amateur press, he became so ashamed and depressed by his situation that he could not bring himself to see them.

A year of this misery was all Lovecraft could stand, and late in 1925 he wrote home to his two aunts that he wished to return to his beloved Providence. This he did on 17 April 1926. In his monograph *Lovecraft: A Study in the Fantastic*, the French scholar Maurice Lévy notes the great significance of this homecoming, which was spiritual as well as physical. He felt settled once again in the familiar surroundings he loved and was no longer distracted by the responsibilities, sexual and otherwise, of being a husband.

In 1929, Lovecraft and Sonia amicably agreed that their marriage could not be sustained and divorce proceedings were undertaken. With immense relief, Lovecraft returned to his bachelor existence, spending all his time reading, writing and travelling not only throughout New England but also as far north as Quebec and as far south as Key West. The pitiable state of his finances compelled him to travel by bus at night, in order to avoid the expense of staying in hotels, and when it was necessary to find overnight accommodation, he stayed in YMCAs.

In this way Lovecraft spent the final 11 years of his life. When at home, he would work either through the night or during the day with the curtains drawn and the lights on, pretending it was night. With a certain pride, he subsisted on as little as $1.75 per week, which he spent on canned beans, spaghetti, chilli and crackers, ice cream and sweets – a diet which could hardly have been good for his already precarious health. With his aunts, Lillian Clark and Annie Phillips Gamwell, constantly watching over him, he quietly produced the astonishing stories and short novels for which he has achieved posthumous worldwide fame. Among the most important of these are 'The Call of Cthulhu' (1926), 'The Dream-Quest of Unknown Kadath' (1926-7), 'The Case of Charles Dexter Ward' (1927), 'The Colour Out of Space' (1927), 'The Dunwich Horror' (1928), 'The Whisperer in Darkness' (1930), 'At the Mountains of Madness' (1931), 'The Shadow Over Innsmouth' (1931) and 'The Shadow Out of Time' (1934-5). In addition, he wrote long travelogues of his journeys to cities such as Philadelphia, Richmond, Charleston and New Orleans, as well as a truly staggering number of letters to his friends and colleagues in the amateur press. In fact, Lovecraft may well be the greatest letter writer in literary history: his output over his relatively short life is estimated at more than 100,000 letters.

The Mechanistic Materialist

His many excursions notwithstanding, Lovecraft continued to live within himself and his dreams; indeed, his journeys can be seen as an attempt to experience, if only vicariously, a past that was now lost, washed away in the first decades of a century he loathed for its uncouth modernism. Lovecraft hated the reality in which he was forced by chance to live and took refuge in the outlandish worlds of cosmic horror and mystery he created.

In Lovecraft's cosmos, space and time are the arenas of incomprehensible beings, and in this respect he is a true pioneer of serious science fiction. The aliens encountered in his stories are not the tame and familiar creatures which populate the worlds of *Star Wars*, *Star Trek* and many other examples of modern science fiction and which are merely human beings in disguise. (There are of course noble exceptions, such as the unseen and inscrutable beings in Kubrick and Clarke's *2001: A Space Odyssey* and the horrifically mysterious creatures in Ridley Scott's *Alien*. In fact, Dan O'Bannon, who wrote the screenplay for *Alien*, conceived of the story as unfolding in Lovecraft's universe and the aliens as 'blood relatives of Yog Sothoth'.)

The idea that extraterrestrials would bear the slightest resemblance to human beings, either in appearance or psychology, was considered utterly absurd by Lovecraft. For him, the humanoid aliens that were already standard fare in the pulp magazines of the 1920s and 1930s represented a lamentable paucity of imagination. The very presence of Lovecraft's aliens is enough to warp the laws of physics – not to mention the sanity of his unfortunate protagonists. As S.T. Joshi notes, it is not even accurate to say that these beings are hostile to humanity: human beings are destroyed almost by accident, 'as we might heedlessly destroy ants underfoot', as the Great Old Ones follow their own unknown and unknowable agendas.

Along with other serious students of Lovecraft, Joshi maintains that these horrifying entities should be seen as allegorical, as symbols for the unfathomable mysteries of the Universe. The numerous occultists who believe in the literal reality of the Great Old Ones are making a grievous mistake based on a total misunderstanding of what Lovecraft was trying to achieve artistically. And yet, as we shall see shortly, interest in the 'Lovecraft Mythos' as a genuine and workable magical system is extremely widespread in occult circles.

As already stated, Lovecraft was utterly contemptuous of any belief of the significance of humanity in the Universe; his stories expressed a philosophy that was utterly non-anthropocentric in outlook. None of the laws, ethics or emotions that characterise our lonely species has any bearing whatsoever on events occurring in the far reaches of the cosmos. The very idea that an extraterrestrial being could have anything in common with a human being (including the notions of love and hate, good and evil) struck Lovecraft as puerile in the extreme.

This philosophy is perhaps best expressed in his own favourite story, 'The Colour Out of Space'. In this subtle and truly frightening tale, a meteorite crashes on the farm of the Gardner family in the remote Massachusetts countryside west of the town of Arkham (Lovecraft's fictional analogue of Salem). The meteorite contains an entity from deep space, a life form so strange, so alien, that its very presence causes everything in the area (including people) to crumble gradually to a grey dust (most appallingly, the people thus affected retain life and consciousness right up to the final moment of collapse). It has other effects, too: effects which are more subtle, yet even more terrifying. In one scene, a character called Ammi is driving his horse-drawn carriage past the Gardner farm.

> There had been a moon, and a rabbit had run across the road, and the leaps of the rabbit were longer than either Ammi or his horse liked. The latter, indeed, had almost run away when brought up by a firm rein.

Truly, as the head of the family, Nahum Gardner, says just before his leached and desiccated body finally succumbs to the effects of the alien presence, 'It comes from some place whar things ain't as they is here.' In fact, we know nothing of the physical properties (apart from its colour, which is like nothing seen before on Earth – 'it was only by analogy that they called it colour at all') of the entity inside the meteorite. It is certainly destructive, but we do not know enough about it even to call it 'evil', or even to say that it is 'alive'. As Joshi rightly states: 'It is the utterly baffling nature of the meteorite and its [inhabitant] – who may not be conscious, organic, or even alive in any sense we recognize – that produces the deeply metaphysical horror in "The Colour Out of Space".'

In stories such as this, we can perceive what is perhaps the central tragedy of Lovecraft's creative life. He was constantly concerned with terrifying his audience, with making the skin crawl. This is all well and good for a writer of horror stories; and yet we can see from stories like 'The Colour Out of Space' and 'At the Mountains of Madness' that at this stage in his career, Lovecraft was moving in a different direction, towards the magnificent cosmological fiction of writers like Olaf Stapledon, whose great novel *Star Maker* displays a similar sense of humanity's insignificance and in which a 'conscious' Universe of the far future attempts to commune with the entity (the Star Maker of the title) which created it, only to fail and to descend into an existential despair for the rest of time. It may not be too glib to suggest that Lovecraft was a great science-fiction writer trapped in a horror writer's body.

Desperate for money, Lovecraft turned his talents to literary revision and ghost writing, although the rates he charged were too low to provide a sufficient income, and when his clients neglected to pay him, he was too polite to send reminders. In addition, the long hours he conscientiously put into this activity left him little time to work on his own original material.

Towards the end of his life, Lovecraft devoted more and more time and energy to his correspondence with other writers of fantasy and weird fiction, including Clark Ashton Smith, Robert E. Howard (creator of Conan the Cimmerian) and August Derleth, who would later found the Arkham House publishing company to preserve his friend's work in hardcover after his death. He also helped a great many younger writers, many of whom would go on to achieve worldwide fame, including Robert Bloch, Fritz Leiber and James Blish.

H.P. Lovecraft died on 15 March 1937 in Jane Brown Memorial Hospital of cancer of the intestine and renal failure. It is likely that the disease first manifested around 1934, with Lovecraft passing it off as indigestion. He did not seek medical treatment, certainly because he could not afford it and perhaps also (as Joshi suggests) because 'he feared a fate similar to that of his mother, whose death was caused by complications following a gall bladder operation'. His very poor diet of canned foods and sweets doubtless also contributed. He was buried in the Phillips family plot at Swan Point Cemetery on 18 March.

Lovecraft's Occult Legacy

The key texts in Lovecraft's work are known collectively as the 'Cthulhu Mythos' tales. However, this phrase was not invented by Lovecraft but by August Derleth following Lovecraft's death. Many critics dislike the phrase, preferring (if anything) the 'Lovecraft Mythos' to describe the worlds and entities he created.

As we have noted, these tales are set in a universe that is far stranger, more dangerous and more terrifying than we can possibly imagine: a universe that was once ruled, in the unthinkably distant past, by monstrous beings, the Great Old Ones. Some of these titanic beings came from distant galaxies in the far reaches of space, some from other dimensions entirely. All follow incomprehensible agendas in which humanity does not figure at all, save as an infestation of the Earth to be annihilated when the Great Old Ones return to reclaim their property, 'when the stars are right'.

Certain modern occultists have devoted themselves to the principal entities in this bizarre and horrific pantheon, maintaining that they are far more than mere literary inventions. They believe that Lovecraft was an unwitting conduit for the influences of the sinister and incomprehensible intelligences existing outside the ordered Universe – much to the bemusement and irritation of serious Lovecraft scholars.

First among these denizens of the Outside is Azathoth, the blind idiot god, whose frightful aspect Lovecraft describes as a gibbering monstrosity, the essence of confusion and madness living beyond the boundaries of the ordered Universe. This 'daemon-sultan' is surrounded by the colossal 'ultimate gods' who dance around his throne to the sound of mad drums and whining flutes.

The faithful messenger of the Great Old Ones, Nyarlathotep, goes under a number of epithets, including 'the Crawling Chaos', 'the Dweller in Darkness' and 'the Howler in the Night'. He can also take on various forms: in ' Dream-Quest of Unknown Kadath', he appears to the protagonist Randolph Carter as a beautiful young man, while in 'The Haunter of the Dark' he appears altogether more unpleasantly as a black bat-like entity with a single huge three-lobed eye. He is worshipped and summoned on Earth by means of a mysterious object known as the Shining Trapezohedron, which pre-dates humanity. The Trapezohedron was fashioned on the planet Yuggoth, which we know as Pluto (Lovecraft having cleverly incorporated the planet into his mythology following its discovery in 1930).

Comparable in power to Azathoth is Yog Sothoth, who is worshipped by cultists on Earth and by the intelligent crustacean-like entities on Yuggoth. Lovecraft describes this entity as being coterminous with all space and time, as being the gate through which the Great Old Ones will one day return to claim the Earth and annihilate humanity.

Most famous of the Great Old Ones is the gigantic and quintessentially violent entity Cthulhu, who came to Earth millions of years ago from the depths of interstellar space. In terms of his physical form, Cthulhu is the most anthropomorphic of the pantheon, although in truth it is only a passing resemblance. While his scaly body is roughly humanoid, his head is shaped like an octopus or squid and is dominated by a mass of writhing tentacles; from his back sprouts a pair of vast, leathery wings. Following their arrival on Earth, Cthulhu and his spawn built the loathsome city of R'lyeh in what is now the Pacific Ocean.

During their heyday, these beings shared the planet with other extraterrestrial beings known as the Elder Things, who built that vast, cyclopean city discovered by the protagonists of 'At the Mountains of Madness'. Due to some unknown antediluvian catastrophe, R'lyeh sank into the sea, imprisoning Cthulhu and his minions within its titanic walls, where they repose to this day, 'not dead, but dreaming'. They are worshipped not only by degenerate cultists on land but by a race of odious beings known as the Deep Ones who live in the lost cities scattered across the ocean floors throughout the world.

Throughout his tales of the Great Old Ones and the hapless humans who encounter them, Lovecraft makes reference to certain forbidden manuscripts and books of occult lore. It is in these that his protagonists find the information and clues necessary to the completion of their dubious and ill-advised quests.

Among these blasphemous, abnormal tomes are Ludvig Prinn's *De Vermis Mysteriis*, the *Liber Damnatus* and the pre-human *Pnakotic Manuscripts*. As the pseudo-mythology of the Great Old Ones developed, other writers in Lovecraft's circle contributed to it with their own tales, adding other worm-eaten tomes to the nefarious list. Clark Ashton Smith created the *Book of Eibon*, penned by the Hyperborean sorcerer of that name; Robert Bloch created the *Cultes des Goules of the Comte d'Erlette* (a play on August Derleth's surname); and Robert E. Howard created the *Unaussprechlichen Kulten of von Junzt*. Within their pages can be found secrets too terrible for the eyes of mortal humanity, telling of events that happened on Earth aeons before the first proto-humans existed; of frightful civilisations existing on different planets and in other dimensions; of the chaotic beings who strode godlike across the intergalactic spaces of the primeval Universe.

Among these books, one stands out as particularly blasphemous and vile, achieving infamous fame in Lovecraft's world, in the world of fantastic literature and in the wider world of occultism and black magic: the *Necronomicon*. In response to the many letters he received from friends and colleagues, Lovecraft, with his tongue firmly in his cheek, composed a short essay on the history of the dreaded book. Written in 1927, the 'History of the Necronomicon' explains that the book's original title was *Al Azif*, the Arabic word *azif* referring to the nocturnal sounds made by insects, which the Arabs attributed to the howling of demons. According to Lovecraft's amusing pseudo-history, the book was composed by Abdul Alhazred, a mad poet and wizard of Sanaá in Yemen, who lived during the period of the Ommiade caliphs around AD 700.

Alhazred, wrote Lovecraft, was a wanderer, a seeker after forbidden knowledge, whose curiosity led him from the ruins of Babylon to the subterranean vaults beneath Memphis; from Irem, the fabulous City of Pillars, to the ruins of a nameless town, beneath which he discovered the records of a long-vanished pre-human race. He spent ten years alone in the great southern desert of Arabia, the Roba el Khaliyeh or 'Empty Space', said to be inhabited by demons and horrific monsters, where he learned many appalling secrets of the Universe. He spent his final years at Damascus, where he composed the *Necronomicon*, the dark testament of what he had learned on his travels. He is said by his twelfth-century biographer Ebn Khallikan to have suffered a particularly awful death: in the middle of a crowded market place, he was seized by an invisible monster and devoured alive.

In AD 950, so the story goes, the *Azif* was secretly translated into Greek by Theodorus Philetas of Constantinople under the title *Necronomicon*. For the next century, those fortunate (or unfortunate) enough to have access to a copy experimented with the incantations contained within its blasphemous pages, with disastrous results. It was finally suppressed and burned by the patriarch Michael. However, Olaus Wormius made a Latin translation in the late Middle Ages, and his text was printed twice, once in the fifteenth century in Germany and once in Spain in the seventeenth century. It was banned by Pope Gregory IX in 1232, and the Arabic original was lost. Some Latin texts were said to exist, Lovecraft informed his readers, in the British Museum, the Bibliothèque Nationale in Paris, the Widener Library at Harvard, the library at the University of Buenos Aires and in the library of Lovecraft's fictional Miskatonic University at Arkham, Massachusetts. These copies were kept securely under lock and key, not only because they were so fantastically valuable but also because reading them could lead to serious mental problems, or worse.

Lovecraft's invented history of the make-believe book was convincing enough to prompt many readers to write to him enquiring as to whether it really did exist. (And since his death, libraries throughout the world have received similar enquiries from people wishing to examine a copy.) That the book is indeed his invention is placed beyond all serious doubt by the many letters he wrote to readers to disabuse them of the notion that the *Necronomicon* was real. It certainly amused and gratified Lovecraft that his literary endeavours were seen to possess such an air of authenticity, although he invariably and conscientiously took pains to point out that what he wrote was fiction.

It is a strange kind of tribute to the power of Lovecraft's vision that, over the years, a number of books have been published purporting to be the real *Necronomicon*, discovered at last after painstaking and dangerous research (and, as the title of a story by the late science-fiction writer John Brunner wryly has it, published in inexpensive paperback editions).

As noted at the beginning of this chapter, it is an ironic testament to the power of H.P. Lovecraft's vision that it has become so influential, not only to science-fiction, fantasy and horror writing in the twentieth century, but also to modern occultism. Is it true that the master was in unwitting contact with some unutterably strange and profoundly terrible astral realm, receiving arcane secrets from the 'Outside' in the form of hideous nightmares which he transcribed into his immortal tales of cosmic dread? Many occultists respond with a resounding 'Yes!' Most (if not all) Lovecraft scholars merely shake their heads in bemusement, preferring to admire Lovecraft for what he was: an immensely gifted teller of tales from the nightside.

28

AN ARTIST IN THE MAGICAL WORLD

The Strange Talents of Austin Osman Spare

To most of us, the talents of a great artist are as mysterious as any enigma of history or nature. Austin Osman Spare (1886–1956) was one of those rare individuals who gained huge fame and admiration at the very outset of his career; and yet the adulation was not to last. His decline in the art establishment was strange and shocking: a near-total fall from grace which ended in abject poverty in a grubby basement in south London. His life was even more extraordinary than his work, and perhaps more extraordinary than any artist of the twentieth century. For not only was Austin Spare a painter and draughtsman of genius he was also a skilled practitioner of that other, darker art – the art of magic.

Spare was born in Smithfield in 1886, the son of a policeman. At the age of 18, he exhibited at the Royal Academy exhibition of 1904, and in 1907 he had his first West End show at the Bruton Gallery. For a short time he attended the Royal College of Art but did not complete the course. Although his exhibitions drew great praise from the art establishment (with some critics comparing his line work with that of Aubrey Beardsley), others were profoundly disturbed by the strange and dangerous visions he set down on paper and canvas. It is said that George Bernard Shaw considered his work too powerful for normal people, as if he were expressing some dark and bizarre aesthetic that had no place in the lives of ordinary humanity.

During the First World War, Spare was conscripted into the Royal Army Medical Corps and became an official War Artist. Some of his work from this period is preserved in the Imperial War Museum. He edited a journal called *Form: A Quarterly of the Arts*, and was a promoter of automatic drawing long before the idea occurred to the Surrealists. After the war, he edited another artistic journal called *The Golden Hind*, 'a luxury production which became known as "The Golden Behind", due to Spare's fleshy taste in female nudes,' according to Phil Baker in his article on Spare in the *Fortean Times*.

Spare's decline into poverty and obscurity is perhaps unsurprising given his total contempt for modern art, artists and art dealers. He was also proudly working class, which didn't help, and he felt utterly out of place in the genteel and rarefied artistic and literary environment in which he found himself during the early years of his career. By the 1920s, he had had enough and decided to return to his roots in the south London where he grew up. He remained there for the rest of his life.

As Phil Baker notes in his article on Spare in the *Fortean Times*, it was a great era to be interested in magic, so Spare thrived. Had he been born a little earlier, he would doubtless have joined the famous occult group the Hermetic Order of the Golden Dawn. In the event, he joined the breakaway organisation created by the magician Aleister Crowley, the Argenteum Astrum, in 1909. Although he and Crowley became friends (there may or may not have been a physical element to the relationship), Spare did not remain in the organisation for long. He saw little point in following the elaborately formulated magical operations developed by Crowley and, since he had already begun to develop his own system of ritual magic, he decided that such research was better conducted in isolation.

In his art, Spare employed a wide range of styles and mediums. In addition to Beardsley, his work has been compared to that of Blake, Dürer and even Michelangelo. Most intriguing from the magical point of view are his occult drawings, which are expressions of his interest in the nature of belief – as opposed to the question of what to believe. Baker compares Crowley's and Spare's attitudes towards magic with Picasso and Marcel Duchamp in the artistic world. He notes that Picasso's position as the greatest painter of the twentieth century has been usurped, according to many, by Duchamp, whose work comments on the nature of art itself. In a similar way, Spare was more interested in the nature of belief itself rather than the subjects upon which belief is focused.

When he was 17, Spare stayed at the home of the Reverend Robert Hugh Benson, author of several occult novels. While out walking one day, Benson told Spare that he was curious about the young man's alleged magical powers and wondered whether he would be kind enough to offer a demonstration. It was summer and the weather was particularly fine with not a cloud in the sky. Would Spare be kind enough to produce rain through magical means?

Spare agreed and took out an old envelope from a pocket, on which he began to draw a magical symbol, known as a sigil. He then held the drawing before him and concentrated on it. About ten minutes later, small clouds began to collect in the sky above them and, before long, the clouds let loose a downpour that drenched them both.

In his book *The Magical Revival*, the occultist and ceremonial magician Kenneth Grant, Outer Head of the Ordo Templi Orientis and one-time disciple of Crowley, describes how Spare had occasion to prove his magical ability again a year later when Benson introduced him to Everard Fielding, Secretary of the Society for Psychical Research (SPR). Like Benson, Fielding was intrigued by Spare and also asked if the young artist might furnish proof of his abilities. Once again, Spare was quite happy to oblige and asked Fielding what he had in mind. Fielding suggested that he think of an object (which he would not divulge) and Spare would attempt not only to state the nature of the object but also to make it materialise out of thin air. In other words, he would produce what is known in parapsychological circles as an 'apport', an object that is created or transported through unknown and apparently non-physical means to the vicinity of the person creating the phenomenon.

Spare succeeded, but not quite in the way Fielding had been expecting. Again, he began by drawing a sigil on a piece of paper. Surprisingly, this drawing did not represent the unknown object but rather one of Spare's spirit familiars, to which he turned for aid whenever mind-reading was required. Presently, Spare received a mental impression of the object in Fielding's mind. He then drew a second sigil, upon which he began to concentrate. At this point there was a knock at the door. Fielding opened it to find his valet standing there holding Fielding's slippers, which was indeed the object in his thoughts.

As if channelling his magical ability through his artistic talents, Spare performed his magic through the practice of automatic drawing whereby the hand is allowed to roam freely across the paper, without the direct influence of the conscious mind. In this way, the subconscious (or perhaps 'superconscious') mind can transmit ideas and magical concepts directly to the consciousness. From these strange, interlocking shapes, ideas could be born, enhanced and developed by the artist. 'By these means,' Spare wrote, 'may the profoundest depths of memory be drawn upon and the springs of instinct tapped.' To illustrate his point, Spare noted how Leonardo da Vinci would often derive artistic inspiration from gazing at the random patterns on dirt-streaked walls, or upon the surfaces of striated stones.

According to Spare, handwriting itself is given distinctiveness and expression by an automatic or subconscious nature acquired by habit; and this is also the case with automatic drawing, 'one of the simplest of psychic phenomena', which relies upon the same mental mechanisms that give rise to dreams. Automatic drawing is the 'manifestation of latent desires . . . the significance of the forms (the ideas) obtained represent the previous unrecorded obsessions'.

This mode of expression serves to undo the mental repression achieved by conventional education, releasing the 'truths' that lie dormant in the unconscious mind. In effect, the practice of automatic drawing is a magical operation designed to liberate the consciousness and re-establish the practitioner's individuality, which has been subsumed in the overriding conditioning which every society aims to impose upon its members. Spare warns, however, against the retention of personal biases, convictions and religious beliefs, which can:

> produce ideas of threat, displeasure or fear, and become
> obsessions . . . In the ecstatic condition of revelation from
> the subconscious, the mind elevates the sexual or inherited
> powers (this has no reference to moral theory or practise)
> and depresses the intellectual qualities. So a new, atavistic
> responsibility is attained by daring to believe – to possess
> one's own beliefs – without attempting to rationalize spurious
> ideas from prejudiced and tainted intellectual sources.

Automatic drawing may be performed either by lengthy concentration upon a sigil or by any means of pleasantly exhausting both the body and mind, in order to achieve a condition of 'non-consciousness'. The important thing is to completely relinquish control over what is being drawn and to complete the drawing with a single, unbroken line. 'Drawings should be made by allowing the hand to run freely with the least possible deliberation. In time shapes will be found to evolve, suggesting conceptions, forms and ultimately having personal or individual style.'

The mind should not be allowed to think or dwell upon any particular subject or thought: it should descend into a state of primal oblivion, unencumbered by the concerns or intentions of the conscious intellect. Thus, a state may be reached in which 'one's personal ideas, symbolic in meaning and wisdom' may be achieved.

There are many tales regarding Spare's skills as a magician, which, as Phil Baker wryly notes, 'make the London Borough of Lambeth seem like H.P. Lovecraft's Arkham County'. One such tale is told by the late scholar Francis X. King, who relates how a young friend of his, an art student, met Spare and got on very well with him. While they agreed that the fashions of modern art were execrable, King's friend could not bring himself to accept the reality of magic.

Spare confided to the young man that he was sometimes possessed by the soul of that other great visionary William Blake, to which the young art student replied (rather undiplomatically) with a mini-discourse on schizophrenia. This was a little too much for Spare, who told him that he believed wholeheartedly in the reality of magic and the occult, and, moreover, he had been a practitioner all his life. If his friend wished to see a demonstration, he added, he would be more than happy to oblige the next time they met.

Somewhat bemused, his acquaintance agreed, and a date was set for the demonstration, which would be performed in Spare's dingy basement flat in Brixton. In the intervening days, the younger man had done a little reading on occult subjects and did not feel quite as confident in his scepticism as he had done previously. The state of Spare's accommodation did little to help; in fact, it was the last thing the young man was expecting. Far from the Persian rugs, antique furniture, book-lined walls and scattered occult accoutrements one traditionally associates with a magician's study, Spare's flat was dank, smelly and noisy, with gurgling pipes, and buses thundering past outside. There were no crystal balls, no cloaks with embroidered stars and half-moons hanging on the wall, no pointed hats, no wands or magic circles drawn on the floor. There were, however, several sheets of paper containing letters and strange symbols – apparently the full extent of Spare's magical toolkit.

Even more out of keeping with the traditional image of the ritual magician, Spare was eating a piece of pie when his guest arrived. When he had finished, he said that the demonstration could now begin. He would, he declared, attempt an apportation: the materialisation of a solid object out of thin air. Spare had decided on a bunch of fresh roses, and began the magical operation by taking up one of the pieces of paper containing the strange symbols and waving it in the air for a few moments. He did this in silence, with a look of fantastically intense concentration on his face and without any of the incantatory mumbo-jumbo the young art student was expecting. In fact, the only word he uttered, at the end of the operation, was 'roses'. The two men waited in silence for a few moments, the air in the dingy room thick with expectation of a supernatural event. When the event happened, it was not what either of them was expecting: one of the pipes in the ceiling burst, showering them with an unpleasant mixture of sewage and used bathwater. Spare's young visitor went away even more bemused than when he arrived.

This event was surely no more than coincidence – unless Spare's spirit familiars had decided to have a bit of fun at his expense. However, another tale of Spare's abilities is told by Kenneth Grant. In *The Magical Revival*, Grant relates how Spare was approached by two dabblers in the occult, magical dilettantes who were seeking thrills in the world of the unseen (never a wise course of action). The two young men had recently attended a series of séances, at which they had apparently witnessed the materialisation of departed spirits. Their interest had been piqued and they asked Spare if it might be possible for him to summon some form of elemental being.

Spare didn't think this a good idea, as such entities existed at deep and atavistic levels of the human subconscious. He believed they were potentially extremely dangerous and difficult to control. Spare suggested that he demonstrate the reality of magic and the occult in some other, more innocuous way. However, the young thrill-seeking dilettantes were adamant that they wanted to see an elemental.

With great reluctance, Spare complied and began the summoning. Gradually a green vapour filled the room and began to coalesce into a man-like figure with glowing eyes and a grinning, idiot face. The entity moved among them, accompanied by an unholy stench. This was more than enough for the two dabblers, who begged Spare to banish the vaporous monstrosity. Without hesitation he did so, and the thing disintegrated before their terrified eyes, leaving a miasma of evil in the room. Grant claims that within weeks one of the dabblers had died of no apparent cause while the other was committed to a mental asylum.

Although this is a fascinating and spine-tingling story, Baker implies in his article (quite rightly) that it is somewhat redolent of the horror tales of Lovecraft, Arthur Machen and Sax Rohmer (creator of Fu Manchu), whom Grant had enthusiastically read. He goes on, however, that late in his life Spare made a curious comment to his friend Frank Letchford. Knowing that Letchford was not interested in the occult, Spare usually steered away from the subject in conversation with him. On this occasion, Spare mentioned that he had become disenchanted with occultism, saying that he'd had a friend who had delved too deeply into its mysteries and been driven insane.

Equally fascinating (although perhaps just a little less chilling) was an episode that occurred in 1955, one year before Spare's death. At this time, Kenneth Grant was engaged in a magical feud with witchcraft revivalist Gerald Gardner, who believed that Grant had 'poached' one of his mediums, an apparently talented but mentally unstable young woman named Clanda.

Gardner went to see Spare and asked him for a magical talisman for the restoration of stolen property. He did not provide Spare with any details so the artist was unaware that the talisman was to be used in a magical operation directed against Grant, who was a friend. Spare drew a strange creature, 'a sort of amphibious owl with the wings of a bat and the talons of an eagle', and gave the talisman to Gardner.

Not long after, Grant and Clanda attended a magical meeting at the Islington home of an alchemist. As the ritual began (apparently to incarnate the goddess Black Isis), Clanda lay upon an altar but almost immediately sensed that something was terribly wrong. She claimed later that she had felt the temperature of the room drop suddenly and became aware of a great bird flying into the room. The entity gathered her up in its great claws and carried her from the house. She could clearly see the roofs below. Eventually the bird lost altitude and approached a 'wharf-like structure'. Overcome with terror, Clanda struggled with all her might – and suddenly found herself back on the altar in the alchemist's house.

Grant later said that a slimy substance was discovered on the windowsill, which – bizarrely – seemed to put forth sprouts or buds.

Spare developed his magical thinking in three books: *Earth Inferno* (1904), *The Book of Pleasure (Self Love): The Psychology of Ecstasy* (1913) and *The Focus of Life* (1921). His philosophy is based on the central concept of the 'Kia', which can be described as the state of 'inbetweenness' sometimes equated with the unconscious, combined with another element known as 'Zos', which represents the human body and mind.

Spare was a fervent believer in reincarnation and maintained that we retain in our unconscious all the thoughts and experiences of our past lives, whether as humans or animals. He further believed that we can actually observe and communicate with the essences of these previous incarnations or selves, and this was a major inspiration for the strange entities populating his art.

In his magical operations, Spare attempted to pass through these 'levels of being', in the words of Kenneth Grant, to 'penetrate the silent regions of consciously forgotten experiences, evoking by its reverberant power the ineluctable memories that abide perpetually in subconsciousness'. In *The Book of Pleasure*, Spare himself describes his intentions to probe deeply into the subconscious of humanity, which, he believed, contained all the levels of evolution through which it has passed to reach its present state. His ultimate goal was to reach what he called the 'Almighty Simplicity', the very essence of life. In so doing, he would gain its properties and power.

Spare believed that this atavistic power could be focused through the use of sigils and other magical formulae composed of words and phrases, which are then either hidden or destroyed, thus banishing their contents into the magician's subconscious mind, where their power can be set to work. It is of the utmost importance not only that the sigil be forgotten but that the initial desire itself also be forgotten. In this way, it can come to dominate the unconscious mind, which nourishes it and increases its power. In *The Magical Revival*, Grant explains that conscious desire takes time to materialise, while unconscious desires can do so very quickly. In fact, consciousness interferes with the empowerment of the desire.

For Spare, this forgetting, this entry into the primal void at the centre of the mind, could best be achieved through exhausting the body through physical activity. To achieve this, he employed yogic meditation, which resulted in a trance state in which his body was completely rigid and immobile. He called this 'The Death Posture', and it appears in several of his drawings.

Spare had nothing but contempt for Western occultism and its elaborate rituals and theatrics: his system, with its solitary simplicity, was more akin to the techniques of shamanism. With his straightforward approach to magic, so very different from that of Crowley (by far the most famous magician of the twentieth century), with its densely written and incredibly complex procedures, it could be argued that Spare's magical legacy is of far greater importance to the contemporary occult scene than Crowley's. The system known as 'Chaos Magic' is the fastest-growing school of modern occultism, and it owes a great deal to Spare's philosophy.

However, like many occultists, Spare nevertheless had a flair for the dramatic and loved to spin a yarn, as can be seen from his assertion that he had studied hieroglyphics in Egypt (plausible), and that he had a letter from Sigmund Freud acknowledging Spare's greater genius (rather less plausible).

A perfect illustration of this is Spare's assertion that his interest in magic stemmed from the childhood influence of Mrs Yelga Paterson, an elderly witch who apparently seduced him when he was a boy. He later claimed that Mrs Paterson had the ability to materialise thought-forms and to tell fortunes with cards. She herself claimed to be descended from one of the Salem witches that Cotton Mather failed to execute. Spare called her his 'second mother' and, although she possessed a rather limited vocabulary, she was able to explain the most arcane principles of magic with ease. She was extremely poor, yet Mrs Paterson would never accept any payment for her fortune telling, probably because of the widespread belief in occult circles that payment results in the loss of the fortune-telling gift.

Mrs Paterson had her own spirit guide, an entity known as Black Eagle, who was the 'control' behind several witch covens, two of which she headed. Black Eagle was apparently of 'Narragansett provenance' and here Grant makes one of his many allusions to the works of H.P. Lovecraft (see Chapter 27), whom he considers to have been in subconscious contact with the Great Old Ones, the race of godlike extraterrestrial and extradimensional beings which figure so prominently in the New England writer's weird tales.

Following Mrs Paterson's death, Black Eagle 'focused' through Spare, inspiring many of his drawings.

In 1980, Grant came into contact with an old woman who claimed to have been a member of Yelga Paterson's coven around the turn of the century and who was able to provide him with information regarding Mrs Paterson's link with the Great Old Ones.

Grant has much to say on the subject of Spare's connection with the Great Old Ones. For instance, it seems that the name 'Yelga' is actually 'Yelder', a blend of 'Ye Elder'. Grant attributes the mistake to Spare's mild dyslexia but concedes that the appellation is an appropriate one, since it was through the aged witch that the artist first began his traffic with the occult entities.

According to occult historians, Paterson had a profound influence on Spare's life and magical work. It was through her that Black Eagle transmitted the influence of the Great Old Ones. The current of magic that flowed from Black Eagle through Mrs Paterson was unconscionably ancient, and it was frequently expressed by Spare in the form of discs and other circular features, which he described as 'Flying Saucers'. This strongly implies a fascinating connection between occultism and ufology, which a number of commentators on the latter subject have suggested over the years. Both Spare and Grant were well aware of this connection.

Carl Jung equated the disc shape of many UFOs with the mandala, the circular archetype denoting wholeness and harmony, which, he argued, modern industrial society woefully lacks.

To Jung, the appearance of discs in the skies, while essentially a psychological phenomenon, nevertheless was a significant expression of human apprehensiveness and uncertainty in the face of the dangers peculiar to modern life (in reference to the Cold War, he said that our world is 'dissociated like a neurotic').

In his book *Outer Gateways* (1994), Kenneth Grant considered the occult connections between the alien forces from beyond Earth and the mythos of H.P. Lovecraft. The Lovecraft Mythos, Grant maintains, reflects 'vastly ancient pre-human lore', an unclassifiable phase of our planet's history. The entities themselves are representative of the subconscious and the cosmic forces existing beyond our narrow awareness, and true creativity occurs when these forces are invoked 'to flood with their light the magical network of the mind'.

Grant envisages the human mind as divided into three 'rooms': the subconscious or dream state; the mundane consciousness or waking state; and the transcendental consciousness. Through a system of 'conduits or tunnels', these rooms are connected with the house that contains them; the house itself represents 'trans-terrestrial consciousness'. In the magical universe of Kenneth Grant and Austin Osman Spare, the forces from 'Outside' (the Great Old Ones) are not seen as evil or destructive but rather as dynamic and liberating energies, 'the functions of which are to blast away the delusion of separate existence (the rooms of our illustration)'. For this reason, the magician must remember that danger is not inherent in the Great Old Ones themselves, but rather in the attitude the magician adopts towards them when performing magical operations.

In one form or another, the Great Old Ones appear in the myths of humanity throughout history. However, Grant maintains that it was H.P. Lovecraft who 'traced in his tales . . . the most significant map of the pre-human Gnosis', despite the author's claims to the contrary.

There is a powerful thematic thread running from Lovecraft's work to Spare's. The power of their imaginations and the nature of the material they produced make them kindred spirits; however, they differed fundamentally in their attitudes to that material. While Lovecraft considered himself a writer of weird fiction and no more, Spare believed unequivocally in the power of his own art to place him in contact with the potent denizens of the outer realms of space and time.

29

AN ERUPTION OF DEMONISM?

Occultism in the Third Reich

The dark history of the Third Reich inspires a perennial fascination in the public; countless books and television documentaries have been produced over the years and the ultimate origin of the horror of Nazism remains the subject of intense debate.

Even in the immediate aftermath of the Second World War, historians were already attempting to address the question, and they were soon joined by psychologists and theologians who began the long struggle to understand where Hitler stood on the spectrum of human nature containing pacifists and philanthropists as well as sadists and killers. Were his crimes explicable in the same terms that are applied to other mass murderers? Or was he, perhaps, something else entirely, belonging to an order of iniquity outside the continuum of humanity?

Unlikely as it may seem (and orthodox historians consider it very unlikely indeed), these attempts to understand the motivations of Hitler and the Nazis have given rise to one of the most controversial and extraordinary claims of the twentieth century. The claim is simply this: that the high echelons of the Nazi regime were in contact with an evil, non-human intelligence with which they attempted to ally themselves in their bid for world domination.

So bizarre is this claim that serious historians have consistently dismissed it as outrageous nonsense. Those who deign to consider it at all have suggested that it is little more than an example of the way in which lurid legends can take on a life of their own, perpetuating themselves in the absence of concrete explanations for history's most extreme aberrations. And yet, many occultists still believe that the leaders of Nazi Germany were black magicians. Could this claim have any basis in truth?

The theologian Emil Fackenheim believes Hitler's crimes were so extreme that he must be considered a radical evil, an 'eruption of demonism into history'. Thinkers like Fackenheim see Hitler's evil as existing beyond the bounds of normal human behaviour.

Historians have rightly concentrated on the many important economic, social and historical factors that influenced the development of Nazi ideology. However, much less attention has been paid to the Nazis' fascination with esoteric belief systems. Humans are great myth-makers, and it is hardly surprising that the known history of the Third Reich should have given rise to the belief that the Nazis were, quite literally, in contact with an evil trans-human intelligence, which succeeded in exerting its influence over human affairs through the magical conduits of Hitler and other high-ranking members of the Third Reich.

The Origins of Nazism

That the irrationality of Nazism should have its roots in belief systems that were themselves irrational and spurious should come as no surprise. The fathers of National Socialism in the late nineteenth and early twentieth centuries were obsessed with occult doctrine and the idea that the blood of racially pure Germans contained magical powers; they also believed that Atlantis was a lost Aryan supercivilisation.

As the Nazis grew more powerful, Hitler's own subordinates dabbled in occult sciences such as astrology, and occultism also played a significant role in the formation and rituals of the SS. It is also a matter of historical record that the Nazis embraced bizarre and ridiculous cosmological theories such as Hans Hörbiger's World Ice theory, which provided them with an opportunity to denounce the ideas of the Jewish Albert Einstein.

However, Nicholas Goodrick-Clarke, one of the few serious historians to have explored in detail the occult inspiration behind Nazism, stresses that although the founding fathers of National Socialism undoubtedly contributed to Nazi mythology, with its weird notions of prehistoric Aryan supermen inhabiting vanished continents, they did not exert a direct influence on those in positions of power.

Nevertheless, Goodrick-Clarke concedes that there is one important exception to this: Karl Maria Wiligut (1866–1946) who greatly influenced Reichsführer-SS Heinrich Himmler (1900–45). Therefore, before turning our attention to the SS and the magical rites it is alleged to have practised, we should pause to examine the life and thought of Wiligut and the reasons for his influence over the leader of the most powerful organisation in the Third Reich.

Wiligut was born in Vienna into a military family and saw action against the Russians in the Carpathians during the First World War. After being transferred to the Italian front, he reached the rank of colonel in 1917 and was decorated for bravery. He was discharged from the army in 1919, after 35 years of service. At around this time, rumours began to circulate in Vienna's occult underground that Wiligut possessed an impressive talent: an 'ancestral memory' that allowed him to recall the history of the Teutonic people all the way back to the year 228,000 BC. Wiligut himself maintained that this incredible clairvoyant ability was the result of an uninterrupted family lineage extending thousands of years into the past. He claimed that his father had initiated him into the secrets of his family in 1890.

Research conducted by Goodrick-Clarke in the primary sources of the period revealed the origin of this information to be a man named Theodor Czepl, who knew of Wiligut through his occult connections in Vienna, which included Wiligut's cousin, Willy Thaler, and various members of the Order of the New Templars (ONT). Czepl visited Wiligut several times at his Salzburg home in the winter of 1920; during these visits, Wiligut claimed that the Bible had been written in Germany and that the Germanic god Krist had been appropriated by Christianity.

According to Wiligut's bizarre account of prehistory, the Earth was originally lit by three suns and was inhabited by a variety of fantastic beings, including giants and dwarfs. It was ravaged by warfare for tens of thousands of years until Wiligut's ancestors, the Adler-Wiligoten, brought peace with the foundation of the great city of Arual-Jöruvallas (Goslar, the chief shrine of ancient Germany) in 78,000 BC. Conflicts broke out periodically over the next several thousand years involving various now-lost civilisations, until 12,500 BC, when the religion of Krist was established. Three thousand years later, an opposing group of Wotanists challenged this hitherto universal Germanic faith and crucified the prophet of Krist, Baldur-Chrestos. The Wotanists destroyed Goslar in 1200 BC, forcing the followers of Krist to establish a new temple at Externsteine, near Detmold.

Wiligut maintained that his own family was the result of a mating between the gods of air and water and, in later centuries, fled from persecution at the hands of Charlemagne, first to the Faroe Islands and then to Russia. His family history was a self-aggrandising mish-mash of genuine cultural traditions (such as those described in the Scandinavian Eddas) and theosophical belief systems that have little or no bearing on mythology.

Wiligut claimed that the victimisation of his family had been going on for tens of thousands of years and was being continued by the Catholic Church, the Freemasons and the Jews, all of whom he blamed for Germany's defeat in the First World War. When his infant son died, bringing the family's male line to an end, his already precarious mental health was further undermined. Wiligut's wife, Malwine, was already singularly unimpressed with his grandiose claims regarding his family's prehistoric greatness, and their son's death placed an even greater strain on their marriage. After becoming increasingly violent and obsessed by the occult, he was committed to the mental asylum at Salzburg in 1924. He was certified insane and stayed there for the next three years.

During his confinement, Wiligut maintained contact with his colleagues in various occult circles, including the ONT and the Edda Society, and five years after his release he decided to move to Germany. He settled in Munich, where he was fêted by German occultists as a source of invaluable information on the remote and glorious history of the German people.

Wiligut's introduction to Heinrich Himmler came about through the former's friend Richard Anders, an officer in the SS. Himmler was greatly impressed with the old man's ancestral memory; SS recruits had to prove their Aryan family history back to the year 1750, but Wiligut seemed to possess an Aryan purity going back quite a bit further than that. Wiligut joined the SS in 1933 and was made head of the Department for Pre- and Early History in the SS Race and Settlement Main Office in Munich. Here, he was charged with the task of writing down the events he clairvoyantly recalled. His work evidently met with Himmler's approval, and the Reichsführer-SS promoted him to SS-Oberführer (Lieutenant-Brigadier) in 1934.

As if his own ravings were not enough, Wiligut introduced Himmler to another occultist, a German crypto-historian named Günther Kirchhoff (1892–1975) who believed in the existence of an ancient grid of energy lines crossing the Earth. Wiligut decided to forward a number of Kirchhoff's essays and dissertations on ancient German tradition to Himmler, who ordered the Ahnenerbe (the SS Association for Research and Teaching on Heredity) to study them. However, the Ahnenerbe quickly realised that Kirchhoff was a crackpot who understood nothing of scholarly prehistorical research (quite an indictment, coming from that particular organisation). When Kirchhoff accused them, along with the Catholic Church, of conspiring against him, the Ahnenerbe responded by describing his work as rubbish and him as nothing more than a fantasist. Nevertheless, Himmler continued to instruct the Ahnenerbe to take his rantings seriously until the outbreak of the Second World War forced him firmly into the background.

Wiligut, on the other hand, made one further contribution to Himmler's SS. While travelling through Westphalia during the Nazi electoral campaign in 1933, Himmler found himself deeply affected by the atmosphere of the region, with its romantic castles and mist-shrouded Teutoburger Forest. In 1934, he appropriated the Wewelsburg castle with the intention of turning it into an ideological training college for SS officers. Himmler's view of the Wewelsburg was probably influenced by Wiligut's assertion that it was destined to become a magical strongpoint in a future war between Europe and Asia. Himmler was fascinated by this idea, which corresponded with his own belief that a future conflict between East and West was inevitable. In addition, it was Wiligut who influenced the development of SS ritual and who designed the SS Totenkopfring (literally 'Death's Head Ring') that symbolised membership of the order.

In 1935, Wiligut moved to Berlin where he joined Himmler's Personal Staff and continued to advise the SS on all aspects of his German pseudo-history. The reason for his eventual decision to leave the SS is uncertain, although it may have been because his health had started to deteriorate. He was prescribed powerful drugs to maintain his mental faculties but these had serious side effects, including personality changes that resulted in heavy smoking and drinking. His psychological history (including his committal for insanity) also became known, causing Himmler considerable embarrassment. In early 1939, Wiligut's staff was informed that he had retired due to poor health and that his office would be closed. Although the old occultist was supported by the SS in his final years, his influence on the Third Reich was at an end. After moving house several times throughout the war years, he was finally sent by the British occupying forces at the war's end to a refugee camp where he suffered a stroke. After his release, he went first to his family home at Salzburg, and then to Arolsen, where he died in January 1946.

Heinrich Himmler: Rationalist and Fantasist

The man who was so deeply impressed with the rantings of Wiligut, who would become most closely associated with the terror of the SS and an embodiment of evil second only to Adolf Hitler himself, was born in Munich on 7 October 1900. Heinrich Himmler was not blessed with a robust physical constitution and this hampered his family's initial intention that he should become a farmer. After serving in the armed forces briefly at the end of the First World War, he joined Hitler's NSDAP (the National Socialist German Workers' Party).

In January 1929, Himmler was appointed head (Reichsführer) of the SS. At that time, the organisation had barely 300 members, but such were Himmler's organisational skills, he increased its membership to over 50,000 during the next four years. By 1937, the three major concentration camps in Germany were staffed by the SS Totenkopfverbände (Death's Head Units), and the following year saw the foundation of the Verfügungstruppe (Action Groups), which numbered 200,000 and which later became the Waffen-SS (Military SS). By the end of 1938, SS membership had reached nearly 240,000, a figure that would later rise to approximately one million.

It has been said of Himmler that he was a curious mixture of rationalist and fantasist: that his capacity for rational planning, the following of orders and administrative detail, existed alongside an idealistic enthusiasm for utopianism, mysticism and the occult. This combination of the mundane and the fantastic led to Himmler's conception of the ultimate role of the SS: to provide bloodstock for the future Aryan race and to become the ideological elite of the expanding Reich.

From 1930, Himmler concentrated on the formulation of his plan for the SS, which included the establishment of the SS officers' college at the Wewelsburg castle in 1933. Two years later, he established the Ahnenerbe with the Nazi pagan ideologue Walther Darré. The Ahnenerbe was initially an independent institute conducting research into Germanic prehistory, archaeology and occult mysticism. It was subsequently incorporated into the SS in April 1940, with its staff holding SS rank. It is likely that inspiration for the Ahnenerbe came from a number of German intellectuals and occultists who had subscribed to the theories of an ancient Germanic super race espoused by the nationalist writers of the late nineteenth century, as well as from the adventures of a number of explorers and archaeologists.

Himmler's vision of the SS required its transformation from Hitler's personal bodyguard into a pagan religious order with virtually complete autonomy, answerable only to the Führer himself. The castle of Wewelsburg was close to Paderborn in Westphalia and near the gigantic stone monument known as the Externsteine, where the Teutonic hero Arminius defeated the Romans.

The principal chamber in the castle was the great dining hall, with its huge oak table around which sat 12 of the senior Gruppenführers – this arrangement owing much to the legend of King Arthur and the Knights of the Round Table. Beneath the dining hall was a circular room at the centre of which was a shallow depression reached by three stone steps (symbolising the three Reichs). In this place of the dead, the coat of arms of the deceased 'Knight' of the SS would be ceremonially burned. Each member of Himmler's Inner Circle of Twelve had his own room, which was dedicated to an Aryan ancestor. Himmler's own quarters were dedicated to King Heinrich I, the

Saxon king who had battled Hungarians and Slavs and of whom Himmler was convinced he was the reincarnation – although he also claimed to have conversations with Heinrich's ghost at night.

Inside the dining hall, Himmler and his Inner Circle would perform various occult exercises, which included attempts to communicate with the spirits of dead Teutons and efforts to influence the mind of a person in the next room through the concentration of willpower. There was no place for Christianity in the SS, and members were actively encouraged to break with the Church. Christian ceremonies were replaced with new ones; Christmas, for example, was replaced with a specially designed winter solstice ceremony. Weddings and christenings were also replaced with pagan rituals.

As mentioned, the Ahnenerbe received its official status within the SS in 1940, and while other occult-oriented groups such as the Freemasons, the Theosophists and the Hermetic Order of the Golden Dawn were being suppressed, the Ahnenerbe was given free rein to pursue its own line of mystical and occult inquiry, with the express purpose of providing the historical validity of Nazi paganism. With more than 50 sections, it covered every aspect of occultism and paganism, including Celtic studies, Scandinavian mythology, runic symbolism, the World Ice theory of Hans Hörbiger and an archaeological research group that attempted to prove the geographical ubiquity of the ancient Aryan civilisation. In addition, at the door of the Ahnenerbe must lie the ineradicable iniquity of the medical experiments conducted at Dachau and other concentration camps, since it was this organisation that commissioned the hideous programme of 'scientific research' on living human subjects.

The mental ambiguity of Heinrich Himmler – rational, obedient and totally desirous of security on the one hand, immersed in the spurious fantasy of Aryan destiny on the other – was demonstrated most powerfully in the final phase of the Nazi regime, when it became obvious that Germany would lose the war and the 'Thousand-Year Reich' would turn to dust. From 1943 onward, Himmler maintained loose contacts with the Resistance movement in Germany, and in the spring of 1945 he entered into secret negotiations with the World Jewish Congress. Himmler's actions at this time indicate what the historian Joachim Fest called 'an almost incredible divorce from reality', one example being his suggestion to a representative of the World Jewish Congress that 'it is time you Jews and we National Socialists buried the hatchet'. He even thought, in all seriousness, that he might lead a post-war Germany in an alliance with the West against the Soviet Union. When the reality of the Third Reich's defeat finally overwhelmed his fantasies, and the idea of disguise and escape finally presented itself to him, Himmler adopted perhaps the worst false identity he could have chosen: the uniform of a sergeant major in the Gestapo. He was, of course, arrested on sight.

Malign Forces and the Spear of Destiny

In the decades since the end of the Second World War, occult writers have attempted to explain the terrifying mystery of the true origins of Nazism by attempting to fit it into an occult context. Perhaps unsurprisingly, these writers have paid close attention to an intriguing statement Hitler is known to have made – 'Shall we form a chosen band, made up of those who really know? An order: a brotherhood of the Knights of the Holy Grail of Pure Blood' – and have attempted to use this statement as a point of connection between the Nazis and the occult.

Although serious historians such as Goodrick-Clarke accept that occult and folkloric concepts played a significant role in the development of Nazi ideas and doctrines, it has been left largely to writers on 'fringe' subjects to push the envelope (wisely or otherwise) and claim that the Nazis were motivated by genuine occult forces: in other words, that there exist in the Universe malign non-human intelligences that seek ways to influence the destiny of humanity for their own ends, and that these forces used the Nazis as conduits.

According to this scheme of history, the Nazis were, quite literally, practising Satanists and black magicians. We have already seen how Nazi ideology was influenced by the ideas of German nationalist occultists in the latter decades of the nineteenth century. But is this as far as the connection goes?

In 1973, Trevor Ravenscroft, a veteran of the Second World War, published a book that caused more controversy than any other on the subject of Nazism and one which is still the subject of heated debate today. Entitled *The Spear of Destiny*, the book chronicles the early career of Hitler, the man who would stain the twentieth century with the blood of millions and whose name would become a synonym for cruelty of the most repulsive kind. Hailed by some as a classic of occult history and derided by others as no more than a work of lurid fiction, *The Spear of Destiny* is still in print today and, whatever its merits or demerits, remains one of the most important texts in the field of Nazi occultism. (And, such is the bizarre and murky nature of this field, to make such a claim for a book is by no means equivalent to defending its historical accuracy.)

Ravenscroft, a commando, spent four years in German POW camps. He made three escape attempts but was recaptured each time. While imprisoned, Ravenscroft claimed to have experienced a sudden apprehension of higher levels of consciousness, which led him to study the legends of the Holy Grail and the Spear of Longinus. The spear in question was the one said to have been used by the Roman centurion Gaius Cassius Longinus to pierce the side of Christ during the Crucifixion, the possession of which (so the legend goes) would allow one to hold the destiny of the world in one's hands.

Ravenscroft claimed that, by rights, the man who should have written *The Spear of Destiny* (and would surely have done so, had he not died in 1957) was a Viennese philosopher and wartime British secret agent named Walter Johannes Stein (b. 1891). An Austrian Jew, Stein had emigrated from Germany to Britain in 1933. His association with Ravenscroft came about as a result of a book Stein had written in 1928 entitled *The Ninth Century: World History in the*

Light of the Holy Grail. Ravenscroft was greatly impressed by the book, which asserts that the medieval Grail Romances and their description of the quest for the Holy Grail formed a kind of esoteric map leading to transcendent consciousness. It was clear to Ravenscroft that Dr Stein had conducted his historical research along rather unorthodox lines, relying on occult methods of mind expansion to corral data rather than the more traditional means of consulting extant medieval texts. In view of his own experience of higher levels of consciousness and his fascination with the Grail legends, Ravenscroft requested an interview with Dr Stein.

During their meeting, Ravenscroft voiced his belief that Stein had utilised some transcendent mental faculty in the course of his research for *The Ninth Century*, adding that he believed a similar faculty had inspired Wolfram von Eschenbach to write the great Grail romance *Parzival* around the year 1200. According to Stein, von Eschenbach based *Parzival* on the key figures of the ninth century. The Grail King Anfortas corresponded to King Charles the Bald, grandson of Charlemagne; Cundrie, the sorceress and messenger of the Grail, was Ricilda the Bad; Parzival himself corresponded to Luitward of Vercelli, the Chancellor of the Frankish Court; and Klingsor, the fantastically evil wizard who lived in the Castle of Wonders, was identified as Landulf II of Capua, responsible for a pact with Islam in Arab-occupied Sicily, and whom Ravenscroft calls the most evil figure of the century.

Stein had first read *Parzival* while taking a short, compulsory course on German literature at the University of Vienna. One night, he had a most unusual extrasensory experience in which he recited long sections of the work in a kind of semi-dream state. This happened three times in all. Stein wrote down the words he had been speaking and, on comparing them with von Eschenbach's romance, found them to be virtually identical. To Stein, this strongly implied the existence of some preternatural mental faculty, a kind of higher memory that could be accessed under certain circumstances.

His subsequent researches into the Grail Romances led to his discovery in 1912 in a dingy bookshop in Vienna's old quarter, of a tattered, leather-bound copy of *Parzival*, the pages of which were covered with annotations in a minute script. Stein bought the book from the shop assistant and took it to Demel's Café in the Kohlmarkt, where he began to pore over its pages. As he read, he grew more uneasy at the nature of the annotations, which seemed to have been made by someone who was highly knowledgeable not only on the subject of the Holy Grail but also on black magic. Stein was repelled yet fascinated by the vulgar racial fanaticism displayed in the annotations, which he regarded as the work of a brilliant but utterly hideous mind, a mind that had inverted the traditional idea of the quest for the Grail as a gradual and immensely difficult awakening to wider spiritual reality, turning it into its antithesis: the opening of the human spirit, through the use of black magic, to the power and influence of Satan himself.

Shaken by what he had read in the pages of the book, Stein glanced up for a moment through the café window and found himself looking into an arrogant face with demoniacal eyes. The apparition was shabbily dressed and was holding several small watercolours that he was trying to sell to passers-by. When Stein left the café late that afternoon, he bought some paintings from the down-and-out painter and hurried home. It was only then that he realised that the signature on the watercolours was the same as that in the copy of *Parzival* he had bought: Adolf Hitler.

According to Ravenscroft, by the time Stein found the annotated copy of *Parzival*, Adolf Hitler had already paid many visits to the Weltliches Schatzkammer Museum (Habsburg Treasure House) in Vienna, which held the Lance of St Maurice (also known as Constantine's Lance), a symbol of the power of the Holy Roman emperors at their coronations. Having failed to gain entry to the Vienna Academy of Fine Arts and the School of Architecture, and growing increasingly embittered and consumed with an increasing sense of his own destiny as dominator of the world, Hitler had thrown himself into an intense study of Nordic and Teutonic mythology and folklore, German history, literature and philosophy. While sheltering from the rain in the Treasure House one day, Hitler heard a tour guide explaining to a group of foreign politicians the legend associated with the Lance of St Maurice: that it was actually the spear Gaius Cassius had used to pierce the side of Christ, and that whoever succeeded in understanding its secrets would hold the destiny of the world in his hands for good or evil.

Intent on meeting the man who had written so perceptively and frighteningly in the battered copy of *Parzival*, Stein returned to the dingy bookshop and this time encountered the owner, an unsavoury-looking man named Ernst Pretzsche, who told him that Hitler pawned many of his books in order to buy food and redeemed them with money earned from selling his paintings. The shop assistant, he said, had made a mistake in selling the book to Stein. He showed Stein some of Hitler's other books, which included works by Hegel, Nietzsche and Houston S. Chamberlain, the British fascist and advocate of German racial superiority who frequently claimed to be chased by demons.

In the conversation that followed, Pretzsche claimed to be a master of black magic and to have initiated Hitler into the dark arts. After inviting Stein to consult him on esoteric matters at any time (which Stein had no intention of doing, such was the loathsomeness of the man), Pretzsche gave him Hitler's address in Meldemannstraße.

Hitler was irate when Stein told him of his interest in the annotations in the copy of *Parzival*. He cursed Pretzsche for selling one of the books he had pawned. However, once Stein had told him of his own researches into the Holy Grail and the Spear of Longinus, Hitler became more amicable. They decided to pay a visit to the Schatzkammer together to look at the Holy Lance. As they stood before the display, the two men responded to it in very different ways. Stein felt a healing warmth emanating from the artefact, filling him with love, humility and compassion. But as he looked across at Hitler, he sensed a hideous and alien euphoria in his companion, who was radiating a wild-eyed evil, as if in the grip of some malign spirit.

The inscrutable occult processes that were set in motion by Hitler's 'discovery' of the Holy Lance were consolidated 26 years later on 14 March 1938, when Hitler arrived in Vienna to complete the Anschluss of Austria. While the Viennese people cheered the German forces' arrival, Jews, gays, Gypsies and opponents of the Nazi regime faced persecution. According to Ravenscroft, Hitler went straight to the Habsburg Treasure House to claim the Holy Lance, believing that his bid for world domination was now a very large step closer to being realised.

In spite of the breathless praise that has been heaped upon *The Spear of Destiny* by occult writers over the years, there are many problems with Ravenscroft's account of Hitler's discovery and seizure of the Holy Lance, not to mention the very idea of Hitler as a black magician.

Let's begin with the lance itself. The existence of a lance that supposedly had been used to stab Christ is first recorded in the sixth century by the pilgrim St Antonius of Piacenza, who claimed to have seen it in the Mount Zion Basilica in Jerusalem. When the city fell to the Persians in AD 615, the shaft of the lance was captured by the victors, while the lance-head was taken to Constantinople, where it was incorporated into an icon and kept in the Santa Sophia Church. More than six centuries later, the point found its way into the possession of the French King and was taken to the Sainte-Chapelle in Paris. The lance-head disappeared (and was possibly destroyed) during the French Revolution. The shaft was sent to Jerusalem in about AD 670 by the Frankish pilgrim Arculf and only reappears in history in the late ninth century, turning up in Constantinople. In 1492, it was captured by the Turks, who sent it as a gift to Rome. It has remained in St Peter's since then.

However, archaeologists have established that this lance, first mentioned in the sixth century, is not the one Hitler coveted in the Habsburg Treasure House. The Austrian lance, known as the Lance of St Maurice, or Constantine's Lance, was made in the eighth or ninth century.

If *The Spear of Destiny* is to be believed, the moment Hitler entered the Habsburg Treasure House upon the annexation of Austria in 1938 and stood before the holy artefact he had coveted for so long, humanity in the twentieth century was lost, locked on to an irrevocable collision course with disaster. And yet there are more problems with this pivotal point in the book. Ravenscroft claims that Hitler triumphantly faced the Viennese crowds on the reviewing stand in front of the Hofburg, whereas Joachim Fest, a great authority on Hitler and the Third Reich, maintains (with photographic evidence to back him up) that Hitler faced the crowds from the balcony of the Hofburg, not from the reviewing stand in front of it.

In addition, Ravenscroft claims that after reviewing the Austrian SS and giving his permission for the founding of a new SS regiment, Hitler refused an invitation for a tour of the city and also declined to attend the civic dinner and reception in his honour because he was afraid that an attempt would be made on his life. This raises the question: if he was fearful for his life, why did Hitler arrive in Vienna in an open car and then stand in full view on the balcony of the Hofburg? The claim in *The Spear of Destiny* that Hitler went to the Treasure House on the night of 15 March also presents problems, since records show that Hitler flew out of Vienna late in the afternoon of 15 March: he was not in the city that evening.

Historians have frequently returned to Hitler's Vienna period in search of a clue to the origin of his evil. With the story of Stein and the down-and-out Hitler, Ravenscroft also follows this tradition. What makes this story so compelling (regardless of its veracity) is its inclusion of incontrovertible facts about Hitler, juxtaposed with highly controversial material. At this time, he was extremely poor and did scrape a meagre living from selling watercolours to passers-by on the streets. *The Spear of Destiny* treats this period as an incomplete canvas onto which Ravenscroft adds his strange picture of the dark forces motivating the Führer-to-be.

Although it makes fascinating reading, it is not satisfactory as a historical work and is crippled by the research methods on which Ravenscroft appeared to rely – namely, the use of occult techniques to enhance the powers of the mind and thus gain access to historical information that has not been preserved in any conventional way. In the final analysis, we must dismiss the book on the grounds that when information gathered through psychic processes conflicts with what has been established through documentary evidence or the testimony of first-hand witnesses, we have no alternative but to abandon it in favour of what can be verified by those who do not possess these psychic talents.

The history of occultism is inextricably intertwined with the wider history of human affairs. This is just as true of the twentieth century as of any earlier period. It is therefore unsurprising that the evil of Nazism should have compelled some to wonder whether Nazis were practising black magicians in contact with malignant supernatural beings. They were not and so we must accept the terrifying fact that the 'eruption of demonism into history' came not from Hell, but from the uncharted realms of the human mind.

30

HORRORS OF THE
INNER EARTH

The Bizarre Claims of
Richard Shaver

R aymond Palmer was used to receiving strange letters. As the
editor of the pioneering science-fiction magazine *Amazing
Stories*, he had more than his fair share of correspondents with
unusual ideas and bizarre theories. However, the letter that landed
on his desk in late 1943 took first prize for wackiness.

The letter was from a man named Richard Shaver, and after
reading it, Palmer was tempted to toss it into the waste-paper basket
where it surely belonged. Yet something stopped him and he reread
it, marvelling at its curious contents, which claimed that the English
language contained hidden concepts and connections unknown to
linguists. Instead of discarding the letter, Palmer contacted the writer
and one of the strangest and most persistent myths in the history of
fringe beliefs began.

Born in Milwaukee, Wisconsin, in 1910, Palmer was something of
a Renaissance man in the fields of the bizarre and unusual, writing
science-fiction stories, editing pulp magazines and founding *Fate*,
the world's longest-running journal of the paranormal. His early life

was marked by tragedies that might have led a lesser man to sink into perpetual despair: at the age of seven he was run over by a truck and his back was broken; two years later, a failed spinal operation left him with a hunchback, and this, combined with a growth-hormone deficiency, resulted in an adult height of just four feet.

Understandably, these misfortunes led him to become something of a loner, with a voracious appetite for reading, particularly the fantastic romances that were becoming increasingly popular in the 1920s and 1930s. Palmer was also a great fan of Hugo Gernsback's pulp science-fiction magazine *Amazing Stories*, the first of its kind. (The term 'pulp' comes from the low-grade paper on which these popular magazines were printed.) Palmer organised the first-ever science-fiction fan club, the Science Correspondence Club, and founded the first science-fiction fanzine, *The Comet*, in 1930. Over the next few years, he wrote a number of stories for the pulps before becoming editor of *Amazing Stories* in 1938. At that time, the magazine was in serious difficulties, but Palmer turned it around with an emphasis on romantic, suspenseful and picaresque adventures. Under his editorship, the magazine's circulation rose by several tens of thousands.

Palmer had an important talent, prized by any editor: he was able to home in precisely on what his readers wanted while being sufficiently thick-skinned to ignore criticism. Many science-fiction fans deserted *Amazing Stories* for the science- and technology-driven 'hard SF' of magazines like John W. Campbell's *Astounding Science Fiction*, which published early work by such luminaries as Robert Heinlein, Isaac Asimov and A.E. van Vogt. But many more readers came to *Amazing Stories*, attracted by the otherworldly romance and cosmic mysticism of its fiction, not to mention the illustrations of scantily clad young women that frequently graced its covers.

Palmer also noticed that the magazine's circulation jumped whenever it featured a story about the lost civilisations of Atlantis or Lemuria, and he was wondering how best to capitalise on this interest when Richard Shaver's letter landed on his desk.

Intimations of a Dark History

Born in Berwick, Pennsylvania, Richard Sharpe Shaver (1907-75) was fond of playing pranks on people. As a child, he had had two imaginary companions, one good, the other evil, who became more real to him than his family. After graduating from high school, he worked for a meat packer and then a tree surgeon before moving to Detroit and enrolling in the Wicker School of Art. In 1930, Shaver joined a Communist group called the John Reed Club (named after the American correspondent who had reported on the Russian Revolution). Like just about everyone else, Shaver fell on hard times with the arrival of the Depression but managed to eke out a living as a part-time art instructor at the Wicker School of Art, supplementing his meagre income by going to a park and selling sketches of passersby for 25 cents each.

In 1933, Shaver married a fellow art student named Sophie Gurivinch, who was originally from Kiev in the Ukraine. They had a daughter in the same year and Shaver took a job as a welder in Highland Park, Michigan. He continued in this job for about a year until he suffered heat stroke, lost the power of speech and was admitted to the Ypsilanti State Hospital for two weeks. In February 1934, Shaver's brother, Tate, to whom he had been very close, died. His brother's death affected Shaver very badly, and he became increasingly depressed and paranoid, claiming that people were following him (and, as a known Communist, he may well have been under surveillance).

Shaver later received another blow when Sophie died in a mysterious accident in her apartment (they were living separately at the time). While Shaver returned to his welding job, their daughter went to live with Sophie's parents (who apparently told her that her father, too, was dead). For the next few years, Shaver led an itinerant existence, travelling between cities across North America, finding the odd job here and there and, eventually, marrying again.

The marriage was short-lived: his new wife left him when she found papers indicating that he had been in a sanatorium. Shaver moved back to Pennsylvania and married for a third time.

In 1936, he came across a curious article in *Science World* magazine. Entitled 'The True Basis of Today's Alphabet' and written by a man named Albert F. Yeager, the article claimed that there were six letters in our alphabet that represented concepts in addition to sounds. These six letters could thus be used as a key to unlock the hidden meanings in words. In response to this article, Shaver wrote to *Science World*, claiming that he understood the hidden concepts behind all the letters of the alphabet. He called this conceptual language 'Mantong'.

After several years of work with the Mantong language, Shaver wrote the following letter to Raymond Palmer at *Amazing Stories* in September 1943:

> Sirs: Am sending this in hopes you will insert it in an issue to keep it from dying with me. It would arouse a lot of discussion. Am sending you the language so that some time you can have it looked at by someone in the college or a friend who is a student of antique times. The language seems to me to be definite proof of the Atlantean legend. A great number of our English words have come down intact as romantic – ro man tic – 'science of man life patterning by control'. Trocadero – t ro see a dero – 'good one see a bad one' – applied now to theatre. This is perhaps the only copy of this language in existence and it represents my work over a long period of years. It is an immensely important find, suggesting the god legends have a base in some wiser race than modern man; but to understand it takes a good head as it contains multi-thoughts like many puns on the same subject. It is too deep for ordinary man – who thinks it is a mistake. A little study reveals ancient words in English

occurring many times. It should be saved and placed in wise
hands. I can't, will you? It really has an immense significance,
and will perhaps put me right in your thoughts again if you
will really understand this. I need a little encouragement.

R.S. Shaver, Barto, Pennsylvania

Enclosed with this letter was the Roman alphabet together with its
associated Mantong concepts:

A. Animal (used AN for short)

B. Be (to exist – often command)

C. See

D. (also used DE) Disintegrant energy; Detrimental
    (most important symbol in language)

E. Energy (an all concept, including motion)

F. Fecund (use FE as in female – fecund man)

G. Generate (used GEN)

H. Human (some doubt on this one)

I. Self; Ego (same as our I)

J. (see G) (same as generate)

K. Kinetic (force of motion)

L. Life

M. Man

N. Child; Spore; Seed

O. Orifice (a source concept)

P. Power

Q. Quest (as question)

R. (used as AR) Horror (symbol of dangerous quantity
    of dis force in the object)

S. (SIS) (an important symbol of the sun)

T. (used as TE) (the most important symbol; origin of the cross symbol)

Integration; Force of growth (the intake of T is cause of gravity; the force is T; tic meant science of growth; remains as credit word)

U. You

V. Vital (used as VI) (the stuff Mesmer calls animal magnetism; sex appeal)

W. Will

X. Conflict (crossed force lines)

Y. Why

Z. Zero (a quantity of energy of T neutralised by an equal quantity of D)

By applying these strange hidden meanings behind the letters of the alphabet, one can perceive even stranger hidden meanings behind various words. The word BAD, for instance, can be interpreted as 'Be a de', to be a destructive force. LADY is interpreted as 'Lay de', a complimentary term meaning to allay depression. The reader will note that in both these examples, the letter D (DE) is used, meaning unpleasant, destructive and detrimental. The letters D and T were of great importance to Shaver, as we shall see shortly.

Palmer was intrigued and decided to publish both the letter and the accompanying alphabet in the December 1943 issue of *Amazing Stories*. Alongside Shaver's material was a caption that read:

> We present this interesting letter concerning an ancient language with no comment, except to say that we applied the letter-meaning to the individual letters of many old root words and proper names and got an amazing 'sense'

out of them. Perhaps if readers interested were to apply his formula to more of these root words, we will [sic] be able to discover if the formula applies . . .

To Palmer's surprise, the December issue prompted hundreds of people to write in claiming that the Mantong alphabet really did release the hidden meanings of words. Encouraged by this response, Palmer wrote to Shaver asking for more information on the Mantong language and how his understanding of it had developed. Shaver responded by sending a 10,000-word manuscript evocatively entitled 'A Warning to Future Man'. Palmer felt that this was the circulation-booster he had been looking for. The article detailed the hidden history of Earth, complete with ancient spacefaring civilisations, lost continents, sex, violence and high adventure. Shaver's writing style, however, was not as impressive as his subject matter, and Palmer decided to rewrite 'A Warning to Future Man', turning it into a 31,000-word story which he re-titled 'I Remember Lemuria!' and published in the March 1945 issue of *Amazing Stories*.

In this story and the many others that followed (all of which were billed as true), Shaver painted a terrifying picture of a world honeycombed with vast caverns and tunnel systems containing enormous cities and advanced technology. Shaver's awareness of this world had begun while he was a welder in Highland Park in 1933. He realised that one of the welding guns was somehow allowing him to read the thoughts of his fellow workers in the factory. As if this were not bizarre enough, he also began to pick up the thoughts of evil creatures living far underground – creatures that apparently had the power to kidnap surface people and subject them to unthinkable tortures in their secret underground caverns. According to Shaver:

> The voices came from beings I came to realize were not
> human; not normal men at all. They lived in great caves far

beneath the surface. These alien minds I listened to seemed to know that they had great power, seemed conscious of the fact they were evil.

This realisation proved too much for Shaver: he quit his job and embarked on the aimless wanderings through North America mentioned earlier. During this time he was tormented by invisible rays projected at him by the evil subterraneans. Eventually, however, he was contacted by a beautiful young woman named Nydia, who was a member of another subterranean group opposed to the evil ones. Inevitably, they became lovers, and with her help Shaver was able to gain entry into the underworld and access the 'thought records' containing the fantastic history of Earth.

These 'thought records of Lemuria' contained some pretty astonishing information, which was at odds with what astronomers had discovered about the Sun. According to them, the Sun was originally a huge planet whose coal beds had been ignited by a massive meteor strike, transforming it into a coal-burning star. Since it burned coal, the Sun radiated clean, positive energy (reader, feel free to mentally insert exclamation marks).

The Earth was then colonised by two spacefaring civilisations, the Titans and the Atlans, who possessed marvellous technological devices 'such as the ben-ray, which broadcast healing energies; the stim-ray, which prolonged and heightened sexual pleasure; the telesolidograph, which could broadcast three-dimensional images; the penetray, used to observe events from vast distances; and the telepathic augmenter or telaug, which transmitted thought'.

The Atlans and the Titans called the Earth Lemuria and lived in utopian bliss until 20,000 years ago, when the Sun's outer shell was destroyed and it entered its current phase, producing harmful radiation, called d, de or dis. This 'disintegrant' energy is the opposite of t or te, the integrative, formative energy in Shaver's dualistic world view. Their immortality under threat, the Atlans and Titans excavated gargantuan caverns and tunnels far below Lemuria/Earth's surface, in which they built fantastically huge cities, the largest of which would dwarf New York or London. These subterranean realms shielded the entire Atlan and Titan populations, some 50 billion individuals. However, the underground cities did not prove a permanent solution and 12,000 years ago Lemuria/Earth was abandoned in favour of younger star systems.

Many Lemurians had already fallen victim to the debilitating effects of the Sun's harmful radiation and were forced to remain on Earth. Some of them moved to the surface (the reader will not be surprised to learn that these were the ancestors of *Homo sapiens*), while the ones who remained in the subterranean realms degenerated into a race of disfigured, idiotic and malicious beings known as the 'dero'. This word is an abbreviation of 'abandondero', and is based on the Mantong words 'de' (meaning negative or destructive) and 'ro' (meaning subservient). Hence the deros were, literally, controlled by negative forces. The group to which Shaver's exotic girlfriend belonged are known as the 'tero', or integrative ro, 'te' denoting positive or constructive energy. The tero, who somehow managed to avoid contamination by the Sun's radiation, are locked in a constant struggle with their unpleasant cousins.

According to Shaver, the fiendish, sadistic and perverted dero kidnap thousands of hapless surface-dwellers every year and take them into their cavern cities where they are tortured, sexually abused, used as slave labour or eaten. Although fundamentally stupid and brutal, the dero nevertheless know how to use the fabulous machinery left behind by their ancient ancestors, the original colonisers of Earth, and are able to spread evil and destruction throughout the world by means of dis rays.

The response to 'I Remember Lemuria!' was truly remarkable. Not only did the March 1945 issue of *Amazing Stories* sell out but Palmer received thousands of letters, many of which were from people claiming to have had bizarre experiences with the denizens of the fabulous subterranean world. One letter, from an ex-Air Force captain, read in part:

> For heaven's sake drop the whole thing! You are playing with dynamite. My companion and I fought our way out of a cave with submachine guns. I have two 9-inch scars on my left arm . . . [M]y friend has a hole the size of a dime in his right biceps. It was scarred inside. How we don't know. But we both believe we know more about The Shaver Mystery than any other pair . . . [D]on't print our names. We are not cowards, but we are not crazy.

While the above may or may not be true (it's possible that Palmer himself may have fabricated it), there is no doubt that many thousands of people were deeply affected by 'the Shaver Mystery' and wrote to Palmer to tell him so. Many had tales of encounters with strange people who may have been deros, while others complained that they, too, were hearing bizarre voices in their heads. Some even claimed to have visited the cavern-world itself.

By now, the phrase 'paranoid schizophrenia' will surely have suggested itself to the reader. To be sure, Shaver's claims sound very much like he was suffering from this condition: the voices in the head experienced in connection with a mechanical device (the welding gun) are classic symptoms, as is the belief that unpleasant influences are being projected at the victim through air ducts, pipes and so on. Paranoid schizophrenics frequently believe that some form of 'ray' is adversely affecting their health, damaging their brains or causing them to hear voices. This sounds remarkably like what the hapless Shaver was apparently going through and yet it falls far short of explaining why the number of letters to *Amazing Stories* jumped from 50 a month before the Shaver Mystery to 2,500 a month during and after, virtually all of which maintained that something sinister and terrifying really was going on beneath the Earth's surface.

Notwithstanding his decision to label each Shaver story as 'true', Palmer was reluctant to commit himself on the veracity of Shaver's claims. While he invariably supported Shaver, he also suggested that the dero caverns might not exist as physical locations in this dimension but rather on the astral plane. However, Palmer did make the perhaps inevitable claim that he himself had heard the voices of the cavern-dwellers while visiting Shaver and his last wife, Dorothy, at their Pennsylvania home. Palmer claimed that he heard five disembodied voices discussing the dismemberment of a human being in a cavern four miles below. For his part, Shaver maintained that the deros and teros did not live on some astral plane but were solid flesh-and-blood beings and that the cavern world was a real place.

Despite its huge popularity with the readers of *Amazing Stories*, the Shaver Mystery prompted a powerful backlash among diverse groups, including hard science-fiction fans who objected to a fantasy being marketed as truth (and who organised a campaign to boycott the magazine) and various occult groups who criticised Palmer for releasing information that would surely prove lethal to anyone inexperienced or foolish enough to attempt an exploration of the caverns. At the end of 1948, the Ziff-Davis Publishing Company, which published *Amazing Stories*, decided the Shaver Mystery was to be dropped from the magazine, in spite of the fact that Shaver's 'revelations' had virtually doubled its readership and enabled it to move from quarterly to monthly publication.

Palmer would later claim that the Shaver Mystery had been sup-pressed by a publisher 'too sedate' for material of this nature. However, Palmer's relations with Ziff-Davis had already become strained, possibly as a result of his having launched *Fate* magazine; Palmer left *Amazing Stories* in 1949 to concentrate on his new publication. According to Jim Probst in his book *Shaver: The Early Years*:

The Queens Science Fiction League of New York passed a resolution that the Shaver stories endangered the sanity of their readers, and brought the resolution before the Society for the Suppression of Vice. A fan conference in Philadelphia was rocked by threats to draw up a petition to the Post Office, asking that *Amazing Stories* be banned from the mail.

This was not the end of the Shaver Mystery, however; it would later inspire a number of people to start their own publications. Richard Toronto published *Shavertron* between 1979 and 1985. Subtitled 'The Only Source of Post-Deluge Shaverania', the magazine reported on the continuing activities of the nefarious deros, such as the time they allegedly interfered with Toronto's car while it was parked on a steep hillside and he was standing in front of it (Toronto barely managed to avoid being run over and killed).

The Hollow Hassle was published by Mary le Vesque between 1979 and 1983 and featured a regular column by the Reverend Charles A. Marcoux, a fascinating and colourful character who claimed to have hunted the deros during his many cave explorations. In the August 1981 issue of *The Hollow Hassle*, he wrote (with typically muddled syntax and howling non sequiturs):

> My experiences in the cavern world began at a very young age with astral experiences in the caverns ever since my birth, and in other worlds from other dimensions too. I joined R A Palmer and R S Shaver's group in January of 1945, and I am one of the few original members left. I still 'SEARCH FOR THE PORTALS' and as far as I know, am the only original member who does.

The Hollow Earth Insider ran for a few years in the early 1990s. Edited by Dennis Crenshaw, the journal included reprinted material by Shaver, in addition to news clippings and conspiracy theories, such as government (and dero) mind control.

Palmer made a final effort to perpetuate the Shaver Mystery in the early 1960s with The *Hidden World*, a trade paperback series which contained reprints of the original Shaver stories together with yet more tales from people claiming to have encountered and been victimised by the fiendish deros. Unfortunately, *The Hidden World* was not particularly successful and publication ceased in 1964. Shaver himself claimed to have discovered pictorial records of the Titans and Atlans hidden within the rocks and stones of the Wisconsin prairies in the 1950s, and for the rest of his life he tried in vain to persuade various scientists that they constituted final proof of the reality of the cavern world. He died of a heart attack in 1975. Palmer continued to publish journals until his death two years later, although none ever approached the success of *Amazing Stories* and *Fate*.

There is perhaps some truth in the assertion that the Shaver Mystery constituted, in effect, a modern mythology, which served a number of functions including escapism from post-war reality and the incipient threat of the Cold War. It explained why there was so much evil and suffering in the world and, of course, was an exciting corollary to the perceived menace of Communism, a new enemy whose very existence could be used to define the contrasting, positive attributes of the American Way. Palmer himself was a clever manipulator (if that is not too strong a word) of the public need both for escapism and for an explanation of the violence and evil that seemed to characterise life on Earth (it was all the fault of the deros). This was further illustrated by his reaction to the rise of the UFO mystery, which came to the world's attention with Kenneth Arnold's sighting of nine crescent-shaped objects over Mount Rainier in Washington State on 24 June 1947. Arnold's sighting was followed by a torrent of reports of strange objects flitting through the skies. In the pages of *Fate* magazine, Palmer instantly provided the answer to the puzzle: some of the UFOs were indeed alien spacecraft but most were vessels piloted by the denizens of the cavern world. Whatever the underlying truth (if any) of the claims of Shaver, Palmer and others about the strange and frightening drama constantly being played out beneath our feet, the Shaver Mystery occupies an important position in the complex network of rumours, speculations, crypto-historical inferences, anomalous events and genuine government violations of public trust that constitutes modern conspiracy theory.

31

CONSPIRACY THEORIES

Who Really Runs the World?

There are several reasons for our fascination with the world of conspiracies. For one thing, we live in an 'information age'. We are constantly bombarded with news from a wide range of sources, which can be extremely difficult to collate and place within an easily understandable and consistent frame of reference. For many people this results in a feeling of powerlessness, of a constant low-level unease in the face of monumental or even sinister events. A belief in conspiracy theories can provide us with a partial (albeit illusory) empowerment allowing us at least to feel that we know what is really happening in the world; that, while we may be the pawns of people and forces we cannot control, at least we are not unwitting pawns.

Of course, the phrase 'conspiracy theory' has become virtually synonymous with the rantings of the paranoid. And yet there is no doubt that conspiracies exist and have done throughout history. For instance, one need only hear the word 'Watergate' to be reminded of the lengths to which politicians will go to realise their aims. Watergate, of course, is a well-known example, but the code word MKULTRA may be more of a mystery to the majority of people.

MKULTRA was the name given to the Central Intelligence Agency's attempts to control the behaviour of individuals through the use of psychoactive drugs such as LSD. The genesis of MKULTRA goes back to the Second World War, when the US Army began looking into the possibility of using barbiturates, marijuana and hypnosis as aids to interrogation. The MKULTRA project itself became fully established after the Korean War, when the CIA began experimenting with more powerful drugs. The intention was to create secret agents who would be able to withstand torture should they be captured and also agents who would be unaware that they were carrying out secret orders. Unwitting recruits were taken not only from the military but from the civilian population. MKULTRA research included the use of ketamine, psilocybin, lobotomy, electroconvulsive shock and electrodes implanted in the brain. Although the US Senate Church Committee exposed these practices (and the CIA solemnly promised not to continue them), it has been claimed many times since that the intelligence agency simply changed the name of the project and moved it to a different department.

In fact, the United States has a long and rather embarrassing history of experimentation on human subjects without seeking their consent. Since the beginning of the twentieth century both the military and private organisations have used groups of citizens to test various substances and theories. Although much information has been made available to the public by means of the Freedom of Information Act, the real extent to which human experimentation has occurred as part of the US biological weapons programme will probably never be known. The following examples are based on information that was declassified in 1977.

In 1900, an American doctor conducting research in the Philippines infected a number of prisoners with the Plague, then induced beriberi in a further 29 prisoners. These experiments resulted in two known fatalities. In 1931, the Puerto Rican Cancer Experiment was conducted by Dr Cornelius Rhoads under the auspices of the Rockefeller Institute for Medical Investigations. Dr Rhoads deliberately introduced cancer cells into the bodies of several dozen human subjects. At least 13 of these subjects are known to have died. The reader may be forgiven for wondering how a doctor could possibly conduct such awful experiments on fellow human beings. The blood-chilling answer was provided by Dr Rhoads himself, who stated his belief that the entire population of Puerto Rico should be eradicated! In spite of his rather appalling ambition (or perhaps because of it), Dr Rhoads was asked to establish the US Army Biological Warfare facilities in Maryland, Utah and Panama. He went on to work for the US Atomic Energy Commission, where he continued conducting radiation experiments on prisoners, hospital patients and soldiers.

During the 1940s, a crash programme was established to develop new anti-malaria drugs for use in the Second World War. Doctors in the Chicago area infected approximately 400 prisoners with the disease, and although the subjects were told they were helping the war effort, they were not told how. The withholding of this information from the experimental subjects was not in accordance with later standards set by the Nuremberg War Crimes Tribunal, and indeed Nazi doctors on trial for truly hideous crimes cited the Chicago studies as precedents to defend their own activities, which they claimed had been aiding the German war effort.

In 1950, the US Navy sprayed a cloud of bacteria over San Francisco in a 'simulated' germ warfare attack. The intention was to develop means of tracking any future attacks by hostile powers, and the Navy claimed that the bacteria were harmless. Nevertheless, many of the city's residents became ill with pneumonia-like symptoms and one is known to have died.

On 9 June 1969, Dr D.M. McArtor, then Deputy Director of Research and Technology for the Department of Defense, appeared before the House Subcommittee on Appropriations to request funding for a project to produce a synthetic biological agent against which humans would have no natural immunity. Dr McArtor requested $10 million to produce this agent over the next five to ten years. According to the Congressional Record, the most important characteristic of the new agent would be 'that it might be [resistant] to the immunological and therapeutic processes upon which we depend to maintain our relative freedom from infectious disease'. Acquired Immune Deficiency Syndrome (AIDS) first appeared as a public health risk ten years later. There are many more examples, but the above should give an idea of what the United States government (and many other governments) have been up to over the last century.

Although a case can be made for saying that conspiracy theories are among the most useful of intellectual tools with which to understand the true nature of life at the beginning of the twenty-first century, the fact remains that such theories possess wildly varying degrees of plausibility, ranging from the entirely possible to the utterly bizarre and fantastic.

One of the most engaging aspects of the subject is that a great deal depends on how one defines words such as 'plausible', 'bizarre' and 'fantastic'. To illustrate this, we can look briefly at the dreadful events that occurred in the town of Tuskegee, Alabama, in the middle years of the twentieth century.

In the 1980s, it became apparent that for more than 40 years the US government had been experimenting on more than 200 poor black men in the town by exposing them to syphilis in order to study the effects of the disease. Most people would surely have regarded such a rumour as bizarre and implausible, until the conspiracy was exposed, the awful experiments on US citizens were established as fact and President Clinton was obliged to travel to Tuskegee and apologise to the survivors and their families.

The history of the twentieth century was profoundly influenced by the activities of a number of clandestine societies and groups. The Bilderberg Group (also known as the Bilderbergers) is one of the most secretive of all such groups. It takes its name from the Bilderberg Hotel in Oosterbeek, Holland, where it was originally convened by Prince Bernhard of the Netherlands, its first chairman, in May 1954.

'Bilderberg' is actually a misnomer, since the group only met there once and, since then, has met in a different location once or twice every year. However, since the group has no other name (at least, none that is known to outsiders), the name 'Bilderbergers' has stuck. As with most secret groups, there are a number of unsubstantiated rumours regarding the Bilderbergers. Since members include international financiers, heads of state and media tycoons, the main accusation levelled against them is that they are our true masters, deciding the fate of entire nations from the fortress-like security of luxurious hotels in remote locations across the world. According to the British journalist Will Hutton, who attended a Bilderberg meeting in 1997, members are the 'high priests of globalisation'. Although no policy is made at the meetings, the consensus resulting from their discussions heavily influences subsequent policy, both national and international.

According to a Bilderberg draft document of 1989, the first meeting:

> grew out of the concern expressed by many leading citizens on both sides of the Atlantic that Western Europe and North America were not working together as closely as they should on matters of critical importance. It was felt that regular off-the-record discussions would help create a better understanding of the complex forces and major trends affecting Western nations in the difficult post-war period.

The group was originally the brainchild of the American Dr Joseph Retinger, who headed the CIA-financed European Movement and who had numerous contacts at the very highest levels of the American establishment. In the 1950s, Retinger came to believe that the course of world events would be conceived and executed not by governments but by multinational organisations. At a meeting with Prince Bernhard, head of Royal Dutch Petroleum, in 1952, Retinger suggested that the problems facing the world might be discussed at a series of secret meetings between the world's elite. Bernhard agreed, so Retinger then took his idea to his immensely powerful friends in America, including the billionaire banker David Rockefeller and Walter Bedell Smith, then-Director of the CIA. This idea met with the approval of those concerned and resulted in the first meeting at the Bilderberg Hotel.

It has been claimed that each meeting is attended by about 120 members, one-third of whom are American and the rest European, and that politicians at the meetings are outnumbered by business people, financiers and media barons by two to one. Interestingly, although the media are heavily represented on these occasions, their viewers and readers are never given any information on the Bilderberg Group, the locations of its meetings or the subjects discussed there. In fact, journalist Lawrence Wilmot stated in an article in the journal *The Spotlight* (published by Liberty Lobby, Inc. in Washington DC) in May 1993, that no journalist will even attempt to cover Bilderberger meetings. When he mentioned this curious fact to some colleagues, he was told by Anthony Holder of the London *Economist* that 'the Bilderbergers were removed from our assignment list years ago by executive order'.

Of course, the suggestion that the richest and most powerful people in the world are actually running it is hardly a revelation of shattering originality. However, conspiracy theorists have long held that the Bilderberg Group, along with the Trilateral Commission and the Council on Foreign Relations, is in the process of overseeing the construction of the New World Order, a secret international government that will transfer all political and economic power into the hands of a small elite. This belief looks beyond the more plausible possibility that the Bilderbergers' fine-tuning of international economic policy could merely be an expression of all-too-familiar corporate greed. In this more extreme and sinister scenario, the Bilderbergers are intent on destroying the sovereignty and economic independence of nations, if necessary through the ignition of civil and international wars – after having sold the necessary armaments to those nations, of course.

It has also been suggested that the Bilderberg Group is actually a front organisation, designed to divert public attention away from the true controllers of world events, the notorious Illuminati. Although the Illuminati was originally founded in Bavaria by Adam Weishaupt in 1776, conspiracy theorists fervently believe that the group still exists today, wields an enormous amount of power and is more than willing to destroy anyone standing in its way. Although in its original incarnation the Illuminati has come to be regarded as the *sine qua non* of conspiracy theory, in recent years the definition of the word has become somewhat looser, and today can be used to describe any clandestine elite believed to be intent on world domination.

There is a yet more bizarre theory which holds that the Bilderbergers are actually under the control of the infamous alien race known as the Greys, whose tactics are to disseminate free market capitalism to the point where social cohesion breaks down utterly in the developed nations. The resulting poverty, desperation and low morale would soften up the entire human race and make the Earth ripe for a full-scale invasion. This is a good example of how conspiracy theories can, in effect, superheat and run completely out of control, spawning wilder and more implausible sub-theories as time goes on.

Conspiracy theories can be extremely complex and tangled affairs, and nowhere is this more apparent than in the works of the doyen of the subject, Robert Anton Wilson. In particular, his *Illuminatus!* trilogy (co-authored with Robert Shea) contains a great deal of material (some of it true, some not) that has found its way into 'mainstream' conspiriology. One of the most entertaining examples of this is the notorious Operation Mindfuck (OM), originated by Ho Chi Zen (aka Kerry Thornley, founder of the Erisian Liberation Front which worships Eris, goddess of Chaos). The underlying philosophy of OM is that adopted by John von Neumann and

Oskar Morgenstern in their book *The Theory of Games and Economic Behaviour,* which states that the only strategy that an opponent cannot predict is a random strategy.

Operation Mindfuck is most closely associated with the Discordian Movement, which some claim is a complicated joke disguised as a new religion, while Discordians themselves counter that it is a new religion disguised as a complicated joke. Discordians are divided into two camps, in accordance with the rule: 'We Discordians Must Stick Apart'. The Erisian Liberation Front (ELF), led by Ho Chi Zen, is an anarchist/libertarian anti-authoritarian movement, while the Paratheo-anametamystickhood of Eris Esoteric (POEE), led by Malaclypse the Younger, follows an altogether more passive, mystical doctrine.

No one within or outside the Discordian Movement has the faintest idea who is involved with OM, or what its ultimate agenda might be. The scale of OM projects varies from the trivial to the massive. An example of the former is a rubber stamp owned by Dr Mordecai Malignatus, which says: 'SEE MENTAL HEALTH RECORDS'. Whenever Dr Malignatus receives mail which he considers to be impertinent or insulting (usually from government departments), he stamps the envelope with this instruction and sends it back unopened. The intention is to puzzle and slightly unnerve the offending bureaucrat. An example of a more serious OM project is Project Jake, devised by Harold Lord Randomfactor to punish public servants who have demonstrated excessive stupidity. When they are selected for a Jake, all Discordian cabals are notified. These include the various branches of the Erisian Liberation Front, the Twelve Famous Buddha Minds, the St Gulik Iconistary, the Earl of Nines, the Tactile Temple of Eris Esoteric, the Brotherhood of the Lust of Christ, Green & Pleasant, the Society for Moral Understanding and Training, the In-Sect, the Golden Apple Panthers, the Paratheo-anametamystickhood of Eris Esoteric, Sam's Café, the Seattle Group, the Stone Dragon Cabal, the Universal Erisian Church and the Young Americans for Real Freedom. On a specified day, known as Jake Day, the target bureaucrat receives mail from all of these organisations, on their wacky official letterheads, asking for help in some hideously complicated matter that defies all rational understanding. If the bureaucrat possesses sufficient imagination, the conclusion will be that he or she is the victim of a conspiracy composed entirely of lunatics.

The paranoia that frequently goes hand in hand with conspiracy theory can result in truly outrageous claims. Many conspiracies fall into the category known as TBTB, or Too Bizarre to Believe (the abduction of Elvis Presley by rock 'n' roll-loving aliens is one of the most extreme examples of this). The bizarre and unlikely conspiracy theory surrounding trailer parks in the United States has its roots in the 1929 stock market crash, in which millions of people were plunged into financial ruin and unemployment. In 1932, Franklin D. Roosevelt won the presidential election and began his huge programme of social and economic reform, including the funding of public services and the creation of social welfare. This much is accepted by historians; however, some conspiriologists believe that Roosevelt secretly came to the conclusion that his country's main problem lay in its chronic overpopulation. Since he obviously couldn't order the mass extermination of millions of Americans and still show his face on the world stage, Roosevelt is said to have settled for an alternative that would remove large numbers of superfluous people without making him look too bad.

Roosevelt (it is maintained) instructed architects and engineers to design a house that was quickly and easily built, and was mobile. The result was the 'trailer home', providing low-income families with decent housing and community life. Trailer parks were created throughout the Midwest – and this is where the conspiracy comes in. The region in which the homes were constructed suffers more tornadoes than the rest of the world put together, and since trailer homes are not the sturdiest of constructions (indeed, they are always the first structures to be obliterated when a tornado hits), entire families would be conveniently eliminated every year without anyone facing the blame.

As we have noted, international finance also plays a significant role in conspiriology and the field is full of rumours and claims regarding the nefarious activities of the hyper-rich. Harold Wilson once denounced the 'Gnomes of Zurich', claiming that they had more power than any government in Europe. While most people at the time naturally assumed that Wilson was merely using the phrase to refer to Swiss bankers, others have claimed that he was actually referring to the Grand Lodge Alpina, the largest Freemasonic society in Switzerland. The Grand Lodge Alpina currently controls the finances of the Western world through the banks they own in Zurich, Basel and Geneva. According to conspiriologist David Yallop, the Gnomes of Zurich secretly backed the legendary Propaganda Due (P2) conspiracy in Italy. Yallop claims that their ultimate aim is to restore the monarchy in France and fascism in Italy.

Governments throughout the world, including those of countries that are pleased to call themselves 'civilised', are very fond of harassing their citizens. The so-called 'black helicopters' have most frequently been seen in connection with UFO activity, flying low over the property of witnesses. However, they have also been known to harass civilians with no known connection to UFO mysteries. There is absolutely no doubt that these unmarked aircraft exist, even if their origin and purpose remain unknown. For instance, on 7 May 1994 in Harrahan, Louisiana, a black helicopter chased a teenager for 45 minutes, while the occupants pointed an unidentified instrument at him. When the incident was reported to the local police, the chief said that the aircraft was owned by the federal government and that he was unable to take the matter any further. In 1995, a black helicopter sprayed an unidentified substance on the rural property of a couple in Fallon, Nevada. The substance also fell on their cattle, 13 of which died the following day. When the couple reported this incident to their local police, all knowledge of the aircraft was denied.

Black helicopters have also been seen in the vicinity of the highly mysterious cattle mutilations, in which farm animals are found by their owners with their blood, internal and sexual organs removed. (It has been suggested by sceptics that these mutilations are nothing more than the result of normal predator activity; however, since no known predator carves up its victims with surgical instruments, who knows?)

In 1976, a hunter in the Red Mountain region near Norris, Montana, had a strange and unnerving encounter with the crew of a black Bell Jet Ranger helicopter. The aircraft, which carried no registration markings (a legal requirement), flew behind a hill and landed. Climbing to the top of the hill, the hunter watched as seven men in civilian clothing disembarked and approached. As the men drew closer and the hunter waved and shouted a greeting, he realised that they were all Asian in appearance. The men then turned and walked back towards their aircraft. When they realised that the hunter had started to follow them, they broke into a run, climbed aboard and took off.

The late Jim Keith, one of the most prolific of conspiriologists, suggested that the reason black helicopters are hardly ever reported in the media (despite the frequency of sightings) is that they are far too sensitive a subject to be given any serious widespread attention. Nevertheless, at least two official agencies are known to operate such aircraft: the Drug Enforcement Agency (DEA) and the Federal Emergency Management Agency (FEMA), which is designed to ensure the continuance of the national administration in the event of a major catastrophe (it was FEMA that swung into action in the immediate aftermath of the September 11 attacks on the World Trade Center and Pentagon, and in the aftermath of Hurricane Katrina). The fact that black helicopters are so often seen in the vicinity of cattle mutilations has led some to speculate that the

US government is conducting some kind of ultra-secret biological weapons experiment in isolated areas and is excising the internal organs of farm animals in order to monitor the effects of these weapons. An alternative (and perhaps more plausible) explanation is that they are monitoring the presence of residual radiation from the atomic weapons tests that were conducted in the late 1940s and 1950s.

In recent years, conspiracy theories have been thrust to the forefront of public awareness, first with the death of Diana, Princess of Wales, and most recently with the September 11 attacks. In the case of Diana's death, it has been suggested that she and her companion Dodi Fayed were the victims of an assassination plot by the British Secret Service or, even more outrageously, by the Prince of Wales. Assuming that the Secret Service did want to permanently remove Diana, to kill her in a car crash would have carried a ridiculously high risk of failure. In view of the fact that she was deeply troubled and had said that she had attempted suicide in the past, it would have been far simpler to arrange her death by means of an overdose. Nevertheless, the affair will remain in the thoughts of millions of people for the foreseeable future.

The attacks on the World Trade Center and Pentagon have likewise spawned a host of conspiracy theories, centred on the claim that the US government either knew they were about to happen and did nothing to prevent them, or actually planned them. Writers as respected as Gore Vidal have gone on record with their suspicions that President Bush and his advisers know something that they are not sharing with the American people. Vidal suspects that the attacks were allowed to happen in order to justify the Bush Administration's plans to conquer the Middle East and secure its oil supplies for America's use, with the invasion of Iraq merely the first phase in that plan. As with the Diana conspiracy, public suspicion regarding the motives and secret knowledge of the US government is not going to go away any time soon and will almost certainly increase as more conspiracy theories are developed and disseminated on the Internet.

Finally, we should take a look at one or two conspiracy theories regarding world leaders. One theory holds that they are actually clones incubated by the CIA, MI6, Mossad and other secret agencies. These clone leaders can be used to do the bidding of the intelligence services and multinational corporations who are the true rulers of the planet. While it would seem to make more sense to kill the original leader and replace him or her with a clone, the controllers have discovered that it is far more useful to use the two together. Once in power, the leader is informed of the existence of his or her clone. There is, of course, nothing that they can do about it and, indeed, they would be fools to rock the boat, since the controllers look kindly on obedient politicians. (Apart from this, they realise that they could easily be killed and replaced by the clone, with the world being none the wiser.)

According to this theory, the publicity given to breakthroughs in cloning technology serves a dual purpose: firstly to prepare the public gradually for the prospect of human cloning, so that it will slowly gain more and more acceptability; and secondly to allow governments to dismiss the allegations of human cloning by pointing out that it is at present 'impossible' to clone a human being.

It is suggested that the cloning technology was first developed by the KGB bent on doubling up soldiers and scientists, but with the collapse of the Soviet Union, the CIA stepped in. Its favoured route was that world leaders should be cloned in order finally to consolidate the power of the controllers behind the scenes and make it absolute. The cloning concept is, of course, merely a more extreme version of the commonly held suspicion that politicians only offer an illusion of democracy while secretly taking their orders from multinational corporations and intelligence services that actually hold the strings of power on Earth.

SELECT BIBLIOGRAPHY AND SUGGESTED FURTHER READING

Anderson, Ken, *Hitler and the Occult* (Amherst, New York: Prometheus Books, 1995)

Baigent, Michael; Leigh, Richard and Lincoln, Henry, *The Holy Blood and the Holy Grail* (London: Arrow Books, 1996)

Baker, Phil, 'Stroke of Genius', article on Austin Osman Spare in *Fortean Times* 144

Barber, Malcolm, *The Cathars: Dualist Heretics in Languedoc in the High Middle Ages* (London: Longman, 2000)

Begg, Ean, *The Cult of the Black Virgin* (London: Arkana, 1985)

Brown, Dan, *The Da Vinci Code* (London: Corgi Books, 2004)

Burstein, Dan (ed.), *Secrets of the Codec* (London: Orion Books Ltd, 2004)

Cavendish, Richard, *The Magical Arts* (London: Arkana, 1984)

Cayce, Edgar, *Edgar Cayce on Atlantis* (New York: Warner Books, 1968)

Childress, David Hatcher, *Lost Continents and the Hollow Earth* (Kempton, Illinois: Adventures Unlimited Press, 1999)

Daraul, Arkon, *A History of Secret Societies* (New York: Citadel Press, 1994)

Donnelly, Ignatius, *Atlantis: The Antediluvian World* (New York: Gramercy Publishing Company, 1949)

Duricy, Michael P., 'Black Madonnas', article at http://campus. udayton.edu/mary/meditations/blackmdn.html

Fest, Joachim, *Hitler* (New York: Harcourt Brace Jovanovich, 1974)

Gardner, Martin, *Fads & Fallacies in the Name of Science* (New York: Dover Publications, Inc., 1957)

Godwin, Joscelyn, *Arktos: The Polar Myth in Science, Symbolism and Nazi Survival* (London: Thames and Hudson, 1993)

Grant, Kenneth, *Outer Gateways* (London: Skoob Books, 1994)

Hancock, Graham, *Fingerprints of the Gods* (London: William Heinemann Ltd, 1995)

Harms, Daniel and Gonce, John Wisdom, *The Necronomicon Files* (Boston, Massachusetts: Weiser, 1998)

Haslam, Garth, 'The Green Children of Woolpit', article on Garth Haslam's website http://anomalyinfo.com/articles/sa00022. shtml

Hay, George (ed.), *The Necronomicon: The Book of Dead Names* (London: Skoob Books, 1992)

Hitching, Francis, *The World Atlas of Mysteries* (London: William Collins & Sons Ltd, 1978)

Joshi, S.T., *H.P. Lovecraft: A Life* (West Warwick, Rhode Island: Necronomicon Press, 1996)

Kennedy, Gerry and Churchill, Rob, *The Voynich Manuscript* (London: Orion Books Ltd, 2004)

Le Page, Victoria, *Shambhala: The Fascinating Truth Behind the Myth of Shangri-la* (Wheaton, Illinois: Quest Books, 1996)

Lovecraft, H.P., *Tales* (New York: The Library of America, 2005)

McCalman, Iain, *The Seven Ordeals of Count Cagliostro* (London: Century, 2003)

Maclellan, Alec, *The Lost World of Agharti: The Mystery of Vril Power* (London: Souvenir Press, 1996)

Martin, Sean, *The Cathars* (Harpenden: Pocket Essentials, 2005)

Morton, Chris and Thomas, Ceri Louise, *The Mystery of the Crystal Skulls* (London: Thorsons, 1997)

Reader's Digest, *Great Mysteries of the Past* (adapted from *Wie geschah es wirklich?*, Germany: Verlag Das Beste GmbH, 1990)

Rickard, Bob and Michell, John, *Unexplained Phenomena* (London: Rough Guides Ltd, 2000)

Roerich, Nicholas, *Shambhala* (New York: Nicholas Roerich Museum, 1978)

Russell, Jeffrey B., *A History of Witchcraft: Sorcerers, Heretics and Pagans* (London: Thames and Hudson, 1980)

Rutter, Gordon, 'Da Vinci Decoded', article in *Fortean Times* 193

Schneck, Damon, 'The God Machine', article on John Murray Spear in *Fortean Times* 158

Shuker, Karl, *The Unexplained* (London: Carlton Books, 1996)

Simon, *The Necronomicon* (New York: Avon Books, 1977)

Spence, Lewis, *An Encyclopaedia of Occultism* (New York: Citadel Press, 1996)

Temple, Robert, *The Sirius Mystery* (London: Century, 1998)

Thomas, Gordon, *Journey into Madness: The True Story of Secret CIA Mind Control and Medical Abuse* (New York: Bantam Books, 1990)

Tomas, Andrew, *Shambhala: Oasis of Light* (London: Sphere Books, 1977)

Trungpa, Chögyam, *Shambhala: The Sacred Path of the Warrior* (Boston, Massachusetts: Shambhala Publications, Inc., 1984)

Underwood, Peter, *Dictionary of the Supernatural* (London: Harrap, 1978)

Webb, James, *The Occult Underground* (La Salle, Illinois: Open Court Publishing, 1974)